THE DU 3⁀ . . . Schlesinger, Jill . R MONEY

"Read *Du* . S . . . . ▸ple ney, and remember t . . . . areer."
. . . . our
—*Forbes*

"A must-read for the many women, in particular, who are allergic to
financial advice . . . This straightforward and pleasingly opinionated
book may persuade more of us to think about financial planning.
It is certainly a pain-free introduction to the subject. And never
boring."

—*Financial Times*

"*The Dumb Things Smart People Do with Their Money* is a powerful,
easy-to-read guide full of commonsense advice."

—*Booklist*

"Jill Schlesinger blends five-star financial advice, colorful real-life stories and her trademark wit, humor and candor in this rollicking
guide to what *not* to do when it comes to your money. Avoid even
one of her mistakes and this book will reward you in spades."

—Leigh Gallagher, director, external affairs,
Google

"Common sense is not always common, especially when it comes to
managing your money. Consider Jill Schlesinger's book your guide to
all the things you should know about money but were never taught.
After reading it, you'll be smarter, wiser, and maybe even wealthier."

—Chris Guillebeau, author of *Side Hustle*
and *The $100 Startup*

"A must-read—whether you're digging yourself out of a financial hole
or stacking up savings for the future. *The Dumb Things Smart People Do with Their Money* is a personal finance gold mine loaded

with smart financial nuggets delivered in Schlesinger's straight-talking, judgment-free style. The book helps you live the life you want, while laughing all the way to the bank—since she's not only wise, but also hilarious!"

—BETH KOBLINER, author of *Make Your Kid a Money Genius (Even If You're Not)* and *Get a Financial Life*

"We don't talk nearly enough about money, which is odd given its central place in most of our lives. And it's shockingly easy for even smart, accomplished people to get tripped up by bad habits or just plain lack of knowledge about money management. Jill Schlesinger has written an eye-opening, practical, and funny book about how we screw up and how we can get it right. I needed this book ten years ago! I'm glad I have it now."

—ALISON GREEN, author of *Ask a Manager* and the Ask a Manager website

"The vast majority of people, including highly sophisticated investors, will recognize one if not several of the thirteen 'dumb things' Jill Schlesinger brilliantly discusses in this engaging and important book. I know I did. Drawing on a highly accomplished career—not just as an astute observer of personal finance, but also a planner and options trader—she arms readers with knowledge and tools to help correct existing financial planning mistakes as well as avoid potentially costly ones in the future."

—MOHAMED A. EL-ERIAN, chief economic adviser, Allianz, and author of *New York Times* bestsellers *When Markets Collide* and *The Only Game in Town*

"Jill Schlesinger is one of the smartest voices in personal finance and money management I know. Ignore her words of wisdom at your financial peril."

—HELAINE OLEN, blogger for *The Washington Post*, author of *Pound Foolish*, co-author of *The Index Card*

THE DUMB THINGS
SMART PEOPLE DO
WITH THEIR MONEY

THE
DUMB THINGS
SMART
PEOPLE
DO WITH THEIR
MONEY

THIRTEEN WAYS TO RIGHT
YOUR FINANCIAL WRONGS

JILL SCHLESINGER

BALLANTINE BOOKS

NEW YORK

2020 Ballantine Books Trade Paperback Edition

Published in the United States by Ballantine Books, an imprint of Random House, a division of Penguin Random House LLC, New York.

BALLANTINE and the HOUSE colophon are registered trademarks of Penguin Random House LLC.

Originally published in hardcover in the United States by Ballantine Books, an imprint of Random House, a division of Penguin Random House LLC, in 2019.

LIBRARY OF CONGRESS CATALOGING-IN-PUBLICATION DATA
Names: Schlesinger, Jill, author.
Title: The dumb things smart people do with their money: thirteen ways to right your financial wrongs / Jill Schlesinger.
Description: First edition. | New York: Ballantine Books, [2019] | Includes bibliographical references.
Identifiers: LCCN 2018039472 | ISBN 9780525622185 (trade paperback) | ISBN 9780525622192 (ebook)
Subjects: LCSH: Finance, Personal.
Classification: LCC HG179 .S285 2019 | DDC 332.024—dc23
LC record available at https://lccn.loc.gov/2018039472

Printed in the United States of America on acid-free paper

randomhousebooks.com

246897531

For Jackie

Contents

Author's note   *ix*

Introduction   *xi*

DUMB THING #1   You Buy Financial Products That
You Don't Understand   *3*

DUMB THING #2   You Take Financial Advice from the
Wrong People   *21*

DUMB THING #3   You Make Money More Important
Than It Is   *39*

DUMB THING #4   You Take On Too Much College Debt   *58*

DUMB THING #5   You Buy a House When You Should Rent   *80*

DUMB THING #6   You Take On Too Much Risk   *96*

DUMB THING #7   You Fail to Protect Your Identity   *112*

DUMB THING #8   You Indulge Yourself Too Much During Your
Early Retirement Years   *125*

DUMB THING #9   You Saddle Your Kids with Your Own
Money Issues   *146*

DUMB THING #10   You Don't Plan for the Care of
Your Aging Parents   *163*

DUMB THING #11   You Buy the Wrong Kinds of Insurance,
                 or None at All   *182*

DUMB THING #12   You Don't Have a Will   *199*

DUMB THING #13   You Try to "Time" the Market   *217*

Appendix: Thirteen Smart *Things Smart People Should Do*   *233*
Acknowledgments   *237*
Notes   *239*
Index   *249*

Author's note

Unless otherwise indicated, the stories presented in this book are real. For privacy reasons, I have changed most names and other identifying details. Please visit my blog, *Jill on Money*, for additional information on the topics covered in this book. And please know that certain conceptual formulations and pieces of advice contained in this book originally appeared there.

Introduction

When it comes to money, we all suffer through our share of "Oh, shit" moments—those life-altering instants in which we realize we've screwed up *royally*. I have witnessed countless of these moments and experienced more than a few myself, first as a gold and silver options trader, then as a financial planner, and now as a business analyst for CBS News and the host of a radio show and podcast. As I've found, we sometimes can take action to save ourselves, and what we thought was a major screwup really isn't. But usually, "Oh, shit" is exactly that, and it's all we can do to mourn our losses and carry on.

In 2006, my former client Randy experienced a genuine "Oh, shit" moment, one that would dog him the rest of his life. During the 1990s and early 2000s, Randy had worked for a large bank as a senior loan officer. It was his job to field applications from small businesses and decide whether to make the loans. By 2003, when he was in his early forties, Randy felt ready for a change. Instead of slaving away for a bank, he thought, he could take his considerable expertise and start his own business, consulting for small companies and helping them with all sorts of finance-related issues. He'd have to travel more, trudging across the country to meet with clients, but his income would jump from $150,000 to $300,000 or more, allowing for a much better lifestyle for his wife and two teenage kids.

With some trepidation, Randy quit his job and opened his own consulting practice. Through his vast connections, he landed a few lucrative contracts straight out of the gate. At around this time, he and I met to discuss his financial plan. In many ways, he was in a great place. In addition to having saved for his kids' college, he had about $800,000 in his 401(k) and about $500,000 in a non-retirement investment account. His challenge, now that he was starting his own business, was to replace the generous benefits his bank had provided him. He budgeted money to pay for private health insurance, which wasn't cheap, and we bolstered his life insurance coverage. "Hey," I said to him, "what about disability insurance?" Previously, his bank had paid to insure him in case he suffered a physical injury that prevented him from performing his job. This kind of insurance, which pays out a certain percentage of your annual salary, is affordable as a corporate benefit, but can be very expensive if you buy it as an individual. Now that Randy was on his own, it would cost him about $8,000 a year to cover 70 percent of his new income of $300,000 until age sixty-five, when he would be able to claim Social Security. Of course, he could tap his non-retirement savings at any time, and his retirement account at age fifty-nine and a half, but replacing 70 percent of $300,000 would cause him to drain that non-retirement account in less than three years.

When I told Randy that he needed to buy the coverage, he balked. "That's an awfully high premium," he said. "And look, there's no way I'm going to need that. I could understand if I had a heart problem or something, but I'm healthy and I have great genes." I pressed him on it, but he refused. "Jill, I'm telling you, I just don't need it. And I don't want to pay for it." I could under-stand Randy's perspective. I was asking him to pay a big bill for something we both hoped he'd never need. Then again, I never hear people complain that they had to buy auto insurance, "and damn it, I didn't even get into an accident this year!" I knew disability insurance was the right move for Randy.

Now, you see where this is going. For the next several years, Randy and I met annually to discuss his finances. Each time, I asked him about the disability insurance. Each time, he declined. Then in 2006, the unthinkable happened. No, Randy didn't have a heart attack. He was right—his ticker was perfectly fine. He was diagnosed with multiple sclerosis. His symptoms had developed gradually over a period of several years. By the time of his diagnosis, they were pretty bad. He couldn't control his balance and would fall easily. Although he could still work, he couldn't log nearly as many client hours as he had anticipated, and he couldn't travel for his job. Instead of earning $300,000 each year, he would eke out only $75,000.

The diagnosis was Randy's "Oh, shit" moment. Of course, the news was a terrible tragedy, devastating to him and his family, and entirely beyond his control. But adding to that grim reality were the financial implications. If he had carried disability insurance, he would have received monthly payments that would nearly equal his annual take-home income. Without the insurance, he was in trouble. His family could cut back a bit on expenses, but there was no way to slash his household's monthly expenditures by over two-thirds. Randy's wife worked, but only part-time—she couldn't bridge the gap. So, month after month, Randy would have to dig into his $500,000 in non-retirement savings. Well before he turned sixty-five, it would be gone.

Although my heart goes out to Randy, he and I both realized that he had made a dumb mistake, one that cost him big-time. How much? Let's do the math. Randy's diagnosis came three years after his former company's disability insurance had lapsed. If he had opted for coverage, he would have paid $24,000 in premiums before filing a claim. Because he had declined coverage, he was forced to deplete his $500,000 non-retirement savings. So, *this one unfortunate mistake cost Randy and his family about $476,000.* And this is to say nothing about the emotional suffering he and his family endured because of uncertainty about their financial future. If Randy had purchased the coverage, he would have enjoyed a steady revenue stream. He could have focused on maintaining his physical health, confident that his and his family's future was secure.

Now, I'll bet you're wondering: How could Randy have made such a dumb mistake? He was a pretty smart guy. In fact, after he started his business, people essentially paid him to think for them. Not only that, the guy was a former banker! If anybody knew money, he did. But still he screwed up.

I wish I could say that Randy is the only smart person I know who made a horrendously costly financial mistake, but he isn't. Ben and Tobias were best friends and engineers in their late fifties who worked for a large technology company. In 1999, they visited my office because they were both thinking of retiring and wanted to understand their options. They were in the exact same financial situation. Each had about $1.2 million in retirement savings, at least 90 percent of which was invested in company stock. On top of that, each was lucky enough to have a pension. They wanted to know if they had enough to retire on, and during my meetings with each of them, my answer was an exuberant "Yes, but . . ." Yes, they had enough to retire on, but from an investing standpoint, they needed to diversify their portfolios to reduce the risk should their company's stock price take a hit.

One of these gentlemen, Ben, loved what I was saying. After our meeting, he went right home and sold his entire position in the company's stock. Two weeks later, he waltzed into my office and announced he was going to give notice of his retirement at the age of sixty, and that he wanted me to manage his retirement account, reallocating his funds and building him a well-diversified portfolio. Tobias was a different story. He felt uncomfortable selling his company's stock. "It's going up every month," he said. "I'll have to think about it." A few months later, he came back in and wagged his finger at me. "My stock holdings today used to be worth $1.2 million, and now they're worth $1.3 million. If I had listened to you, it would have cost me $100,000." I congratulated him on the extra hundred grand but cautioned that he might want to look at it from a different perspective. Yes, there was an extra $100,000 in his account, but to gain it, he had been exposing himself to risk. How would he have felt if the market had moved in the opposite direction? "Look, Jill," he said, "I'm a big boy—I can take it."

A couple more months went by before Tobias contacted me again. By this time, his account was worth $1.4 million. "Sorry," he said, "I've decided I'm not going to work with you. You would have cost me $200,000."

"Well, not really," I said, "because you would have made $50,000 had I invested the money for you."

"Okay, fine," he said, "you would have cost me $150,000. I'm still not going to work with you. I'm not selling the stock, and you know, I decided I don't want to retire. I like the money I'm making." He reminded me that he was a few years younger than his buddy Ben.

Again, you can probably see where this story is going. In March 2000, the tech bubble burst. Almost overnight, the company stock plummeted. A couple of years later, I asked Ben how his friend Tobias had made out. (Schadenfreude alert!) Had he sold his stock before the crash? Unfortunately, he hadn't. Whereas Ben's account had largely held its value and was worth $1.3 million, Tobias had sold the stock when it had lost almost $1 million in value. His account was now worth $400,000.

Ben was enjoying his retirement, secure in the knowledge that he had enough money. But Tobias now had no choice but to work.

He wound up staying at his job for another nine years—much longer than he had envisioned the last time I'd spoken with him—retiring at the age of sixty-eight. His one dumb move had cost him about $1 million and almost a decade of his life.

Failing to buy the right insurance or to invest wisely are just two of the many dumb mistakes that smart people make. I've seen renowned heart surgeons, well-regarded attorneys, distinguished scientists, and senior corporate managers all commit blunders that have you shaking your head and saying *"Huh!?"* The costs of these mistakes can be staggering: lost homes, broken lives, abandoned dreams. One friend of mine wouldn't exercise stock options he had received from an employer because he "didn't want to pay the taxes" on them, which were about $100,000. No amount of cajoling could convince him to change his mind. When the financial crisis hit, his company's stock sank, and by the time his options expired, they became worthless. His pointless delay cost him and his family $750,000 of their nest egg, although he was right—he didn't have to pay Uncle Sam a dime.

Then there was the elderly couple I met who purchased a reverse mortgage they didn't need, costing their heirs tens of thousands of dollars. Or the doctor who despite my ardent advice refused to get a will, and whose family upon his death faced an avoidable tax bill of over a million dollars. His heirs had to sell the family home on Martha's Vineyard because of his stubbornness—an outcome he hardly would have imagined or desired.

Even if you don't suffer a financial disaster, chances are you're either wasting your hard-earned money, missing out on a significant chunk of wealth you might otherwise be accumulating, or subjecting yourself or your loved ones to unnecessary emotional distress. Ever wonder why you're not as well off as others around you with comparable careers, or why you can't seem to achieve the financial goals you've set for yourself, despite all your focus and effort? It might be bad luck, but it could also stem from a dumb decision you've made, despite your high IQ, your graduate degrees, or your brilliance in other areas.

Please know that I'm not casting judgment. As I'll describe later in this book, I once made an epic investment blunder that left me ashamed and embarrassed (even to this day, it's hard to talk about it). During the early 2000s, as the stock market recovered from the dot-com bust, I was too slow to invest in riskier growth companies. I waited for "just the right moment" to jump in, thinking I was smart enough to know when that was. Guess what? I wasn't. I made only 12 percent on my money that year, while the market rose over 20 percent.

I've had a lot of time to think about why I made this particular mistake, and why many other smart people continue to make similar ones as well. As I now realize, I fell prey to my emotions and, in particular, my aversion to risk. I'm a conservative investor, always have been. I owe it to a childhood experience I had watching my dad lose a *ton* of money. He was an options trader on the floor of the American Stock Exchange (AMEX), and he liked to place some crazy bets. In 1982, when U.S. Steel bought Marathon Oil, one such bet came to bite him, and my dad's entire trading account was wiped out—and then some. I'll never forget looking through the crack in my parents' bedroom door and watching my father cry as he recounted to my mother what had happened. When they emerged from the bedroom, Dad announced to my sister and me, "Girls, we're going to California with the last $5,000 in my account." And we did. Fittingly, it rained for the entire ten days we drove down the Pacific Coast Highway.

Scary childhood experiences like this will shape your relationship with money and color specific decisions, quite often for the worse. But more broadly, we're all emotional animals, not just rational ones, and hence prone to financial miscues. Randy's "Oh, shit" moment arose because he felt invulnerable and couldn't imagine that something bad could ever happen to him. Tobias's million-dollar disaster hinged on his assumption that his company's dazzling financial performance would continue indefinitely, an assumption that in turn was a result of his unwavering—and unrealistic—faith in his company and in the massive bull market in tech stocks. He was also egotistical, blind to flaws in his logic, even when his well-meaning Aunt Jill (as some of my radio and podcast listeners call me) pointed them out.

In most cases, two emotions in particular hamstring us when it comes to money: fear and greed. We're afraid of losing what we have, and we're eager to have much more. Further, we have any number of built-in cognitive biases that cloud our judgment, convincing us that down is up and left is right. There is confirmation bias—our tendency to seek out information that bears out what we already believe; or restraint bias, our inclination to think we can resist a temptation, when really we can't; or optimism bias, our tendency to engage in wishful thinking. Such biases can lead us to make a whole slew of bonehead decisions that seem innocuous at the time but that cost us dearly. I've seen people do it—again and again and again.

At this point, I've provided financial planning and investment advice to individuals for almost three decades. I've talked with thousands of people. Like a psychologist, I've seen just about every dumb thing that smart people do. And on far too many occasions, I've shed tears with people (both literally and figuratively) upon hearing about the consequences of their mistakes. But unlike a shrink, who attempts to guide and encourage people as they explore their psychological tendencies, I have had the opportunity to tell these folks exactly what to do. Beyond my clients, I have provided financial advice to the masses by hosting a weekly call-in radio show, by appearing on CBS News, by hosting a podcast, and by writing newspaper columns and blogs.

For a long time, I thought that this on-air work would be

enough, allowing me to get the word out and help save individuals from needless suffering due to their financial behavior. But a decade has passed since the Great Recession of 2007–2009, and I'm still hearing smart people ask the same questions and make the same tragic mistakes. I'm still seeing lives ruined and retirements postponed because otherwise intelligent people are stymied by their emotions and biases, and because a few unscrupulous actors in the financial industry actively exploit these blind spots. I've concluded that we all must have an honest conversation about the most common financial missteps, so that we can avoid them or get back on track if we've made them.

If you've suffered through one of those horrible "Oh, shit" moments with your money—whether it's investing, purchasing a home, planning for retirement, or something else—please don't despair. You're not the only one messing up—lots of people do it. Also, please know that there's no shame in making a financial mistake. The only shame is in failing to learn from it and in not taking steps to avoid other dumb moves.

In the following chapters, I'll explore a series of surprising errors that smart people make with their money—mistakes that could cost you tens, even hundreds of thousands of dollars, not to mention untold sleepless nights. I'll unpack these mistakes, explain the underlying psychology that might be causing you to make them, and offer guidance on how to do better. At the end of these chapters, I'll provide you with simple tools to help you avoid these mistakes with a minimum amount of effort. What I don't do is provide a comprehensive guide to personal money management. Such books exist, and you should consult them if you'd like to take a deeper look at topics like mortgages, investing, estate planning, and so on. My goal here is simply to explore mistakes that otherwise intelligent people make. Sifting through dozens upon dozens of such miscues, I've identified the most costly and common ones and collected them in a slender, easy-to-read volume. If you can mitigate just one dumb error, and prevent some others, then this book will have been well worth your time.

Some popular money books offer get-rich-quick advice or dumbed-down financial guidance. Not this one. As I've found, most people prefer straight talk, usable money tips that help you navigate your financial journey, with common sense and an insider's perspective on how to manage your emotions. I've also found that as Julie Andrews says, "Just a spoonful of sugar makes the medicine go down," so we're going to spend just a little time laughing at our own folly. How could we not? We're all flawed human beings who make terrible choices (hello from the woman with two failed marriages under her belt!), including financial ones. And while these choices hurt, many of them are also pretty damn funny, so long as you can come to accept your flaws and forgive yourself for them.

That's what I've done. And that's what I wish for you. Are you humble enough to admit your vulnerability to emotional traps? Are you flexible enough to change your ways? Then let's get started! Thirteen chapters. Thirteen "dumb things." Some much-needed chicken soup for your financial soul. And a heckuva lot of fun.

THE DUMB THINGS
SMART PEOPLE DO
WITH THEIR MONEY

You Buy Financial Products That You Don't Understand

Let's say you've got $800,000 in a low-cost retirement account, and you're also lucky enough to have a pension. One day, your investment guy calls you up, invites you to golf, and suggests that you put your $800,000 nest egg into a variable annuity. As he explains, this is a "unique" kind of investment that resembles an IRA but offers special tax benefits. You will pay no tax while your money grows. Later in life, when you're at or near retirement and in a lower tax bracket, you can take withdrawals and pay Uncle Sam his due. Not only that: You'll have many options for accessing the money and for creating an income stream later on when you need it. If the stock market falls, you'll be protected, and you'll be able to leave the money to your heirs in a seamless fashion. Your very own, personal pension! Sounds great, right?

You drain that Arnold Palmer you're drinking, and without a second thought you tell your adviser to transfer all of your money into that shiny new annuity. You go about enjoying your life, confident that your nest egg is not only secure, but growing. A year later, you glance at your account statement and receive an unpleasant surprise: It's got only $786,000 in it. How could that be? The market is up, yet your account is down.

You look into it, and discover that this annuity your golfing buddy/adviser recommended actually came with some pretty serious fees—about 2 to 3 percent a year, as compared with a quarter of a percent for the plain vanilla index mutual funds in your IRA. An annuity might have made sense if the money flowing into it came from a taxable account, but in your case, the money was already coming from a tax-advantaged retirement account. What you did, in effect, was pay for a tax benefit you didn't need. You took money from a retirement account that had relatively low fees and plopped it into an expensive retirement product you didn't understand. Not such a great move after all. In fact, a $14,000 mistake.

Smart people get snookered into financial products they don't understand all the time. It's not just annuities, but any number of other products. Smart people sink a hefty portion of their savings into gold bars or coins, thinking it's a "safe" investment that will allow them to ride out tumultuous markets. The truth is that precious metals are volatile investments, can lose value, and are hard to get out of if prices fall. Smart people take out reverse mortgages, looking forward to a beautiful little income stream coming to them every month from the equity they've built up in their homes. A few years later, when they realize they need to move, they face high interest and fees they hadn't expected. In some cases, because they and their heirs didn't understand the fine print, they lose their ability to pass on property to the next generation. And then there's hedge funds. Those big boys sound sexy, and they are—for billionaires and institutional investors who have access to the 10 percent of hedge funds that actually perform well. The rest of us schmucks would do much better sticking with our boring old index funds.

In this chapter, I'll probe the hidden downsides to these financial products, parsing some of the small print you might not have taken the time to read, and frankly, that your broker might have hoped you'd gloss over. I'll also present a sophisticated method you can use to prevent yourself from ever again buying a financial product that you don't understand. You won't learn about this method anywhere else—not at Wharton, not at Stanford, not at Harvard. Are you ready? It's called . . . *asking more questions.* I know, obvious, but so many smart people don't do it! We spend more time researching our upcoming vacations, or a restaurant for next Saturday's date night, or the organic, dry-aged, grass-fed steak we eat at said restaurant than we do the financial products on which our futures depend. If you value your money, you'll start asking tough questions right now—not because you want to, but because it's in your own best interest.

NO MORE LOOKING FOR MR. GOLDBAR

Let's talk gold. On late-night television, you'll often see commercials with faded actors hawking gold coins or bars. The first thing you say to yourself is: "Is that guy from *Knots Landing* still alive?" Then you hear him warn that it's a dangerous world out there, and you need a way to keep your money safe, no matter what might transpire. Buy gold coins and gold bars, and you can rest easy. If the stock market crashes, gold will still retain its value.

Do me a favor: Don't make investment decisions late at night from the guy on *Knots Landing*. Just don't. And this comes from a former gold trader, so pay attention!

Gold *sounds* like a reasonable investment. We do need to protect ourselves against unstable financial markets, and particularly against inflationary periods when money loses its value and prices rise. For generations, our forebears have turned to assets like land, oil, and gas, or commodities for such protection, since the prices of these assets rise as prices in general rise. Of all these assets, gold has long reigned as the ultimate "safe harbor." Entire countries used to link their currencies to the price of gold, or as it's known, the "gold standard." So why not put some sizable portion of your nest egg into gold?

I'll tell you why. Gold isn't nearly as "safe" as it seems. All commodities are volatile. Gold can stagnate or lose value over long stretches of time. In fact, over the past two centuries, there have been many five- or ten-year periods in which gold proved a poor investment. The period 2012–2017, for instance, saw its share of economic difficulties, as well as of traumatic moments when the stock market lost value. Politicians in the United States took us to the edge of disaster with their negotiations over raising the debt ceiling, the eurozone nearly collapsed under the weight of the Greek debt crisis, British voters elected to leave the European Union, and as recently as the beginning of 2016, stock markets corrected early in the year as crude oil plunged on worries that the global economy was slowing. Despite these vicissitudes, the S&P 500 rose 82 percent during this period, while gold was down 47 percent. If you had listened to the doomsayers and plowed, say, half your portfolio into gold, you would have gotten shellacked!

On a number of levels, gold is just so *wrong*. Unlike stocks or bonds, gold doesn't create income by paying interest or a dividend (nor do other precious metals, like copper and silver). On that basis alone, most investment pros steer clients away from it. If you want to protect against market instability, you're better off buying an exchange-traded fund (ETF) that places bets against the stock market, so that when it falls, you make money. Wealthy investors with large portfolios can also buy options to protect against dangerous markets. If inflation is your concern, any of us can buy inflation-protected bonds, like I Bonds or Treasury Inflation-Protected Securities (TIPS). There just isn't any need to invest in gold.

If despite my dire warnings you absolutely must buy gold, do yourself a favor and limit your exposure to less than 5 percent of your total portfolio. And for goodness' sake, stay away from bars or coins. Infomercial pitches for these products have *big* commissions built into them. There is insurance and storage to pay for (what, you think you're going to store that gold in your mattress?). Also, if you ever want to sell your gold, you likely won't get the actual market price for it, since it's not easy for ordinary people to access large secondary markets like the New York Stock Exchange or a commodities exchange, where financial products based on gold are bought and sold. You own the physical metal, also known as the "underlying," not a financial product based on that product. So instead of trying to get the competitive best bid for your gold, all you can do is walk into a dealer's place of business and try to unload it. It all adds up to a seriously bad deal.

Invest instead in a gold exchange traded fund. An ETF is an investment that looks like a mutual fund, because it is a pooled investment. Yet it trades more like a stock, because you can sell an ETF at any point during the trading day, rather than having to settle for the end-of-the-day price, as most open-end mutual funds require. The first-ever gold ETF ("GLD") was introduced in 2004, and it allowed investors to participate in the gold market by purchasing a pooled asset that reflected the price performance of gold bullion. If you buy into a gold ETF, you can't redeem your shares for a pirate's trove of gold bullion. On the other hand, you escape the underlying costs and logistical problems that come with owning a precious metal. As an alternative to an ETF, you could also invest in a gold stock (equity in a company that mines precious metals). At least you can sell those easily if they are losing their value. But remember, no more than a smidge of your portfolio.

Look, as I said, I'm a former gold trader, and I still wouldn't touch the stuff. Did I mention that gold saved my step-grandmother's life? Valerie, or "Valley" as we called her, grew up in Hungary after

World War I. During the early 1940s, when the Nazis were marching into her village, her mother handed her a pile of gold jewelry and said, "Hide this, and get out of town!" Hawking the gold bit by bit, Valley managed to buy her way out of Europe, making it to London and then Australia before migrating to the United States after marrying my grandfather. Gold protected her during tumultuous times. But that doesn't mean it offers the best protection for you. Back away. It's usually a crappy investment.

WHY YOU SHOULD PROBABLY BACK OUT OF THAT REVERSE MORTGAGE, TOO

While you're up watching late-night television (probably because you're worried about money and can't sleep), you might also spot commercials for another financial product that has ensnared its share of intelligent people: reverse mortgages.

Let's say you own your home outright or carry just a small mortgage balance. Reverse mortgages, available to homeowners over the age of sixty-two and overseen by the Department of Housing and Urban Development, will pay you a portion of your equity either in a lump sum or monthly installments. You can access your equity now, without having to sell your home. Down the road, when you die or no longer live in your home, the bank recoups its money (usually by the sale of the house), as well as interest and finance charges.

Reverse mortgages can work well for older people who might have accumulated significant equity in their home, but don't have a lot of other retirement income to draw on month to month. With a reverse mortgage, you don't need to move out of your home and find something cheaper; you can stay and age in place. When death comes knockin' at your door, your home is sold, and your heirs get whatever equity remains in the house after the lender is paid off.

So, what's the problem? A couple of things. Sandy Jolley, a consumer advocate and national expert on reverse mortgages, can tell you hundreds of horror stories of consumers preyed upon by predatory lenders who assess extravagant fees or go to extraordinary (and sometimes illegal) lengths to foreclose on borrowers' homes. Even when lenders are behaving reasonably well (and the industry has been cleaning itself up of late), many borrowers or their heirs suffer massive losses because they don't understand the complex terms and requirements of these loans.

One Florida woman, whom I'll call Bonnie, learned that her recently deceased mother had taken out a reverse mortgage on her home.[1] Bonnie's mother had intended for Bonnie to pay back the loan upon her death and keep the property in the family. Bonnie wanted to do so, but she didn't realize that she had to file papers and become formally recognized as a legal representative of her mother's estate before the bank would even tell her the loan's outstanding balance. According to the terms of the reverse mortgage, Bonnie had exactly six months after her mother's death to pay off the loan if she wanted to keep the house. Becoming a legal representative was a costly process that took months. Once Bonnie had finally taken care of that and the bank told her the payoff amount, Bonnie had to apply for a loan herself in order to pay it off, since she didn't have the money. The loan didn't come through within the six-month period, and the bank foreclosed on her mother's home. There was nothing Bonnie could do.

Besides running afoul of the terms and requirements, many people take out reverse mortgages without analyzing whether they really should stay in their homes. What if you suffer a health setback and wind up needing expensive care? Would your income stream with the reverse mortgage suffice, or would you still need to move?

Maybe your home truly is more than you can afford. Or if it

isn't, maybe you'll want to move anyway so that a relative can care for you. If you want to extract yourself from a reverse mortgage after just a few years, you can, but you'll have to repay what the bank has already lent you, and you'll incur thousands of dollars in fees and penalties.

Before taking out a reverse mortgage, slow down and do your homework. To avoid a situation like Bonnie's, Sandy recommends talking to a qualified estate attorney about whether or not you need a trust for your home and other assets. She also recommends creating a detailed financial plan for yourself, seeking counsel from an adviser you trust, and exploring other options, like selling or leasing your home or refinancing your current mortgage (see her website, www.elderfinancialterrorism.com). Reverse mortgages are complex—pages and pages of small print. Make sure you understand fully what you're getting into, and why it makes sense—or doesn't.

CHOP DOWN THAT HEDGE FUND

One summer day in 2005, Jim, a prospective client, strolled into my office and gushed about the $300,000 of non-retirement assets he had invested in a hedge fund. Jim might have thought he was impressing me. "Ooh, a hedge fund," he probably expected me to say. Hedge funds are investment vehicles that wealthy people (the SEC has a special designation for them—they're called "accredited investors") and institutional investors traditionally use to "hedge" against losses in the main portions of their portfolios. Managers of hedge funds can purchase pretty much any asset inside the fund, including complex derivatives (remember those from the financial crisis?) that accelerate the bets managers are taking. These managers claim that their intricate strategies, based on sophisticated algorithms, will deliver superior performance.

About ten to fifteen years ago, these funds changed, no longer marketing themselves primarily as "hedges," but rather as exclusive opportunities to extract dazzling returns. The masses put their money into mutual funds or bonds. Those in the know gained special access to a private hedge fund managed by a genius investor.

"You know," I told my prospect, "hedge funds seem attractive, but what if you want to get your money out fast?" Unlike mutual funds, hedge funds have complex rules about when you can withdraw money. You can't just sell and receive a check three days later.

"Oh, I'm not worried," he said.

He never did become a client of mine. But a few years later, in 2008, we happened to run into each other at the grocery store. "Oh, my God," he said, "I should have listened to you. I just got clobbered!" His $300,000 investment lost two-thirds of its value, leaving him with only $100,000 in his account. He saw it happening, but couldn't get out. When he finally was able to access his money, his account was worth only $80,000. Panicking, he decided to close his account and put his money in cash rather than waiting to see if the fund's value would rise again. Because his money was in cash, he missed out on a portion of the upside as the broader market rose again.

If this guy had invested in a plain vanilla portfolio of mutual funds, like the rest of us, his account's value probably would have eroded as well—it was 2008, after all. But at least he would have been able to access the money. He probably wouldn't have panicked and put his money into cash, a move that cost him thousands of dollars. And quite possibly, he wouldn't have lost so much to begin with. Despite their aura of sophistication, hedge funds *just aren't that great.* Only about 10 percent of hedge funds significantly outperform the S&P 500. The rest do about as well or worse. And try getting into that golden 10 percent. You can't— they're usually restricted to billionaires and institutional investors.

Even if you happen to own a hedge fund that generates income, the IRS might treat a portion of the income as ordinary income rather than capital gains, taxing it at a higher rate. In addition, hedge funds levy high fees that eat into their returns. They charge "two and twenty"—2 percent a year just to own the fund, plus 20 percent of any returns the fund earns. Nice work if you can get it, right?

Hedge funds are like guys and gals on Tinder: Their profile pics look totally hot, but spend five minutes with them, and they fail to impress. Warren Buffett issued a famous challenge to hedge fund managers back in 2007, offering to bet each one $1 million that his or her portfolio of hedge funds couldn't outperform the S&P 500 over ten years, with the winner donating the $1 million to charity.[2] Guess how many hedge fund managers took the bet? One guy, from a firm called Protégé Partners. When the bet concluded at the end of 2017, the hedge fund portfolio had delivered a dismal 2.2 percent compounded annual return. The S&P 500? A 7.1 percent annual gain over ten years. That was great news for Girls Inc. of Omaha, Nebraska, the recipient of the $1 million proceeds.

FEAR: THE ENEMY OF UNDERSTANDING

Why do so many intelligent people get lured into money-losing hedge funds, reverse mortgages, or gold? For that matter, why do they buy into other potentially dangerous financial products that they don't understand, like floating rate funds or junk bond funds?* Part of the problem is that we take advice from the wrong people— a "dumb thing" we'll discuss in the next chapter. But another part of the problem is that most financial products are boring, and

---

* Many smart people buy these funds as alternatives to savings accounts, thinking that they're just as safe and that they'll earn somewhat higher returns—maybe an extra couple of percentage points. That's what salespeople often tell them. In fact, floating rate and bond funds are not just as safe as savings accounts. Floating rate and bond funds can and often do lose value. Those higher returns come with higher risk.

some can be quite complex. The "simple" math on an investment or insurance policy is not so simple when it comes buried in a hundred-page disclosure document, known as a prospectus. And most smart people are busy. We don't want to spend more than a few minutes perusing such documents. Admit it—would you actually read all of the closing documents associated with a home purchase financed with a mortgage? I sure wouldn't! What so many of us don't realize is that this lack of oversight leaves us vulnerable, in many cases, to the twin emotions of greed and fear. Your broker might assure you that an annuity is safer than investing in the stock market. But when you really analyze it, is an annuity the smarter move? Quite possibly, no.

If you ask me, there's a bit more at play here than just boredom. As Professor John Eastwood of York University has noted, two sorts of people tend to become bored. You have your adrenaline junkies who are constantly seeking out novelty and aren't receiving the stimulation they need. On the opposite end of the spectrum, you find that highly fearful people also tend to become bored. To avoid pain, they close themselves off from the world, relegating themselves to environments that might offer more safety and comfort, but that also come to seem quite dull.[3]

I've long suspected that fear lurks under the surface when people purport to be "bored" by their finances. They're afraid, perhaps, that they won't be able to achieve their financial dreams. They don't want to face financial "reality." And so, they wall themselves off, putting up a barrier and calling it "boredom." As I've seen repeatedly as a financial planner, when you take the time to explain financial matters and address people's fears, money suddenly ceases to be so "boring" to them.

To avoid Dumb Mistake #1, overcome your boredom and spend more time reading the fine print. Don't hate me for saying that—you know you should! And then take it further—ask tough, critical questions. So many smart people hesitate to ask questions of financial salespeople and advisers, even though they behave quite aggressively in other areas of their life. Fear plays a role here, too. Many smart people are quite accomplished in their careers. They're used to being the experts, and when it comes to a subject about which they know little, they can fear looking ignorant or foolish. It's psychically easier for them to nod their heads and pretend they understand rather than risk embarrassment. Have you ever done this? I know I have!

Some of us, especially those of us with tinges of gray around our temples, might also fear offending a broker or other financial professional by asking "too many questions." The idea of expertise has taken quite a beating lately, with some observers even proclaiming its death.[4] But many of us still tend to venerate experts and shrink from questioning their judgment. My dad was like that. Throughout his life, he had always been a cynical, rebellious, critical person—some might say "a pain in the ass." You know that parent who hollers at the referee for making a stupid call at his kid's basketball game? That was my dad. Indeed, when I was in junior high, Dad got kicked out of a gym during one of my games for just that.

But in 2013, when he was in the hospital with a serious illness, he refused to ask the doctors any questions. On one occasion, after he had spent almost two months in and out of intensive care, his doctor proposed giving him yet another slate of invasive tests. When I politely inquired whether the testing was really necessary, my father shot me an icy look. Later, after the doctor had left, he ripped me a new one. "What were you doing just now?" he said. "How dare you question him?" In his eyes, I had committed an act of gross disrespect.

During my career as a financial planner, I often wished clients would ask me more questions, not fewer. By asking questions, clients weren't disrespecting me. Rather, they were implicitly accepting a portion of the responsibility for the decision-making. I wanted clients to feel good about the decisions *we* were making together, and if they didn't ask questions, I had a harder time addressing their fears or correcting their misconceptions. As *Wall Street Journal* columnist Jason Zweig explains, "There's no reason to be afraid of asking a lot of questions. Good financial advisers have nothing to hide and welcome the opportunity to tell you everything you want to know. Dozens of advisers have told me over the years that they wish clients would ask more questions, not fewer, before signing on."[5]

If they don't ask questions, smart people risk fooling themselves into thinking they understand a financial topic when they really possess only superficial knowledge of it. In late 2017, I was talking to a room of senior television producers about the Republican tax legislation then pending in Congress. These producers were incredibly smart people—they had attended top colleges and grad schools and earned hundreds of thousands of dollars a year. Yet some of them were reluctant to ask me questions about specific parts of the legislation. They nodded their heads and said, "Yeah, we understand what that is." Suspecting that they didn't, I challenged them to explain these features of the legislation to me. Silence. They really didn't know. They thought they knew, but they didn't understand the legislation in any detail or nuance. They knew enough to be dangerous, but not enough to make smart financial decisions.

Please, please, please: Ask more questions. Familiarize yourself with the relevant facts—all of them. You might understand that an annuity is an investment vehicle sold by insurance companies that allows you to inject money up front. You might know that the insurance company invests these funds for you, paying you an income stream down the road, in effect allowing you to create your own private pension. But make sure you also know the details about how much the product costs, how long you have to wait to access the money, and whether it's cheaper or more expensive than other options out there. If you do, you'll discover that a product that might have seemed fairly straightforward is actually quite a bit more complicated, in ways that disadvantage you. You'll also quite possibly discover that instead of paying a lot of money for that annuity, you could replicate the features of the product yourself at a much lower cost by opening up a retirement account and investing it in a diversified portfolio of index mutual funds.

An adviser discussing a financial product with you might not cue you into the details if you don't ask. This isn't necessarily because they're shady. An insurance company representative selling you an annuity might believe wholeheartedly in her product. But as a salesperson, she's trained to focus on its advantages, not on providing a critical analysis of it. Yes, some salespeople do communicate the downsides of their products, but you can't count on them to do that. You've got to step up and ask questions, so that you can elicit facts that might not be especially convenient for your adviser to relate, but that are essential for you to know.

If you're not working with a salesperson, get in the habit of asking questions *of yourself*. Let's say you've got half of your non-retirement savings invested in the stock market. You know that diversified investing makes sense, so you want to put the other half of your money into bonds. You look up the returns for intermediate-term bonds and you find they're pretty low—only 2.25 percent, say. You scroll down the list of bond offerings, and you find a high-yield bond fund that's paying 5.75 percent. "Wow," you say, "that's a bond fund, and it's paying 3.5 percent more. I'll take that!" The question to ask yourself here is: "Why am I getting a higher return?" If you dig around, you'll find that the reason is that this bond fund is higher-risk. By purchasing that bond fund, you're essentially loaning your money to corporations that have been deemed risky borrowers. If these corporations default, you could lose some of your money—even though this is supposed to be the "safe" part of your portfolio.

Bond funds are *not* all created equal. Junk bonds act a lot more like stocks when the shit hits the fan in the economy. Ask questions, and you'll know!

THE BIG FIVE

There are five questions you absolutely *must* ask anyone who is trying to sell you a financial product, including yourself:

Question #1: How much will this financial product cost me?

Most financial products either require that you pay an up-front commission or that you pay an ongoing fee. For a mutual fund, you might pay an up-front commission of as much as 5.75 percent, as well as an annual management fee of up to 1 percent. Now you see why hedge funds are so ludicrously expensive—the annual fee can be at least twice as high, or more! The difference between fees of 1 percent and 3 percent might not seem so great, but it can mean thousands of dollars each year. Saving on those fees is like amassing risk-free returns. If you're working with a broker, make sure you ask how much he personally makes by selling you the financial product. If he's incentivized to sell you some products over others, you need to know that. This leads us to the second question.

Question #2: What are the alternatives to this financial product?

To get the best deal on financial products, you have to comparison-shop and aggressively explore alternatives. These might be alternatives within a class of product, but can also be different kinds of financial products that could help you better achieve your goals. It might even be possible for you to achieve your goals without buying a financial product. If you want to age in place, for instance, a reverse mortgage might be for you, but as Sandy Jolley points out, you might be able to achieve your objective by refinancing, or by forgoing a loan entirely and renting out your spare bedroom. If you're working with a financial professional, ask him or her the cost for each alternative, as well as how much they personally are making on each.

Question #3: How easy is it to get my money out of this investment? And if I have to do so, what fees or penalties would I pay?

Some financial products tie up your money for a long time—you can't get at it at all, or without paying a steep penalty. That might be fine, but you need to understand how "liquid" a financial product is and analyze it within the context of your larger financial plan. In most cases, you'll want a mixture of liquid assets (such as an emergency cash fund) and longer-term investments that are harder to liquidate. Be realistic about your cash needs. If you think you might need the money you're investing, make sure the penalties or fees are not unduly steep.

Question #4: What tax consequences will this financial product carry for me?

To calculate an investment vehicle's total costs, you must understand how you will be taxed while owning it, and upon its sale. The last thing you want is to get hit with a hefty tax bill you never expected. This is obviously important with any transaction made outside of your retirement account. Imagine if you were smart or lucky enough to buy a winning investment in your brokerage account, and you quickly sold it to lock in the profits. If the sale took place within a year of purchase, you would owe Uncle Sam money, and the tax rate applied would correspond to your ordinary tax bracket. Now, how good was the after-tax return, given the risk you took to make it? Maybe not as good as you initially thought.

Question #5: What's the worst-case scenario I face with this financial product?

This is a great question, because in one stroke it helps you pierce all the happy-talk a salesperson might be sending your way. You've heard about the benefits of a product. Now ask about the most disastrous scenario you might face if the product doesn't work out as you'd hoped. Comparing worst-case scenarios across your array of options will give you a better idea of which one to choose.

It's not easy admitting that you don't understand a financial product, especially when you're used to performing well in other parts of your life. I get that. But look at it this way: The truth is the truth. You can "own" your lack of knowledge now, before you buy in, or you can own it later, once you've made a horrible mistake and have to pick up the pieces. Do your research. *Assume* that you don't know everything about a financial product, and look at the sales process as your opportunity to become educated. Be as engaged and as deliberate as you might be when making other big purchases, like a car or a house. After all, you'll be living with the consequences for years to come.

Once we admit we lack knowledge, we often rely on brokers,

insurance agents, certified financial planners, and other financial counselors to help us make decisions. And yet, as we'll see in the next chapter, not all financial advice is created equal. Some operators out there have a legal obligation to give you advice that serves your interests, while others don't. Despite their intelligence, smart people often neither understand this distinction nor realize when they should pay for solid advice. As a result, they all too often wind up taking advice from the wrong people. And it costs them dearly.

You Take Financial Advice from the Wrong People

My friend Mike, an orthopedic surgeon who practices in New York City, asked me how he could best save for his kids' college education. Easy, I told him—open a 529 plan. All fifty states offer these special educational savings accounts, which provide great tax incentives. Here's how they work: When you put money into a 529, it's protected from federal, and usually state, income taxes. Later, when you access the money for qualified expenses (which now includes up to $10,000 of tuition for K through 12 schooling as well as college and graduate school), there's no tax due—it's like a Roth IRA for education! In most cases, you can sign up as a nonresident, but some plans offer special tax incentives to state residents, and some allow salespeople to enroll consumers and charge commissions (as opposed to others that allow you to buy into the plan directly through the state, bypassing commissions). At the time of my conversation with Mike, New York State offered a particularly strong plan, so I suggested he try that one. "Well," he said, "I don't have a New York plan. My adviser told me to get a Rhode Island plan."

"He did?" I said. "That makes no sense. Rhode Island's plan sucks, especially if you're out-of-state." I explained that if he were to use the New York State plan, he and his wife, Mandy, could get a state income tax deduction of up to $10,000 a year, which given their tax bracket would save them $1,300 each year that they contributed to the New York 529 plan. "Think of what you could do with that extra money. You could plow it into a supplemental retirement plan for you and Mandy. Over time, you'll sock away a ton more and maybe even be able to quit your job sooner." In addition, the investments in Rhode Island's plan were inferior and costlier.

He fell silent. "Well," he finally said, "I'm sure there's a reason my guy told me to do it."

I nodded. "I'll tell you the reason. Your guy gets a commission if he sells you a Rhode Island plan. If he had told you what was best for you—buying a 529 directly from New York State—he can't get one." I went on. "Not for nothing, but I suggest you get out of your Rhode Island plan and transfer to New York. I'd get my tax deduction if I were you."

Mike ignored my advice. In his mind, acknowledging that his adviser was screwing him would also mean acknowledging that he himself was making a dumb mistake. So, rather than acknowledge this misstep and take steps to remedy it, Mike felt better pretending it didn't exist.

Many smart people make the mistake my orthopedic surgeon friend did: taking financial advice from someone who is trying, first and foremost, to sell you something that will make him or her money, rather than help you. It's an easy mistake to make. We might be doing business with insurance brokers or investment advisers who seem knowledgeable and likeable. They might be old friends of ours, or come highly recommended by people we trust. What we don't realize is that many of these professionals lack any legal responsibility to serve our best interests. And that's a problem.

Not long ago, after my friends Kim and Peter had their first child, I advised them that they needed life insurance. They decided to buy it from a childhood friend of Kim's whom they wanted to "help out." Two weeks later, they called, giddy with excitement. They had bought insurance—wasn't I happy for them?

I sure was, until I heard that they'd bought a fancy whole life policy. A simple term life insurance with $1 million in coverage would have cost them $700 a year. The whole life policy they bought cost them *$8,000* a year. That more expensive policy might have made sense if Kim and Peter had needed a way to save more for retirement, or if they had needed to keep the policy for their "whole lives." In addition to providing insurance, the type of policy they purchased offered what is called permanent coverage, providing a death benefit as well as the chance to accumulate money inside the policy. But as it stood, Kim and Peter weren't even maxing out their contributions to their employers' retirement accounts.

Why do you suppose their old friend got them into this policy? Do you think it might have had to do with the fat 80 percent commission he earned on the first year's premium? I think so! (Parenthetically, I almost drove into the median on the Long Island Expressway when they told me this story.) Taking advice from the wrong person would have cost them tens of thousands of dollars or more over a period of years, without giving them an added benefit. I urged them to cancel their new policy immediately, which they could do within a thirty-day window mandated by their state. They did, and bought term life insurance, which was the more appropriate and cheaper coverage. (Psst: State governments regulate insurance, which means that each state gives consumers a slightly different window in which they can change their minds. Ask your insurance salesman how much time you have for your "free look"—in most states it is ten to thirty days).

Kim and Peter were buying only one financial product. What if, in addition to insurance, their adviser told them that they needed help with their retirement investing? "Instead of funding your retirement plan at work," he might have said, "you should open up an IRA with us." Sounds good, but is it really? The retirement account at work might have cost them a half of a percent in annual expenses, while this new mutual fund inside of the IRA might have cost 2.5 percent up front, and then another 1 percent a year for as long as they kept the fund. If Kim and Peter were contributing, say, $5,000 a year toward their retirement, within a few short years they'd have funneled thousands into their broker's pocket for no good reason, except maybe to pay his country club dues. These kinds of shenanigans happen *all the time* to very smart people.

I'm certain your financial adviser is just lovely. He or she is probably great at explaining complex financial products to you in plain language, and more honest than Abraham Lincoln himself. But is this person legally obliged to give you advice that's in your best interest? If a conflict of interest arises, is he or she required to tell you about it?

When we visit a car dealership, we assume that the person selling us a car is trying to earn a commission, and we factor that information in when evaluating the advice we receive. When we visit a doctor's office, by contrast, we assume that this medical professional is acting first and foremost in our interests, not those of pharmaceutical companies, say, or insurers. That's because doctors work according to professional standards mandated by law. If your doctor isn't acting in your best interests, she could lose her license.

The good news is that there are tens of thousands of advisers out there who have to put your interests first. When we seek out financial advice, it's on us to determine which kind of adviser we're speaking with, and what we'll have to pay for their help. Let's take a moment to navigate this gray area together, so that you can consult the adviser who's right for you and know when you need to pay for professional advice. Because before I can help you address more specific money mistakes you might be making, I really do need to get you thinking about financial advice properly. If you're not, who knows what additional mistakes you'll make by virtue of confusing a sales pitch with good advice?

THE "OTHER" F-WORD

You know how people talk about pork as the "other white meat"? Well, it turns out there's something called the "other F-word." I'm talking about "fiduciary," as in "fiduciary responsibility." What in God's name is *that*? Well, lawyers and other professionals have codes of ethics that say they have to put your interests first. They are held to "fiduciary standards." Some financial professionals— the ones with designations like CFP, CFA, CPA-PFS, or CPA—have a fiduciary responsibility to act in your best interest, but many others don't. They're selling products for their firms, and they aren't obligated to disclose whether these products are in their client's best interests. Instead, they're bound by a "suitability" standard: to dispense advice that's "suitable" for their clients, but that might not be in the client's best interests.[1] A 529 account from Rhode Island that charges my friend Mike a commission and doesn't give him tax benefits might be "suitable," in the sense that it provides Mike with what he's seeking: a way to save for his kid's college. But it sure as heck isn't in his best interests.

Decades ago, before I became a financial adviser, the vast majority of advisers didn't formally adhere to the fiduciary standard. They didn't need to, because they almost always did right by their customers—it was a strongly entrenched social norm. During the 1980s and 1990s, brokerage firms experienced more financial pressure, and informal community standards of decency and professionalism eroded. Big firms began trying to sell people financial products they didn't need, and individual advisers discovered that they could make a good living selling you products that were pretty good for you but not the best. In that context, the notion of a premier class of advisers who would act in customers' best interests because they were legally obliged to do so took on new relevance.

After the financial crisis, fiduciary responsibility ballooned into an even bigger issue, because many consumers felt that advisers hadn't leveled with them about risky investments, or in general put their interests first. The Obama administration's Department of Labor proposed new regulations mandating that *all* advisers overseeing retirement accounts had to adhere to the fiduciary standard. Oh, how the financial industry hated that! They feared that if these regulations were adopted, they'd bear legal responsibility for the thousands of advisers who worked for them. Clients could sue them when they felt they'd received advice that was merely "suitable," but not in their best interests. In a flash, the big investment firms and insurance companies would no longer be able to sell expensive variable annuities inside of IRA accounts without a lengthy explanation of why that advice made sense. They would no longer be able to blithely recommend that an individual roll over an old employer's retirement account into an IRA, when the new employer's plan was the best alternative. When I spoke out on-air in support of the fiduciary requirement, the number of heated calls and nasty emails I fielded from the suitability suits was over the top. One critic, a commission-based insurance salesperson, suggested that I had "put the douche in fiduciary." I took that as high praise!

Not content to simply lob insults, the financial industry fought the new rules, spending millions on lobbying. They claimed that the regulations would hurt small investors with less than $250,000 in assets, because it would no longer make economic sense for large firms to serve them after factoring in the higher legal and compliance costs. I called bullshit on that. I said to an executive at one of these firms, "Are you telling me that you want to publicly state that you do *not* want to put your clients' interests first? What's all of that nonsense in your marketing materials?" He demurred. "Off the record, Jill . . . I'm not legally held to that marketing crap."

How would it possibly hurt small investors to put their interests first? That's what I wanted to know. In any case, it's a moot point. As of this writing, the U.S. government has announced that it is undoing the Obama-era regulation, backtracking on this consumer protection. I still firmly believe we need this protection, because so many people—including many very smart people—don't realize that they're receiving advice that's not in their best interest.

In November 2017, I moderated a focus group of investors on behalf of the Certified Financial Planner Board of Standards and the AARP that touched on fiduciary issues. It was stunning. Focus group participants were happy with their advisers, perceiving them as "honest," "trustworthy," and "informed." But when we dug into it, they didn't really know whether their advisers had fiduciary responsibilities. They just assumed it. One participant said it was a "given" that advisers were required to act in customers' best interests, and I had to remind her that it wasn't at all a given. Other participants agreed with me. "There are a lot of blind spots in this space; people just don't know what questions to ask," one said. Another remarked: "I really hope there are some kinds of regulations about this, because a lot of people are just uneducated about all of it."

That we don't have these regulations makes me want to drop an F-bomb—the old-fashioned, down-and-dirty kind. But I won't. Instead, I'll offer some advice that you should follow before getting into bed (not literally) with any financial adviser.[2] In addition to the questions presented in the last chapter, be sure to inquire about the following:

- Is your prospective adviser legally obliged to put your interests first at all times? Ask him or her this point-blank. If the answer is yes, get that in writing, and be prepared to pay a fee of some sort for the advice. Be sure to inquire how he or she earns that fee. Do you pay hourly, is the advice part of an annual management fee, or does he or she receive a commission?

- What professional certifications does your prospective adviser have? If she is certified by the CFP Board of Standards, is a member of the National Association of Personal Financial Advisors (NAPFA), is a CPA Personal Financial Specialist, or is a Chartered Financial Analyst, then she has fiduciary responsibility and also must meet some fairly strict standards regarding testing, continuing education, and experience levels. In the case of the NAPFA, advisers are prohibited from receiving compensation from companies for recommending their products, and they must submit the financial plans they create for peer review.

- Has your prospective adviser ever been sanctioned for unethical conduct, and is he or she properly licensed and registered? If a team of people is working on your account, meet with these individuals, inquire about other professionals with whom they do business (lawyers, accountants, and so on), and call these people to check on your prospective advisers.

- Would others stand to gain from any financial advice your prospective counselor would dispense? Your planner should disclose his or her conflicts of interest to you—and you should get it in writing. For example, if your planner wants to sell you bond funds or annuities, you want to know if he or she maintains a commercial relationship with the original suppliers of those bond funds or annuities.

You might feel squeamish asking pointed questions like this, but as we saw in the last chapter, you have to lose that hang-up.

This is your future at stake here. A good, upstanding financial adviser will understand your concern, and happily clarify his or her level of responsibility and professional certification. If your prospective adviser does take offense, that's a big warning sign. Stay away. If you discover that your financial guru is a salesperson, then you might still wish to work with that person, but be sure to subject anything she says to a whole new level of scrutiny. The burden is on you to research your options and verify whether your financial guru's advice is really worth taking. On the other hand, depending on your situation and needs, you might consider paying someone for *real* help.

WHEN THE LAME-ASS ADVISER IS YOU

You might be reading this and thinking that you don't want to pay anyone for their two cents on your financial situation. You're pretty smart, you think. Surely you can figure it out.

That reasoning often does make sense—many smart people who are currently paying for financial advice probably shouldn't be. But many should, and if they fail to, they're again falling victim to Dumb Thing #2. They're taking financial advice from the wrong people—themselves.

A friend of mine, Paolo, is a young guy (married, three kids) who earns a living running a small graphic design business. Not long ago, he experienced cash flow issues. Customers owed him money, but in the meantime, he had a $50,000 tax bill to pay. Rather than consult a financial adviser, he figured he'd handle the situation on his own. He had about $50,000 in an old retirement account. He withdrew the money, planning to pay it back within sixty days, once his customers paid him. If he did that, he wouldn't be subject to taxes, nor would he fork over 10 percent as a penalty for early withdrawal. (The IRS allows you to take money out of a retirement account, but you must put it into the same account or a different IRA within sixty days—and you get only one sixty-day rollover per year.)

You know what happened. Paolo couldn't repay the money in time, because his customers were late in paying him. With taxes at his high tax bracket and the penalty, he now owed the IRS an additional $25,000. What a dumb-ass move! He eventually came to me for advice on how to dig himself out of this mess. As I told him, if he had received professional financial advice sooner, he would have learned about other, more attractive options, like refinancing his home and using the proceeds to pay the taxes. Now, he'd have to refinance his house anyway, because his customers still hadn't paid him, and he owed the additional $25,000. In addition, he told me that he was communicating directly with the IRS, instead of through his accountant or attorney. Why handle that communication himself? He was only opening himself up to additional problems.

Another friend, Annie, made a similar mistake, with even greater consequences. The owner of two small coffee shops, she owed $80,000 in state sales tax, but this was during the recession, and she lacked the cash, so she decided simply not to pay. She figured that if she waited a couple of years, business would improve and she'd have the money then. With respect, what she didn't realize is that *not paying your taxes is about the worst fucking decision you can make*. Why? Because in addition to the taxes owed, fees and penalties also accrue.

Within a few years, Annie didn't owe just $80,000, but close to $150,000. To pay it, she eventually emptied her retirement account, with no illusions that she'd manage to replace the money at a later date. Again, really dumb move. Like Paolo, she owned a home—in fact, a very nice one. She didn't want to borrow against the equity, because the house was almost paid off. If she had paid for financial advice from a fiduciary, he or she would surely have run her through the math, convincing her that a mortgage, a home equity loan, or the outright sale of the home was far preferable to accruing penalties and fees, and then draining her IRA. Oh, and that adviser would have told her to *never* go radio silent on the IRS or any other taxation department. I mean never. Because they'll find you.

WHO SHOULD–AND SHOULDN'T–
GET PROFESSIONAL ADVICE

I hope I've scared at least a few of you die-hard DIYers to get professional advice if you need it. But how do you know if you need it? Let's first be clear about who *doesn't* need to pay for a financial adviser, and more specifically, a customized financial plan. In general, you don't need a customized plan if any one of the following holds true:

1. You have consumer debt, including credit card debt, student loans, and auto loans.
2. You aren't maxing out your retirement contributions (presuming that you are in a high enough tax bracket for that to make sense).
3. You don't have an emergency account with enough money in it to cover six to twelve months of expenses.

I can't tell you how many times people at work ask me for a referral to a financial adviser. I offer to sit down with them over a cup of coffee to hear what's going on. Nine times out of ten, they don't need to pay a financial adviser, because they haven't ticked off these Big Three, and I'm able to answer their questions within fifteen minutes. You need to take care of these three big-ticket items before you worry about doing anything fancy with your money. You can easily do each of these three on your own.

Some smart people who haven't yet tackled the Big Three will often consult financial advisers because they're having trouble reining in their spending, and they want the adviser to serve as a coach and hold their hand. Usually, that's excessive. Advisers might consult with you once or twice, helping you spot areas of runaway spending and sharing ideas about how to cut back. But most people don't need an adviser standing next to them every minute of the day. They need to learn to control their own spending, and beyond a point, it's not complicated: You track your purchases, and you say no more often. What, you need to ask me or anyone else whether you can buy a $20,000 engagement ring when you have $18,000 of credit card debt? Come on!

It's like hiring a personal trainer at the gym. An initial package of training sessions might help you organize your physical activity, and you might want to work out with trainers periodically to check in and recharge your motivation. But to get in better shape, you need to eat less and exercise on your own. In the same way, many smart people waste their money by soliciting financial advice that they really don't need.

There's an important caveat here: No matter where you are financially, be sure to seek out advice when you're confronting a complex and extraordinary situation in which you truly do lack expertise. When a taxing authority contacts you, for instance, get advice immediately. If you're negotiating your compensation with a new employer and the company gives you a choice between more stock or more cash, get advice. If you're inheriting a large sum of money and aren't sure what to do with it, get advice. If you're hounded by creditors or you're risking foreclosure on your house, get advice, preferably legal advice. As much as you think you might know how to handle these kinds of situations, you really don't. You've never done the relevant calculations. You don't know all of the legal, tax, or financial nuances. And most important, your emotions are likely to seep into the process, clouding your thinking. Overcome your ego or embarrassment or whatever other emotional wackiness might be hindering you, and get on the phone with a fiduciary.

HEED THE WARNING SIGNS

Let's say you've met the three criteria, but you're still not sure if you really need to consult an adviser. Nothing dramatic has happened in your financial life. The tax man isn't knocking on your door. You (sadly) haven't inherited $10 million from your long-lost uncle Sidney. You're clear on your goals, and you've got some financially savvy friends you can call on when you have specific questions. So, should you hook up with a fiduciary adviser and pay for a personalized financial plan?

Honestly, I can't say for sure. Everyone's situation is different. Sometimes you need financial advice because you're your own worst enemy: You think you know more than you do, and you have to come clean with yourself. Sometimes you need financial advice because you manage your money in a way that your romantic partner finds abhorrent, and the two of you need to get on the same page. Sometimes you need a financial adviser because you just don't want to do the work of managing your affairs. Of course, you could do it yourself, but you'd rather pay someone ten grand a year on your million-dollar portfolio, because you *can*. All of these reasons are legitimate, so long as you go in understanding what you're paying for.

My concern is that you get the help you need, but only if you really need and/or want it. To make sure you're getting the help you need, cast a critical eye on your life. Smart people tend to miss a number of warning signs that should send them racing to the nearest fiduciary. Let's run through these one by one:

- *You get a significant tax refund every year.* "Wow," you might say, "a tax refund every year—that's fantastic!" Not really. If you're getting tax refunds, you're prepaying your taxes throughout the year, which means Uncle Sam is benefiting from the use of that money, not you. You may be patriotic, but not that patriotic! Let's say you're getting a $10,000 tax refund. You could be earning, say, 5 percent on that money every year. Do the math. You're leaving money on the table, and because you're using money inefficiently in this way, you might be doing so in other ways. An adviser can help you sort it out.

- *You're obsessing about money.* If you're worrying about money more than once a week, and certainly if you're frequently losing sleep over it, something about your financial situation might be beyond your capacity to handle. Get professional help—and if not a financial adviser, then a shrink!

- *You and your spouse fight constantly about money.* You know those patterns of conflict spouses fall into: They fight and never reach a consensus—the same issue keeps cropping up. If that's happening to you in relation to retirement, saving for college, out-of-control spending, or any other financial issue, seek professional advice. Doing so can help you and your spouse talk through the issues more productively. Working with a financial planner can also help you get your spouse more engaged in money issues, in cases where he or she refuses to have much to do with it.

- *You don't know how much you pay for investments.* Not knowing is a sign of overall lack of clarity about your financial situation. A professional adviser can help you get your affairs in order, so that you're working toward long-term goals.

- *You're scared to run your retirement numbers.* Why are you so scared? Chances are, you haven't thought through your retirement situation closely enough, and your financial life isn't fully under control. Get a solid financial plan in place, and your fears will evaporate under the bright light of knowledge (poetic, aren't I?).

- *You're not tracking your cash flow.* You should know roughly how much you're taking in each month, how much you're spending, and where that spending is going. If not, you have work to do, even if you think you're living within your means.

- *You know you have financial problems, but you can't seem to discipline your spending.* It's like the alcoholic who says "I know I drink too much, but I can't stop drinking." Although I've said that I wouldn't generally advise people to turn to professional advisers as coaches, there's an exception for people who have a serious, ongoing problem, and who could probably use every nudge in the right direction they can get. Returning to the gym analogy, some people really do need regular appointments with their trainers just to get them into the gym week after week. Similarly, it's worth paying for someone to help keep you honest and on plan.

Just because you spot one of these signs doesn't mean you should throw down this book and rush over to your nearest fiduciary adviser. Look for patterns. If you see more than one of these signs cropping up, and if they're not going away, that's when you'll want to acknowledge that you're in over your head, and get some help.

PULL YOURSELF ONTO THE SCALE

When I was growing up, I was an avid athlete, really good at soccer, basketball, and by my college years, lacrosse. I played college sports until my second year, when a nasty back injury ended my athletic career, and frankly, sent me into an emotional tailspin. I didn't quite know what to do with myself, so I took refuge in food. Studying abroad in London my junior year, I ate my way through Europe—oh, the scones, the croissants, the spaghetti Bolognese, the Wiener schnitzel (I could go on). Until then, I'd never had a problem with my weight, because I promptly worked off any excess calories I consumed. This time, when I returned home I just *knew* I was livin' a bit too large.

By the time senior year began, I was disgusted with myself. I had two very skinny housemates, and at one point that autumn I proclaimed to them that I would attend Weight Watchers. I went to the first group meeting, and when it was time to step on that scale for the first time, I had a mini anxiety attack. My heart was pounding in my chest, and I could barely breathe. I called it quits for the day, but eventually went back and was able to get on the scale. I weighed 167 ½ pounds, which was more than I'd ever weighed in my life. But at that moment, upon seeing that number, something clicked for me. I understood what I needed to do to lose the weight, and I resolved to do it. Over the next few months, I jumped into action, eating better and exercising around my compromised back. My housemates marveled at the miles I logged on a stationary bike as I listened to Janet Jackson's "Control." "Schlozz," they said to me, "you're riding to California on that damned bike!" Yes, I was, and the weight just melted away.

When I've sat down with clients to run through their retirement numbers, I've often seen the same fear and embarrassment in their faces that I know I had on mine that first time I tried to get on the scale. It's embarrassing to admit that you've worked yourself into a corner, and scary to think that you might not get yourself out of it. Precisely because my clients harbored such embarrassment and fear, they had ignored their financial problems. They'd failed to track their expenses, put off thinking about and contributing to retirement. They'd made excuses for themselves, telling themselves that they were "bad at math." Conversely, they'd convinced themselves that they were experts and could handle their financial situations themselves, even when they couldn't.

Negative feelings prevent so many of us from getting the financial advice we need. We just don't want to admit to others or to ourselves that we've messed up. And then, when we do get advice, we stumble headlong into that gray area of fiduciary advisers and salespeople, not understanding how to evaluate what we're told. If this is you, I really do feel your pain. As some female clients have told me, "Getting financial advice can be harder to do than walking into the gynecologist and getting a Pap smear." I respond: "But I won't pinch, and it won't be cold." Yet still they're reluctant.

Don't give in to your negative emotions. Take a step back from your daily routine, and try to assess your current financial life more objectively. Do you really need to pay for professional advice? If after considering the warning signs you just aren't sure, then take the conservative route and get the advice, even if it costs you a bit of money. Find an adviser who really will put your interests first. And then, find someone you like, whose working arrangements, fees, and general approach to money feel reasonable to you, and who handles the financial products you need. Even if you *could* do this yourself, wouldn't you rather spend your time on the things you enjoy? I pay someone to clean my house even though I'm quite good at it; I would rather spend my time with my family and friends or riding my bicycle. Amazing financial advisers are out there. And when you find this person, he or she will change your life.

As we've seen, one warning sign that you need to pay for professional financial advice is your tendency to obsess over money. Are you constantly checking your brokerage account balances? Are you so concerned about your spending that your refuse to buy *anything*? Do you endlessly research every last financial decision you face, paralyzing yourself? Obsessing about anything is terrible for your quality of life. But unlike some other obsessions, worrying about money and giving it too much importance in your life can lead to terrible and costly financial decisions. Let's take a closer look at the excessive meaning many of us attribute to money, as well as steps you can take—beyond consulting an adviser—to rein it in.

You Make Money More Important Than It Is

How much money must people make each year in order to maximize their happiness? Is it $300,000? $400,000? More?

Actually, less. Analysis of a global survey found that individuals feel happiest day to day when they make somewhere between $60,000 to $75,000. Yes, that's all! And they feel best about their lives overall when they make around $95,000.[1]

Money just isn't as important as many smart people think it is. Sure, life is tough when you can't afford the basic necessities of life, and having more money can make it easier. But once you provide for your basic necessities, accumulating more money can weigh you down in new ways. You might enjoy nice cars, expensive dinners out, and other luxuries, but you also start to compare yourselves against others, and you feel compelled to buy more just to keep up. You become plagued by that nagging feeling that you don't have enough. You become attached to your lifestyle, and the thought of not having enough or of losing what you have stresses you out. You might wind up working too much in order to earn more, neglecting your relationships and other important parts of your life. So many of my former clients used to lament that they felt wealthier when they were making $100,000 than when they were making three times as much. I know it seems hard to believe—maybe you're even rolling your eyes. But I heard this complaint over and over again.

An excessive emphasis on money leads not only to unhappiness, but ironically, to financial losses. If we start to overvalue money, we can easily get stuck and behave obsessively, making subpar decisions in specific financial situations. I once had a prospective client in his early sixties who strolled into my office with a huge binder of data about his retirement plan; I mean, there were four hundred pages of spreadsheets in that bulky thing, organized with pencil-tabbed notes. Jim had done months of research, poring over the numbers for a dozen possible investment strategies that could generate the income he needed for retirement. He researched mutual funds as well as a bevy of individual stocks, while all along keeping his money in cash.

In his heart, he already knew what the right answer was—because frankly, the decision before him of what kind of retirement plan to fund wasn't *that* complicated (see Chapter 6). But he was so freaked out by the need to have a certain amount of money in retirement that he refused to act. Jim wanted to find the "best" stocks and the "best" mutual funds, and he felt anxious about making the wrong decision. So, he fell back on endless research and analysis as an excuse for doing nothing. Whereas he might have retired two years earlier with a comfortably diversified portfolio, he continued working at a stressful job while ostensibly figuring out what to do. He also lost out on the tens of thousands of dollars his money might have earned had he invested it over that period. Smart move? *Not.*

There are many ways in which an unhealthy attachment to money can cause paralysis. One woman I know was so concerned with bolstering her finances that she wouldn't sell her stock be-

cause she feared the tax consequences. By the time she finally over-
came that barrier, the stock had declined in value, costing her
hundreds of thousands of dollars in potential profit, all because
she didn't want to pony up 20 percent of her gain to Uncle Sam!
Another client, equally enthralled with money, had taken out a
balloon mortgage on her house to get a cheaper monthly payment,
thinking she'd sell before the adjustable interest rate "ballooned"
upward. As the years ticked by, she had no plans to sell, but she
couldn't bring herself to refinance her mortgage. She just ignored
the fact that one day, her interest rate would balloon and the
monthly payment would become unaffordable.

Six months before that happened, she finally snapped to attention and realized that she had to sell her house. By then, home
prices in her area had dropped, and her $800,000 home only com-
manded $600,000. She was forced to go through with the sale, and
was left with only $100,000 in equity, not enough to buy another
house.

Please don't make money more important than it is. Pay attention to it, respect it, appreciate it, but don't become so enthralled
with it that you wind up postponing necessary action, or making
brash moves that run counter to your best interests. Now, I know
it's easy for me to tell you to chill out and get some perspective,
and much harder for you to actually do it. I can't snap my fingers
and prompt you to rethink the outsized emphasis you might be
placing on money, nor can I sit you down on a couch and delve
into the elements of your personality or life history that might
have sent you veering off course in the first place. What I can do is
help you recognize when you might be giving money too much
headspace, and offer some simple strategies that will allow you to
put money in its proper perspective. Just a bit of progress in this
area will enable you to put aside that huge binder of research,
ditch that balloon mortgage, and make other financial choices that
really do work for you.

MY $64,000 QUESTION

I've often wondered: Why do so many smart people tend to give money outsized significance? As I've come to conclude, this is a $64,000 question. Not because nobody knows the answer, but because our sense of money and its importance comes from about 64,000 different places. The underlying causes of our tendency to overvalue money are many, complex, and interwoven.

For starters, many of us carry around a minivan of baggage from our childhoods that affects how we behave around money. I'll describe in Chapter 9 how parents might screw up their kids' attitudes toward money by letting their own emotional issues intrude. For now, let's acknowledge that parents do have this capacity, and that we might be victims of it ourselves. Our parents might have instilled in us the notion that money is all that matters in life. As an adult programmed with this worldview, you might become overly concerned with amassing as much wealth as you can, worrying that you don't have enough, and sacrificing the other joys of life in the process.

Our broader childhood circumstances can factor in as well. Corina, a friend of mine, is a public school teacher, makes good money (including a sweet pension that will pay for most of her retirement needs), and is incredibly happy with her lot. She never feels jealous of her two siblings, each of whom are worth north of $10 million; she's simply happy for them.

Corina's husband, Jeff, is a whole different story. He works in sales, and with a salary of about $200,000 is by far the most successful of anyone in his blue-collar family. Together, Corina and Jeff bring in $300,000 and enjoy what most people would regard as a comfortable and financially blessed life. But Jeff is never happy. Money means way too much to him, to the point where it shapes his identity and sense of self-worth. He compares himself with Corina's parents, who are wealthier than he and Corina, and feels that he's never good enough. Because of his upbringing, he has something he needs to prove when it comes to money and his career. I've tried everything—I even prepared a detailed planning analysis for him proving that he and Corina had more than enough money to fund a thirty- or forty-year retirement. Yet still he couldn't regard himself as a "success," nor could he stop comparing himself with others.

Past traumas can also cause us to overvalue money, or at least to skew our thinking in unhelpful ways. I've described how as a young girl I saw my dad lose everything on the trading floor. That was pretty scary, and ever since I've been too damn cautious with my money, even when I knew I was decades away from retiring. It's gotten so bad that I developed my own hashtag to describe myself: #JillIsAWimp. Likewise, many of us have known Depression-era folk who, having lived through that great calamity, spend the rest of their lives maniacally scrimping and saving, even when they don't have to, or when they would actually be better off spending some of their money. Would it kill them to save a thirty-minute trip to the grocery store across town and buy orange juice that wasn't fifty cents off?

Abrupt *positive* changes in our financial circumstances earlier in our lives can also cause us to attach ourselves too intensely to money, and behave obsessively as a result. Dr. Jim Grubman is a consultant and psychologist who works with wealthy families and their advisers. As he notes, many of his ultra-wealthy clients grew up in more modest circumstances. When they became wealthy as adults, they faced the same challenges that immigrants experience when they're suddenly thrust into a new and quite foreign country. On the one hand, these newly rich might behave like misers because it's emotionally difficult for them to part with the world of hardship and scarcity they've left behind. Maybe that world has become an inextricable part of their self-conception, or maybe they feel guilty knowing that friends or family members are still struggling, while they're not. Whatever the case, these people give money so much importance that they're clipping coupons for three dollars off a haircut, when they could probably buy the whole friggin' chain of salons in cash.

On the other hand, some of these newly wealthy *do* buy the whole chain of salons. Their overvaluation of money causes them to go overboard in the opposite direction, as they totally abandon the values that had grounded them when they were poor or middle class, and spend profusely. As Dr. Grubman notes, they spend in addictive ways, trying to fill a void inside caused by rupture from their earlier upbringing. Just as the immigrant from the "old country" might try to scrub him or herself clean of an accent in order to fit in, so, too, do some of the newly wealthy spend ostentatiously to prop up an identity that feels perennially insecure.

If these root causes might distort your perceptions of money's importance, psychiatric conditions or hang-ups can pile on as well, worsening obsessive thinking and behaviors. As a psychologist friend of mine likes to observe, money often is the vehicle through which psychological disorders express themselves, precisely because it's such a tangible and important part of our lives. Anxiety figures prominently here. So many money obsessions I encounter originate not just in an overvaluation of money, but in fears people have.

In the fall of 2017, for instance, when the country was debating a big Republican tax reform plan, a guy at work whom I'll call Bill pulled me aside and said, "Can I ask you a quick question?"

"Sure," I said. (Psst: It's never "a quick question," and it's usually posed when I'm between television appearances, not the most opportune time.)

Bill was worried that the value of his house would plummet, since the projected tax reform would limit the ability of residents in New Jersey, where he lived, to deduct state and local taxes. "I couldn't sleep last night," he told me, "because my property value is gonna tank 10 percent." Now that he mentioned it, he did have some pretty nasty bags under his eyes.

"Bill," I said, "are you planning on selling your house anytime soon?"

He shrugged. "No. I hope to leave the place feetfirst!"

"So why do you care if your property value declines 10 percent?"

He shot me a puzzled look. "It doesn't bother you?"

"No! I'm not planning on selling for years into the future, if at all. Even if I were looking to sell decades from now, I'm not going to let myself get into the position where I need to get a certain price to make the rest of my financial life work." I looked him hard in the eye. "Look, none of us know what's going to happen with the housing market. So, why are you making yourself crazy? Is this really something to lose sleep over?"

He didn't seem terribly reassured. I could have mustered a hundred arguments, and he still would have worried. Because his fears weren't rational. Money mattered to him quite a bit more than it needed to, leading him to stress about it too much. Any general or unrelated anxieties he might have had only fed the fire.

Bill is hardly alone. At the studio where I record my radio show, a big glass window separates the booth where I sit from the area where the engineers are working. All day long, some of these guys are checking their retirement accounts. They could be getting sucked into a Facebook vortex or swiping right on Tinder (and then right again). But no, they're scanning financial data. For some reason, they need to watch every small market blip and then fantasize about how it might affect them. They research every last mutual fund—the ones they own, the ones they think they should own. They're obsessed! My colleagues and I in the booth always laugh about it.

Now, you might think it odd that radio engineers, who earn a decent income and hardly live on the edge, are making themselves so crazy. But remember, the more money you have beyond a certain point, the less happiness you experience. As Dr. Grubman told me, his super-rich patients are often plagued by something tantamount to an anxiety disorder, which in turn causes them to get stuck in their financial lives. Their symptoms are "based upon a deep-seated series of feelings that are largely related to anxiety."[2] As an example, he told me about a woman who refused to transfer any of her vast wealth to her adult children. She had all sorts of fears, ranging from a concern that she wouldn't have enough money as she aged to a worry that any gifts she'd give to her kids would sap their motivation to work hard. None of her concerns really justified her parsimony, which caused great tension in her family. Her kids just couldn't understand why she was being so miserly with them, given that she was worth tens of millions of dollars. They came to suspect that she didn't trust them with money—or worse, that she was trying to control them by dangling the prospect of money but never giving it. Her husband was "tearing his hair out" trying to get her to loosen up, but nothing he did worked.

As research has shown, there's something special about money that triggers our anxieties; it has to do with how our brains process uncertainty. In 2017 and again in 2018, I had the pleasure of interviewing Mithu Storoni, MD, PhD, neuro-ophthalmologist, and author of the book *Stress-Proof: The Scientific Solution to Protect Your Brain and Body*. Dr. Storoni described a fascinating study that casts light on why smart people sometimes make dumb money moves. Researchers in the UK asked participants to predict how likely they were to find a snake hiding under a rock on the video screens in front of them. (Just hearing about anything snake-related makes my skin crawl, but this is really cool, so stay with me.) If participants found a snake, they received a painful electric shock to their hand. (I know, isn't the snake shock enough?) Even if participants didn't have a snake phobia, they came to fear receiving a shock when spotting the snake. Researchers charted how stressed participants felt as they altered the likelihood that a snake would appear.

You might think that participants were most stressed if they knew they had a higher likelihood of discovering a snake, but that wasn't the case. As Storoni told me, participants' stress levels peaked when they had a fifty-fifty chance of spotting a snake. For participants, the *uncertainty* of suffering pain made for a more stressful experience than the certainty that they would suffer it.[3] Uncertainty itself is apparently quite stressful!

This experiment and related research that Dr. Storoni described blew my mind, because our financial lives are *rife* with uncertainty. Even people who have good jobs and money in the bank can feel extreme stress and anxiety because of the perceived uncertainty of their financial futures. This uncertainty amplifies any other anxieties they might have about their money, and it can lead them to obsess about money, to the point where they drive themselves and others around them totally bat-shit crazy. At the root of it all lies a basic tendency to overvalue money and grant it much greater meaning than it should have.

To make the situation even more complex, relationship issues can become superimposed onto our underlying anxieties, causing us not merely to think about money excessively, but to engage in all kinds of wacko behavior.

A client of mine, Bernie, once sat down in my office and said, "Jill, I've got something to tell you, and you can't tell my wife."

Uh-oh—big warning sign right there.

It turned out that on three separate occasions, Bernie had written checks of about $25,000 to help out his adult son. The kid wasn't in any trouble, but he wanted a car and needed help with other bills, so just like he had always done, he turned to Daddy for help. Bernie hadn't checked with his wife before handing over the money—she knew nothing about it. I advised Bernie that his wife—let's call her Sharyn—needed to know about these transactions, so one day in my office, he told her. Sharyn freaked out. How could he have spent that money without consulting her? But it got worse. Bernie also confessed that he had taken out an additional $50,000 loan against his 401(k) so that his son could buy a house. All told, he had given their son $125,000—not an insignificant sum, given their $2 million net worth.

As Sharyn sat there fuming, Bernie said, by way of explanation, "I didn't ask you because you never would have agreed to it."

She turned an even deeper shade of red. "Goddamn right I wouldn't have agreed to it!"

How could a man betray his wife like this? What issues in their relationship, likely coupled with Bernie's own pathology, had compelled him to keep money secrets? Further, what compelled him to help out his son to an irrational extent (it's irrational to borrow against your 401(k)), risking his retirement savings so that his son could buy a house when he just as easily could have rented? I have no idea—that was for Bernie, Sharyn, and their shrink to work out.

The good news is that they did work it out. Just like couples sometimes remain in their relationship after marital infidelity, so Bernie and Sharyn felt committed enough to stick with one another and try to grow together through their challenges. In the short term, Bernie gave his wife total control over their assets. Rebuilding her trust was much harder, requiring years of effort on his part. Wow, talk about getting stuck around money and giving it too much meaning. Which leads me to a very important question . . .

ARE *YOU* OVERLY PREOCCUPIED WITH MONEY?

"Oh, no," you say, waving me away, "certainly not! I'd never do anything like Bernie did." You laugh. "Come on, Jill. I'm not like these other people."

Are you sure about that? A tricky feature of unhealthy thinking is that it's often unconscious. Yes, Bernie might have known on some level that he was doing something weird—and frankly, being a jackass—by not telling his wife. But my colleague Bill, who was losing sleep over his possibly declining home value, certainly didn't recognize his own wackiness. Likewise, you might think it's perfectly normal to procrastinate for years before investing in the stock market. You keep all your money in cash, making all kinds of excuses for not investing—"It's not the right time," "I haven't quite figured out where to put my money," and so on. Guess what? *It's not normal.* You might think it's perfectly normal to keep track of every single dollar—every *cent*—even when you're not in any kind of financial jeopardy or have some other reason to scrutinize your spending so closely. Again, *not normal.*

We all must become as self-aware as possible about our money-related attitudes and behaviors, so that we can identify our excessive concern with money before it causes us serious harm. Here are my Top Five Warning Signs that you might be giving money a much more important place in your life than it deserves:

- You're keeping secrets around money from your spouse.

- You're losing sleep on a regular basis because of money issues (i.e., once a week or more).

- Other people whom you respect tell you time and again that you've got issues around money. (What do they know, right?)

- You adopt a perfectionist stance in regard to your financial affairs. For instance, you can't invest until you know every last detail, have talked to every last expert, and so on.

- You are constantly and unhelpfully comparing your financial affairs with those of others. Does it really help you to know whether your neighbors are getting laid more than you? Ditto for whether they make more money than you.

I could go on and on with warning signs. Come to think of it, I will! Here are five more:

- You check your investment accounts on a daily or even weekly basis. (P.S. I do this money crap for a living, and I only check my accounts quarterly.)

- You find yourself ruminating about your financial life at work, and asking your colleagues for reassurance.

- You overthink your budget, even when your financial position is just fine. It's like the person who once needed to lose weight and now doesn't (who, *moi*?), yet still counts every one of those seventy calories in a delicious Tate's chocolate chip cookie. Why are you doing this?

- You are incapable of spending money on fun stuff, even though you had planned to do so. Some clients of mine wouldn't take vacations, even though they'd budgeted for them, saying they want to save even more money. I say, "NUTS!"

- You keep moving your financial goalposts. For instance, you crunch the numbers and determine that you need $3 million to retire, and when you save that much, you decide that you need $5 million, and so on.

Do any of these behaviors sound familiar? Be honest! I'm here to help you. And I can't help you unless you're willing to swallow a big, fat honesty pill.

GETTING RIGHT WITH MONEY

Let me emphasize: The stakes here are potentially ginormous. During the mid-1990s, I worked with an engineer whose previous financial adviser had told him to allocate 70 percent of his investments to stocks and the remainder to bonds. He was too scared to invest.

He felt that he needed a certain amount in his account to feel happy and fulfilled in life, and he couldn't bear the thought of losing even a small portion of what he had amassed. So, he preferred to keep his money entirely in cash. He came to me seeking a different answer, which I did *not* give him. I told him over and over: He needed to get out of cash and into a diversified portfolio. If he couldn't stomach doing it all at once, he could commit to slowly putting a certain percentage of his money to work every month—what is called "dollar cost averaging."

For years, he refused. But by the late 1990s, with the stock market booming, it was clear to him—finally—that he'd been obsessed with avoiding risk. So he jumped in and moved his entire $300,000 portfolio from cash to growth stocks. Why should he miss out when his friends were becoming millionaires?

Unfortunately for him, the technology bubble was about to burst. When it did, his $300,000 account lost two-thirds of its value. He freaked out, yanking all of his money out of his brokerage account and putting it back into cash. He resolved never to invest again. And he never did.

If this client hadn't been so personally attached to his bank balance—and thus obsessed with eliminating risk—he might have followed a long-term, diversified strategy, one that would have allocated a smaller amount of his total assets into stocks. In that case, he likely would have been just fine. Sure, he would have lost some money when the dot-com boom went bust, but with a smaller allocation to stocks, he might have been able to bear those losses, maintaining his game plan long enough to recover and then make new gains. The excessive importance he attached to money didn't ultimately prevent him from investing. Rather, it prevented him from investing in a way that would allow him to stick with a plan and make some money. The result: hundreds of thousands of dollars in actual losses and opportunity costs, extending over years and possibly even decades.

Given what's at stake, you really must take the time to fire up your engines of self-reflection and begin to correct for it. What should you do, exactly? I'm glad you asked! First, if your overvaluation of money is causing you to become stuck in any way, get yourself "unstuck" by leaning into the obstacle. As I've often found when working with clients, just running the numbers and coming up with a plan can give you a reassuring sense of control. Remember how in the last chapter I was so nervous about my weight that I couldn't get on the scale? When I actually got on the scale, and later, when I formed a plan in my mind to lose the weight, I felt much better, and more able to confront the reality that I'd become a bit too large. If excessive attachment to money or a lifestyle has caused you to postpone saving for retirement or for your kid's college, just hold your nose and craft a plan. And don't force yourself to come up with "the" plan—a provisional plan will do just fine for now. Put it in place and start to implement it, and the sense of momentum you trigger might surprise you.

A second strategy is to get unstuck by taking baby steps. When helping that wealthy woman who couldn't bring herself to gift money to her kids, Dr. Grubman didn't crack the whip and urge her to fork over a million dollars to each kid right away. He asked her the minimum amount she might feel comfortable giving, and to start with that. Her answer: $10,000. Once she made this gift, she would see that her world didn't come tumbling down around her. That success would likely spur her to make larger gifts, and over time, to loosen her underlying anxiety. In the face of uncertainty, proceeding slowly can dramatically ease the stress you feel, giving you a new sense of power and control.

Third, be a "kind asshole." On the one hand, be kind with yourself as you confront financial sticking points and the problematic thinking that underlies them. Dr. Grubman told me that when treating people for money-related problems, he first takes care to show them empathy, to let them know that he understands. You can do this, too, for yourself. Acknowledge your concerns and how real they feel to you. Acknowledge how hard it is to break with familiar ways of thinking and behaving. Give yourself credit for working at it, and celebrate when you make smart financial decisions that would've previously eluded you.

But don't *just* be kind with yourself. When you catch yourself making the same dumb mistakes with your money, push yourself gently but firmly to make a change going forward, and to challenge the assumptions and perceptions underlying your behavior. Be uncompromising. Tell yourself the truth about what you're doing, in fairly blunt terms (if you're me, you'll throw an F-bomb in, but that's optional). Be an asshole with yourself—a *kind* asshole who has your own best interests in mind.

Fourth, go deep in your introspection. Don't just notice the excessive value you grant to money, and the unhealthy behavior patterns that result. Challenge yourself to understand your money hang-ups as fully as possible. If you suspect that you're locked into ways of thinking learned during childhood, scrutinize your childhood. Were your parents obsessed with money? Did they or others in your family use money as either a carrot or a stick? Did either of your parents ask you to lie about money to the other parent? Was money used to express love? Did you experience any specific traumas around money? These are just a few of the questions you might pose. By exploring experiences in the distant past that you might not have thought about, you'll cast new light on your present-day behaviors. That in turn will empower you, enhancing your ability to break with these behaviors. Be sure also to examine and address other stressors in your life, such as unhealthy relationships or a bad work situation, since these might be feeding your unhealthy financial habits and making them worse.

Fifth, listen to that little voice inside of you. Sometimes when we're locked into unhelpful behavior, we know on some level that we're indulging in it, but we keep indulging in it anyway. Make a habit of asking yourself: "Is what I'm doing *really* in my best interest?" Tune into that voice in your head that says "I should be keeping better track of my money and not spending extravagantly," or "I shouldn't be spoiling my kids the way I do," or "I shouldn't be making these withdrawals from our joint account behind my partner's back." Admit your bad behavior to yourself. Bring it to the forefront of your mind. And then, applying the "kind asshole" suggestion, take action to change it.

Sixth, bring in a third party to help you. It could be a financial planner, but if you're dealing with hard-core psychological or relationship issues, you might need a therapist to help you explore past experiences, identify and understand your unhealthy ways of thinking, and devise tactics for changing your behavior. A therapist can also support you during a potentially lengthy behavior change process, motivating you to stick with it, and catching you when you falter.

THE BEST KIND OF MONEY TO HAVE IS *ENOUGH*

I've highlighted the financial costs of thinking too much about money, but in truth the costs go far beyond that. Caring about money and focusing on it too much can drain your life of joy. It can impoverish your relationships. It can cause you so much stress that it compromises your physical health. In so many ways, it can make life *harder*. Left unchecked, an excessive concern with money doesn't go away. It only intensifies, leading you to make increasingly poor decisions.

On the other hand, looking at money in a balanced way can lead to deep and enduring happiness. Joanne, a friend of mine who owns a small chain of hair salons, grew up under difficult circumstances. Raised by a single mom, she was forced to pinch pennies and often couldn't afford luxuries that her friends at school enjoyed. As an adult, she was determined to live a much more comfortable life, and to show the world that she had "made it." Working extremely hard, she relished her successes and always clamored for more. She also sought to "look the part" of the owner—driving a fancy car, wearing expensive clothes, and living in a nicely furnished house.

She was so attached to financial success that in her daily business dealings, she tried to claw every last penny for herself. She presumed that every employee, vendor, and even client was trying to screw her, because as her mother used to say, "You better protect yourself, because nobody else is going to!" That attitude led her to behave poorly at times. She treated her hairdressers ungenerously, cut off longtime vendors over small misunderstandings, and brushed aside legitimate customer complaints when they arose.

One day, her best hairdresser pulled her aside and told her that she was leaving to start her own business. Joanne was shocked. "I don't get it," she told the hairdresser. "You essentially have your own business here. You come and go as you please, and you make a lot of money. Why would you want to leave?"

"Well, for starters," the hairdresser said, "you nickel-and-dime me on nonsense. Really, Joanne, how much money do you really need to make? Is the few hundred bucks over the course of the year worth it?"

Joanne rejected her hairdresser's observation. She didn't think she was miserly or selfish—just a savvy business owner. That night, she groused about her hairdresser to her husband, expecting that he'd validate her point of view. Instead, he took the hairdresser's side. Listening to his wife's complaints, he said quietly, "Honey, she has a point."

She harrumphed a bit, but as she told me once, "That was the moment when I realized I was not my mother and I needed to make a change to make me happier and to help my business grow."

Ever since, Joanne has maintained a financial equanimity that is nothing short of inspirational. Realizing that she was putting too much emphasis on money, she stopped trying to negate her childhood by accumulating fancy things. Once she shed her spending habits, she found that she wasn't thinking about money all the time, and that she wasn't pegging her sense of self on having a certain net worth. That in turn prompted her to change how she treated people—she didn't need to nickel-and-dime them anymore.

She also became a bit more laid-back in general about business success. No longer did she take it for granted that she had to make the most amount of money possible. Rather, she thought about the lifestyle that actually made her happiest, and how much she would have to earn each year to support that lifestyle. Rather than eke out every last dollar, she contented herself with making what she needed in order to live the life *she* wanted, and forgoing the rest in order to enjoy more leisure time. When fellow entrepreneurs urged her to open more salon locations, she shrugged her shoulders and said, "You know what? I don't need the stress. Life is to be enjoyed. I have enough, and I'm happy."

Can you say the same? Do you know how much money is enough for you? If you suspect that you might be taking money too seriously, please take steps to address it. And if you don't think you are, but wonder why you're not more prosperous and happy, then please take a good, hard look at your attitudes and behaviors around money. You might not be as healthy in this area as you think.

When people get stuck around money, they tend to impoverish themselves by limiting their options. Little by little, their actions place constraints on their lives. In the story that began this chapter, Jim had fewer options open to him in retirement after two years of obsessively mulling because he had lost tens of thousands in potential investment earnings while his nest egg sat in cash. As we'll see throughout this book, smart financial decisions usually help us to keep our options open, while poor ones close them off.

In the next chapter, we'll explore a common trap that limits the options of even the smartest people. Many of us assume that paying for a college education will create wonderful new opportunities for ourselves or our kids. It often does, but paying too much for the wrong kind of college can also leave us in an extended postgraduation nightmare—forced to live with our parents, and/or to work a crappy job that we absolutely hate—or, if we're parents ourselves, to push back our retirement age. Let's examine the financial pitfalls of higher education, and then learn how to pick a school that gives us or our children access to a great career without ruining our finances in the process. We're smart people here. Isn't it time we got smart about higher education?

You Take On Too Much
College Debt

once had an acquaintance, Brooke, who back in the day looked very much like Janice Joplin—long tangly hair, psychedelic hippie dresses. She had a taste for weed to match—which, by the way, she diligently accounted for when I asked her to list her monthly expenses. When she hit her thirties, she got her act together, becoming a well-paid corporate manager at a large consumer products company in the Midwest. And that's when her troubles began.

Before getting her big job, Brooke had bought a two-bedroom condo, taking on a decent-sized mortgage. The condo needed work, and it wasn't in such a great neighborhood, but Brooke liked it well enough, and it was all she could afford. After she had been living in the condo for about a year, she met a nice girl named Chris, fell in love, and soon after, like the joke goes, rented a U-Haul and moved in with her. The two bought a three-bedroom ranch house in the burbs, since Brooke's place was too cramped for them, Chris's daughter, and their requisite two dogs.

But rather than sell the condo, Brooke retained it as an investment property, figuring she could rent it out. Bad move. Since she was also paying off large education loans for her college and MBA degrees, Brooke couldn't make the monthly payments on the condo, despite earning $150,000 a year. When I met her, her credit score had taken a serious hit, she was drowning in debt, and she was on the verge of losing her condo.

So many smart and successful people make the mistake of assuming too much college debt. Americans owe about $1.4 trillion in outstanding student loans, and about 40 percent of people who borrowed through the government's primary student loan program are behind in their payments or in default. In recent decades, the number of people with crushingly large loan burdens has skyrocketed. According to the Brookings Institution, in 1992 only 2 percent of borrowers had federal student loans of more than $50,000. By 2014, 17 percent did.[1] In 2017, the average borrower owed almost $35,000, a figure that is 62 percent higher than a decade ago.[2]

All of this excessive borrowing is exacting a terrible toll. Some people, like Brooke, can't embrace career or investment opportunities that come along because of burdensome debt. Others have monthly loan payments so onerous that they have to work jobs they hate (often multiple jobs at a time), or push back their retirement age by many years. When one of my friends reached her midforties, she had to leave her exciting and fulfilling job practicing environmental law at a nonprofit for a soul-sucking but highpaying job as a corporate attorney. She had lagged way behind in her retirement savings, thanks to all of her monthly student loan payments, and her husband had lost his job to boot. Making the big bucks at a mega law firm was the only way she would catch up.

Other people with abundant student debt are forced to live with their parents through their thirties (rarely good for the kids or the parents), or delay purchasing a home or starting a family. Still others see their quality of life suffer—vacations not taken, new cars not purchased. They might accept lower pay from employers, failing to bargain as hard as they could because they feel too financially vulnerable. And then there are the less tangible costs. In one study of working professionals, 80 percent of those who carried educational loans regarded that debt as "a source of 'significant' or 'very significant' stress."[3] Even some high school students are worrying about the debt they'll have to carry when they go to college. One high school sophomore was quoted as saying, "Thinking about college debt makes my hair want to fall out. It's insane."[4] Survey research has linked higher debt levels with diminished well-being, including physical health.[5] If you're a parent in your thirties or forties and are still worried about paying off student debt, think, too, about the untold effects your financial stress might be having on your kids. The problems caused by student debt are every bit as insidious as they are rampant.

In rehearsing this litany of horrors, I'm not at all contesting the value of higher education. College degrees can create amazing opportunities. Individuals with bachelor's degrees enjoy higher wages and lower levels of unemployment than those with only a high school education. According to one study, the bachelor's degrees awarded by most schools deliver an annual income boost of roughly $6,500 a year, amounting to a $200,000 "wage premium" over a thirty-year career.[6] I myself was fortunate enough to attend a great school—Brown University (and also to graduate debt-free because my grandparents had set aside money to help my sister and me go to college). At a number of points in my career, my degree has helped me.

And yet, education costs have skyrocketed over the past few decades, so that the overall value of higher education for individuals has eroded. That means you have to work harder to make sure that the degree you seek makes sense for *you,* given your financial circumstances and career aspirations. Many smart people fail to do that work. They assume that *any* undergraduate or professional degree is worth it at any price, which simply isn't true. In so many instances, people take on debt that closes off the very opportunities they're striving to create.

If you're an intelligent, ambitious high school kid applying for your undergraduate degree, or if you've been out in the workplace and are thinking about returning to school for a graduate degree, I beg you to read this chapter. If you're a parent of a student, then please turn off *Game of Thrones* or *The Crown* and pull up a chair as well, because this nonparent has an important message for you: We need to talk. What are you *thinking,* nodding your head yes when your kids ask to go to these pricey private schools? Is it worth consigning your kids to lives of poverty to attend a pricey second-, third-, or fourth-tier private school your family can't afford? And is it worth compromising your own future by pumping money into these unaffordable schools rather than into your retirement accounts?

THINK IT THROUGH, PEOPLE!

Barb, a friend of mine from Rhode Island, called to give me the great news: Her daughter Kelly was going to St. Michael's College up in Vermont. "Whoa," I said. "Wasn't Kelly going to attend URI?" The University of Rhode Island is the big state-supported university in the Ocean State. The total cost of a year there, including expenses, would run about half the price of St. Michael's.

"Well, she was," my friend said, "but she really wanted to go to St. Mike's."

"Why?" I asked. "What for?"

My friend didn't have a clear answer. She muttered something about how Kelly really wanted to go to school out of state, meet more diverse kids, yadda, yadda, yadda.

"You realize you can't afford St. Mike's, right?"

"We know," she said. "Kelly's going to have to take on loans."

Fast-forward four years. Kelly graduated from St. Michael's, majoring in anthropology. She tried to get a job in a major metropolitan area, but couldn't break in, despite having excellent grades. Within a year after graduating, she returned to Rhode Island to live with her parents. A few months after that, she did get a job, and good thing: She had to start making interest payments on the $70,000 in school debt she now carried. Was it her St. Michael's degree that had landed her the job? No. Her father had a mid-level job in finance, and he had used his personal connections to get her an entry-level position at a local bank.

Think about this situation. If Kelly had sucked it up and gone to URI, her father could probably have used his connections to get her *the exact same job* that she now had. She had racked up $70,000 in loans and would likely be making payments for decades—for what? It's like paying six bucks for "Asparagus Water" at Whole Foods when you could have just poured tap water into a jar, dropped in a few cents' worth of asparagus spears, and let it sit for a while. Who does that???[7]

Keep in mind, smart people and their families don't just get snookered on college, but on graduate school as well. Another friend of mine had a son, Vince, who graduated in the top of his class from Princeton, and then didn't know what to do with himself. So he did what every brilliant, budding something-or-other would do: He enrolled at Cornell Law school, and hated every minute of it.

When Vince graduated, he joined up with some college buddies to launch a start-up venture. He didn't need a law degree for that, and in fact would never work as an attorney. Three years of Cornell Law plus expenses cost him $250,000. If you count what he might have earned had he spent those three years working at an entry-level job that paid, say, $50,000 a year, his short-lived dalliance with the law cost him and his family at least $400,000. For nothing.

Why do smart people make such dumb-ass moves? There are a number of reasons, but first, many students and their parents just don't spend enough time thinking through their higher education decisions. When I hear that someone's spending $70,000 more so that they can "go to school out of state," it's obvious—they didn't think it through. Ditto when I hear that someone is going to business or law school not because they're burning to practice in those fields, but because "it's great training for whatever you might want to do."

I've met families that spend more time deliberating over and researching next year's vacation than they do college. It's fun to daydream about the white sand beaches in Bora Bora, or that chic Left Bank condo you found on Airbnb. Running the numbers on St. Michael's College versus University of Rhode Island? Not so fun. Researching and applying for federal grant money to help fund your education? Even less fun. But life isn't all fun and games, and this is your (and your kid's) financial future we're talking about. Do you, Mr. or Ms. Student, want to pay $500 a month for your student loans for the next *twenty-five years* because you rushed to send in your deposit to the fancy private school rather than doing a proper cost-benefit analysis? Do you, Mr. or Mrs. Parent of Said Student, want to push back your retirement ten years because you didn't do the proper cost-benefit analysis?

I didn't think so.

IT MIGHT NOT BE A NETWORK YOU'RE GETTING, BUT A NOT-WORK

Even when students and parents do spend time working through their higher education decisions, they often go astray by overestimating the value of a high-priced private college. I hear it all the time: "It's important to go to a name-brand school, because it opens doors once you graduate." Some schools do open enough doors to justify the high price. If you or your child gets accepted at an Ivy League school or at another top-twenty school like Stanford, University of Chicago, or MIT, it might make sense to take on significant debt so as to tap into the magic of these schools' alumni networks. And if your household income falls below $250,000 or so, most of these institutions have massive endowments, which will provide the funds necessary for you or your kids to attend. But other name-brand schools in the second or third tier won't deliver nearly enough networking gold to make taking on the debt a good deal, and neither will they provide comparable financial packages.

One smart, ambitious young guy I know, Jesse, went to college and then got a great job in the marketing department of a medical device manufacturer. After several years, he had worked his way up to a middle-manager role, but decided he wanted to go into investment banking. To make the transition, he went for his MBA, enrolling in a program outside of Boston that was middle-of-the-pack at best. He tried for months to get a job with one of the big New York investment banks, but couldn't score a single interview. Nobody gave a crap that he'd graduated from the particular MBA program that he had—it wasn't Harvard Business School or Wharton. To these elite employers, he might as well have attended "Whatsa Matta U." He finally did land interviews, but that was because members of his extended network of family and friends called in favors for him. For Jesse, the job search process was essentially a DIY proposition. The cost of his education had been full-service all the way.

Here's the dirty little secret we rarely admit: Most smart, successful parents already have networks their kids can access, so it would behoove them to spend time selecting colleges that are affordable. Consider, too, that the job market has changed in recent decades. Back when John F. Kennedy was President and Bob Dylan was releasing his eponymous debut album, having a degree might have gone a long way toward helping you snare a job, simply by virtue of the school's brand name. That doesn't happen so much in our era of Donald Trump and Bruno Mars. Actual work experience matters much more than it used to, as well as your ability to demonstrate the "soft skills" employers seek, like problem-solving talents, the ability to collaborate, or creativity.

Survey data has documented the relative importance of work experience over academic pedigree. The National Association of Colleges and Employers (NACE) releases an annual survey that asks employers what they're most seeking in new hires. When employers choose between two candidates with similar profiles, what makes the difference? The top answer in 2018 wasn't an applicant's alma mater, but whether an applicant had worked an internship with the employer. Coming in second was whether an applicant had completed an internship in the wider industry. An applicant's alma mater was actually the *ninth* most important factor in the survey. In most cases, employers want some indication that you have the skills to actually do the job.[8] The much-lauded "brand name" of schools has become less compelling. So why pay big bucks for it?

THE COLLEGE CONVERSATION THAT WASN'T

Yet another reason so many brainiac students are up to their clavicles in debt is because *their parents didn't stop them*. Parents often don't have the cojones to speak honestly with their kids about what the family can afford. Overachieving parents feel that they must do everything possible to ensure the happiness and success of their offspring. Anything less than that, and they're bad parents—or so they think. I hear it a lot: "I just can't say no to my kids." These parents went to name-brand schools themselves, so they can't bear the thought of denying their kids the same privilege. They either pretend the family can afford this opportunity, compromising their own futures to pay the tuition bills, or they affect a lackadaisical attitude toward school debt, compromising their children's futures. "My father earned less than I do now," they say, "even accounting for inflation, and he was able to pay for my four years at Penn. Why is it so hard for me?" I'll tell you why: Tuition has risen at about two times the general rate of inflation since you got your boogie down in West Philly.

There are many other reasons parents fail to level with their children about what the family can afford to spend on education. Maybe you feel you somehow screwed up your own career, you're embarrassed about your lack of means, and you don't want to admit it to yourself or your children. Or maybe you made one of the other twelve dumb mistakes in this book and don't see yourself as a good financial role model for your kids. Feeling that you lack authority, you're not about to take a hard line and say no to your children's educational requests. Maybe you and your spouse disagree on how to handle college, so it's easier to just punt on a conversation. Maybe you're disorganized and don't know what your family can afford.

Whatever the case, you're probably not doing your child or yourself any favors by going along to get along. My client Gail was a single mom with three kids living in a Philadelphia suburb. She sold cars at a Jaguar dealership, making $120,000 a year. Her kids all went to public school through twelfth grade. When it came time for them to attend college, she didn't spend too much time thinking about it, nor did she sit each of them down, relay how much the family could afford for his or her education, and use that as the basis for subsequent decisions.

Her eldest daughter attended college, and happily, she didn't have to take on much debt—only around $20,000—because Gail footed most of the bill. Then her next child, a son, went off to college. He had to borrow more money—about $60,000. You see, Gail hadn't planned carefully enough, hadn't taken into account potential risks to her own spending power. Midway through her son's college career, the market for high-end cars contracted, and Gail's take-home pay declined almost overnight by about $25,000. Taking on more school debt was the only way to make up the difference.

Gail felt guilty that her son had to take on more debt than her daughter, so she told him she would pay off his debt. When I heard that, I almost lost my marbles. "How can you do that?" I asked. "You can't afford it!" Gail proceeded to make a mistake so terrifying, so awful, so monumental that I'm devoting a whole upcoming section of this chapter to it: She borrowed $50,000 from her retirement account to pay off her son's loans. Oy vey. And then Child Number Three, a daughter, crossed the high school graduation stage. The larder was bare, so to speak, for college, but Gail couldn't tell her daughter not to go to school. So her child enrolled, becoming the family's school loans champion with a staggering $105,000 of debt.

Midway through her younger daughter's junior year, Gail got hit with another cut in pay. She could no longer support herself and had to start over in a new line of work. She wound up selling her house and moving to a town in Florida with a much lower cost of living than suburban Philly. She got a new job as a medical device rep and stabilized her finances. Still, because she had dug into her retirement and non-retirement savings, and because she decided that she had to pay off her younger daughter's loans, she wound up working more than a decade longer than she had hoped to before retiring, and subsisting on a smaller amount of retirement income than she'd planned for.

If Gail had been honest with herself about what the family could safely afford, and if she had sat all of her children down individually when they were still in high school and adjusted their expectations about college, her entire financial future might've unfolded differently. She would have realized that while loans might make three private school educations possible, they were just too risky for the family. She might have resolved to fund only state school educations for her children, or if they insisted on private schools, she might have put the onus on them to find grant money.

She might also have tailored her financial support to each of her children's individual needs and desires. If one of her children was a serious student, maybe he or she would have gotten to go to a more expensive private school, while a sibling who was more social and likely would spend college chugging beer would only get to go to a state school. Who says college has to be even-steven among siblings?

The point is that if Gail had proceeded more thoughtfully and strategically and if she had communicated honestly, all three of her kids would probably have found themselves with career opportunities that were comparable to what they in fact found after college, with much less debt. The whole family would have been better off.

DUMB THING #4(A)–YOU FUND COLLEGE BEFORE RETIREMENT

Let's take a closer look at Gail's epic error of taking money out of her retirement account to pay for her kids' college. On one level, I get why she did it. If you're a parent of school-aged children, you probably pride yourself on doing the very best you can for them. You're socking away money for their college education, perhaps taking advantage of a 529 plan. In fact, you're probably such a good parent that when allocating money for savings, you prioritize your kids' education over every other financial goal you have, including retirement.

Many people think and behave in these ways. A recent study found that almost half of middle-aged Americans are "willing to overextend themselves financially" to help their kids live more comfortably. Almost 20 percent said that they would willingly borrow six figures to fund college for their kids.[9] And more middle-aged parents *are* borrowing. As of 2017, individuals in their sixties and older were "the fastest-growing age segment of the student loan market," according to a report from the Consumer Financial Protection Bureau.[10] The vast majority of these borrowers weren't paying off their own school debt, but their kids'. And in many cases, this borrowing was unaffordable. One study found that almost 40 percent of seniors paying off student loans were scrimping on their basic needs, such as visits to the doctor.

Now, I know that a good mathematical case exists for doing two things at once: saving for retirement *and* college.[11] But in my experience working with families, that approach requires discipline that some might not have. More significantly, it assumes that parents will earn as much money later in their careers, after the kids are done with college, as they do while their kids are small. In the current economy, we can't necessarily make that assumption.

Please listen close to Aunt Jill: *You simply must fully fund retirement before attending to your kids' college.* Take care of the Big Three first, including retirement, and if you have money left over, then save for college or help your kids out with their tuition bills. You know how when you're on an airplane you hear messages telling you that if something bad happens, you should place an oxygen mask on yourself before you place it on your small children? Well, something similar holds true for retirement savings. You can take out parental loans or help your kids pay off loans that they assume to help pay for college. But there are no loans, other than the thorny reverse mortgages that we've already discussed, to fund retirement. Retirement comes first.

If you're a parent, you probably hate hearing this advice. The parents who attend my live presentations certainly do. Hyperfocused on education, and rightfully so, they feel selfish funding their retirement first and asking their kids to either go to state schools or take out more loans. But that's not selfish. Once you reach retirement age without enough savings, your adult children will be paying to take care of you anyway! Wouldn't it be better for you to lock down your retirement now, taking advantage of the magic of compound interest, than burdening your kids later? Which course really is more selfish? As playwright Tony Kushner said, "Sometimes self-interested is the most generous thing you can be."[12]

Because college precedes retirement, many of us assume we should focus on college first and largely forget about retirement until later. As one caller on my radio show declared: "I'm a psychologist, so I'll have many years after my kids graduate to address my retirement funding. I'll figure it out." That logic seems to make sense, but it's wrong. You might well have many years to save for retirement, but will those years really suffice?

I'm not saying you're inevitably screwed if you underfund retirement now to pay for college. Maybe a parent who does this really will figure out retirement later. Much of the time, parents manage to make retirement work after paying for college, saving more toward the end of their careers or making changes that allow them to spend less in retirement. But in some significant percentage of cases, parents run into the kind of trouble that Gail did. Someone loses a job. Someone experiences a health crisis. A family member has unexpected needs that you want to help fund. In such cases, people nearing retirement find themselves in situations that are unexpectedly precarious. Lacking good options, they have to make painful sacrifices, like working seven years longer than they'd like in a job they can't stand, or moving away from friends and family to live in a locality with a lower cost of living.

Do you want to risk putting yourself in such a position? Do you want to depend on "working longer" at a time when robots are poised to make millions of jobs obsolete? And do you want to enter your fifties or sixties dealing with the stress of having money issues? If you slow down, get serious about your retirement needs, and make tough decisions now about prioritizing retirement over your children's college, you might be able to reach retirement age feeling calm, peaceful, and in control of your destiny.

My clients Judy and Don did. When they first contacted me, they wanted to know how to save for a four-year private college for their two kids, aged ten and twelve. The family lived in Maryland just outside of Washington, D.C., and Judy and Don were in their early forties and earned a combined annual income of $250,000. Yeah, I know—$250,000 should be enough to fund everything. But it's not. As they quickly discovered, the money they were planning on saving for college needed to go into their 401(k) plans if they were to hit their retirement goals.

Our initial couple of meetings left Judy and Don feeling defeated—Judy especially. An engineer by trade, she had attended a community college for the first two years of college, and had finished up at what she described as "a middling state college." As someone who valued education highly, she had dreamed of sending her kids to private universities. Sitting across the table from Judy and Don, I could tell their emotions were going haywire, and I wondered if they were absorbing what I was advising.

By the next couple of sessions, however, Judy and Don had accepted their situation, and they were more willing to rethink their plans for their kids. When they asked me to lay out feasible alternatives, I proposed that they follow a combination plan. "Tell your kids that you can afford the lion's share of a public college education," I said, "but they will need to work a little and take out small loans to graduate. If all goes well with your plan, you might be able to help them repay the loans, but they shouldn't count on it." If Judy and Don followed that approach, they would be able to save enough to reach their reasonable retirement goals.

Judy and Don decided to go with this plan. As soon as their kids entered high school, they explained what the family would be able to contribute to college. Their daughter wasn't thrilled about attending a public college. "If I can figure out a way to pay for the rest of the tuition at a more expensive private school, I can go, right?" she asked. Her parents agreed. And incredibly, their daughter pulled it off. She worked hard at school and landed a merit-based scholarship to attend Haverford College. Their son attended the University of Maryland, and both kids graduated with *zero* debt. Meanwhile, Judy and Don are on track to retire at age sixty-five, two years earlier than expected. They're reaching the end of their careers feeling what all of us want: peace of mind about our financial future.

Unlike other clients of mine, Judy and Don didn't resist when I told them the number—or at least, they didn't resist for very long. They didn't insist that they would pay the full ride for college now and then "work longer" or "save more later." They were willing and able to process the information at hand, come to grips with reality, entertain new ways of thinking, and adjust their expectations. If you can overcome your initial emotional response like they did, you'll allocate your savings in ways that really do serve your best interests. You'll save hundreds of thousands of dollars more for retirement than you would have if you had gone all in on college. You'll enter your retirement years feeling confident and in control. And quite likely, without cumbersome debts of their own, your kids will be better off, too.

SMART COLLEGE DECISION-MAKING 101

Whether you're a parent of college students or a student yourself, I hope I'm inspiring you to take a new, more realistic look at college, one grounded in careful analysis of your financial circumstances and the value that specific educational options can deliver. I hope, too, that you've begun to set aside the strong emotions you might feel—"I just *have* to go to that cool private school," or "I have to give my kids the exact same education I had," or "I have to

treat all of my kids exactly the same," or "My kid's college education is more important than anything else." You really do need to
start seeing the college decision for what it is: a hard-edged business decision, one of the biggest and most important that you and
your family will ever make.

Looking at college in this way, you'll realize that there's actually a great deal you can do to maximize value for your family. Did
you know that some $2.7 billion in federal financial aid goes un-
claimed every year? That's incredible! According to Kelly Peeler,
the founder and CEO of NextGenVest, a service that provides students with the help they need to navigate the financial aid, scholarship, and student loan process, many families assume they won't
qualify for these grants, and leave this money on the table.[13] In
truth, if they make $200,000 or less annually, they very well might
qualify.

If families were approaching higher education in a more rational, businesslike way, they would make it their mission to know
what state grants might be available, or what grants and scholarships particular institutions might offer, or how to use investment
vehicles like 529 plans or Coverdell Education Savings Accounts
to save for college.[14]

More important, many families haven't bothered to explore the
full array of lower-cost schools available to them. In addition to
the standard college rankings, you should pay close attention to
Money magazine's annual rankings of "The Best Colleges for Your
Money."[15] Also, you might want to research individual academic
departments at low-cost schools that offer outstanding values for
the money. If you live in Virginia, for instance, and you want to
major in business as an undergraduate, you could attend an expensive, name-brand school like New York University. But you could
also choose University of Virginia or University of North Carolina-
Chapel Hill, both highly regarded institutions. If you paid out-of-
state tuition at UNC, you would still have saved $15,000 per year

as compared with New York University, and living expenses would probably also have cost you less.

You simply *must* do your research if you want to win the college financing game. You should also do what very few students do, and *negotiate* when possible. Not long ago, a young colleague of mine decided to ditch network news and attend law school. She gained admission to Georgetown, which would have cost her $60,000 a year. She also got into a lower-ranked school, Fordham, which had awarded her $35,000 in grants (that's TAX-FREE money, people), bringing the yearly cost down to only $25,000. As a bonus, she could attend law school right next to Lincoln Center!

Despite the cost differential, she really wanted to go to Georgetown. At my urging, she called up Georgetown and told them she wanted to attend, but had received an offer of $35,000 a year from Fordham. Guess what? Georgetown came back and awarded her $25,000 per year, slicing her tuition down to $35,000 a year. She wound up choosing Georgetown. That one phone call, which she almost neglected to make, saved her $75,000 over three years, plus the interest she would have had to pay had she borrowed that money.

If a school has awarded you grants or scholarships, and if your grades or background make you an attractive candidate, don't be afraid to ask other schools to match it. After all, the worst that can happen is they say no. Do the asking yourself rather than relying on your parents (good advice for almost everything in life). Colleges aren't that impressed by helicopter parents who take care of everything for their kids. They *are* impressed by ambitious students who advocate articulately and confidently for themselves.

Long before you engage in any negotiation, sit down with your parents and calculate exactly how much debt you can afford. College experts I've interviewed for my radio show have suggested an easy benchmark to keep in mind. It's a good idea, they say, to borrow no more than what you anticipate your first year of salary will be when you eventually hit the job market. If you're studying engineering, this formula would allow you to take on more debt than, say, if you were an art history major, since your first-year salary would likely be appreciably higher. But either way, you'll assume an amount of debt that you would likely be able to pay off within ten years.

If you dig into the numbers, as I have, you'll find that it's really after ten years that education debt starts to limit your opportunities. If you're in your twenties and paying off debt, that's a whole lot different from being in your thirties and still paying it off. Of course, this formula is of limited use if you don't have a clue what kind of career you want. But most people have at least some idea, so for them, this formula serves as a useful point of orientation.

What if you already stagger under loads of student debt? Don't panic—you can still take action to pay back the loans efficiently and mitigate the burden on yourself. I advise people with debt to get organized as quickly as possible. Create a spreadsheet listing all of your loans, the loan ID number, the name of the lender, its phone number, and other pertinent information, including—critically—the amount you borrowed and the interest rate. Then arrange for your bank to make automatic payments on these loans each month. This will save you the fees and interest that might accrue from missed payments, not to mention the stress of having to arrange for these payments each month.

If you calculate your budget and find that you have extra money each month, begin paying down your loans more quickly, starting with the most expensive one first. It might feel more satisfying psychologically to "just take care of" a small loan you have as opposed to a larger loan with a higher interest rate, but you're accruing greater overall interest costs that way. If you have federal loans, apply for deferments or forbearance, or investigate income-based repayment plans.

If you're a parent, help your kids get organized in navigating the loan repayment process. You want them to shoulder the responsibility, but that doesn't mean you can't serve as an informational and emotional resource to them. If you're able to help them financially without unduly compromising your future, feel free to do so, but don't let them off the hook entirely. Rather than gifting them the money for the loan, you might pay off some or all of their loans and have them pay you back over a period of time with lower or no interest. You want your kids to feel like they have "skin in the game." How else will they ever learn to be responsible for their financial well-being?

If your children are still in high school, start talking to them honestly about college financing early—like, during freshman year. Also, get to know your kids' ambitions and work ethics. Will all of them really make the most of a high-cost education at a prestigious school, or are some better off at a more affordable school, where they tap kegs in exactly the same way as at the fancy places? Are all of your kids emotionally ready to go to school out of state? Are they all equally clear about their career directions? A friend of mine had to pull her son out of a pricey out-of-state school because he partied like a rock star his freshman year. He moved back in with her and enrolled in community college. If he could demonstrate that he was serious about his studies, then they would explore other, more expensive options. The more honestly you can appraise your kids' capacities early on, the less likely you are to confront these kinds of unpleasant surprises, wasting tens of thousands of tuition dollars in the process. It's okay if your child doesn't know yet what he or she wants out of life. But please, let him or her experiment at a cheaper school.

TURN YOUR KID INTO A GO-GETTER

A high school student I know, Jocelyn, lives in a small town in Oklahoma. From a young age, she knew she wanted to write and direct movies. When she was still in middle school, she dreamed of attending college at the University of Southern California, one of the country's top film programs (and incidentally, one that is also popularly known as the University of Spoiled Children). Jocelyn's parents strongly encouraged her to attend college and follow her passion for film, but they weren't about to mortgage their future to send her to USC. They were very clear that with three other kids in the family, they could only afford a public university or in-state college, which would cost about $12,000 in tuition and fees. If she wanted to live in a dorm on campus, she would have to take on loans and pay for it herself. Otherwise, she could live at home, commute, and graduate debt-free.

The last time I checked, the University of Oklahoma's film studies program didn't rival USC's. In fact, the two programs weren't on the same planet. But that was reality, and Jocelyn would have to accept it. Her parents didn't forbid her from applying to USC. But they did tell her that if she wanted to attend that school, she would have to figure out how to pay about $60,000 a year— the school's $72,000 a year of tuition and expenses, minus the $12,000 her parents would contribute.

To her parents' surprise, Jocelyn accepted the challenge. The summer before she entered high school, she spent hours researching what it would take for her to get into USC, and more important, how she could apply for grants, scholarships, and yes, even loans. Over the course of her freshman year, she scoured the school's alumni directory, searching for anyone from Oklahoma who had attended USC. When she found local alumni, she called them up, asking them about their experience at the school and what she could do to get admitted and obtain funding. She also applied herself to her studies, earning straight A's.

Now, I don't know if Jocelyn will reach her college goal. But what I do know is that her and her parents' clear-eyed assessment of her college finances didn't discourage her. Rather, it emboldened her to reflect on what she wanted, to work hard for it, and to look for creative solutions. Whatever Jocelyn does with her life, she'll have the benefit of the scrappiness and persistence she has cultivated while contemplating her college future. And she'll benefit from the knowledge of financial reality she has gained. Many people who don't have college handed to them realize similarly hidden benefits. They become laser-focused on their career objectives. They discipline themselves to make their monthly payments, becoming great savers once they've paid off their loans. They come to appreciate the career goals they achieve all the more—because they've earned them. Ultimately, they become more mature financially, more accepting of limits and of personal responsibility.

I wish that everyone could afford the college of their dreams. But we don't live in such a world. Still, I take some comfort in knowing that all the struggle and hardship and disappointment people feel can in many cases bring enhanced personal growth. I also take comfort in knowing that it's not a black-and-white world out there. The choice before us isn't between attending an expensive school and taking on loads of debt, or avoiding debt but consigning yourself to lower levels of career opportunity. In most cases, you still can achieve your career ambitions without burdening yourself under a crushing debt load. But you do have to set aside outdated assumptions and some of your own emotions, do your research, and, of course, endure those tough conversations. You have to be as smart about college as you are about other areas of your life.

Learning to make better decisions about college has another upside that often goes unremarked. In the process of "getting real" about college, you put yourself in a better position to resolve a range of other important financial issues. Within a decade or so of graduating from college, many smart people start to think about settling down. Should they buy a home, or continue to rent? These same people might later contemplate whether or not to buy a vacation home or investment property. All too often, emotional decision-making combines with conventional wisdom about the joys of ownership to induce people to buy property they can't afford or that in some other way doesn't fit their circumstances. The result: tens of thousands of dollars in losses, and in some cases much more. Let's examine the common mistakes smart people make in real estate, as well as some strategies for ensuring that any property you buy really does bring you enduring joy.

You Buy a House When You Should Rent

You're in your early fifties, and your kids are almost out of the house. After working your butt off for thirty years, you've been fortunate enough to amass wealth above and beyond your retirement income needs. All you want to do when you retire is hike the Sonoran Desert for as long as your creaky old body lets you. After many vacations at Canyon Ranch or Miraval, at several thousand dollars a crack, you decide it's finally time to get a place of your own in Tucson. What do you do, buy or rent?

In 2004, clients of mine, John and Mary, faced this predicament. Because real estate values were rising, they decided to jump in and buy a place. They felt they could afford it: They had $1 million in savings, with $650,000 of that in 401(k) plans and the remaining $350,000 in a non–retirement investment account, which they could tap at any time. Their primary residence was worth about $300,000, with a $150,000 mortgage balance on it. To round out this picture, John and Mary had a combined annual income of $300,000.

Initially, they bought a plot of land, spending $100,000 out of their available savings. They had $250,000 left that they could use in case of an emergency. A year later, having saved an additional

$50,000, they began building their dream home, spending $300,000 on the project and borrowing another $250,000 to complete it. They knew they had depleted their liquid savings, but real estate prices were soaring and so, too, was the cost of construction. They did some homework and figured they could use the house for a couple of weeks a year and rent it out for the remainder. The rent would pay for the cost of the house, they thought, and before they knew it they would have replenished their savings.

I know what you're thinking: Where were you, Jill? How could you let them do this? One of the frustrating parts of being a financial adviser was that I could only provide advice, not force clients to do what was best for them. When John and Mary first proposed the idea of building a house, I waffled between freaking out and *really* freaking out. "You'll drain all of your cash," I gasped. "You're going to wind up responsible for two mortgages, with all of your money tied up in real estate. What if you need that money for something?" I didn't question their love of the iconic saguaro cactus, but I asked them to consider renting for a while. "We're throwing money out the window if we rent," they told me. Maybe, but they were also keeping their options open. They could explore different communities and housing situations and see which ones they preferred.

They didn't want to hear it. The real estate market was too hot, and they couldn't contemplate that home prices would ever drop. But drop they did. In mid-2006, the housing crisis was in its early stages, especially in the Southwest. It started with the no-money-down house flippers, who were suddenly flooding the market with tons of inventory for sale (read Michael Lewis's book *The Big Short* for more on this). When they found no buyers, many tried to rent out their properties, flooding the rental market. As a result, my clients couldn't rent out their new house as they planned. In 2008, when the financial crisis hit, John lost his steady job. Needing cash, and burdened with two mortgages, Mary and John were forced to sell their Arizona house at a $50,000 loss. Not a huge disaster, but one they could have avoided.

Many smart people make mistakes with real estate, buying when renting would have been a much better move. In 1999, I counseled a pair of medical students, married and in their twenties, who wanted to buy a house to live in while they finished their degrees and were applying for residencies in their medical specialties. They couldn't bear the thought of "throwing their money away" paying rent, and their parents were willing to chip in for a down payment.

"What if you don't get accepted into residencies in the area and have to move?" I asked.

"Oh, we'll just sell," they said.

"Okay," I said, "but what if you can't sell, or what if you can't get a decent price?"

They brushed me off. "We don't think that's going to happen."

Ah, the optimism of youth.

They plunked down $250,000 for a ranch-style home in a nice neighborhood. Had they held on to the house for a decade or more, they would have made a substantial profit. But a few years later, in 2002, they finished medical school and, as I'd feared, got accepted into residencies in another state. In the wake of the dot-com bust, the real estate market was shaky. They managed to sell their house, but at a loss of tens of thousands of dollars. Now, if the timing had worked out differently and they were selling in 2006, just before the real estate market crash, they would have looked like geniuses. So did they really make such an unwise move? I would argue they did. Because it was likely that this couple would need to sell in just a few years, the most prudent course was to rent. Buying amounted to a roll of the dice—and as these clients found out, sometimes you lose.

Be careful about real estate. If you're buying your primary residence, can you really afford to take on a mortgage and the other costs of owning a property? Maybe renting is the better option. If you're thinking of buying a vacation home, you're years away from retirement, and you're not independently wealthy, it will almost always make sense to hold off on buying, since you'll have more liquidity that way, and therefore less exposure to risk as well as more options. You're not "throwing money out the window" by renting. Rather, you're *buying flexibility*. Every rent check you write purchases you the freedom to grasp opportunities as they arise, or the ability to adjust to unforeseen setbacks that smack you in the face. Renting might not be nearly as sexy as buying, especially for older generations steeped in notions of the "joys of real estate" or "buying a piece of the American dream." But if your goal is a safe and secure financial future as well as a life you can actually enjoy, renting might be the way to go. Save sexy for another time.

THE ETERNAL WISDOM OF THE BULGARIAN OPTIMIST

Why do so many bright people make such rotten real estate decisions? Quite often, it's because they're clinging to overly rosy outlooks about the future. Cognitive scientists have a name for it: "optimism bias," the tendency of human beings to think bad stuff can happen to everyone else, but not us. Without realizing it, we zip through life thinking about best-case scenarios, and making decisions on that basis. When reality bites us in the ass, as it has a tendency to do, it comes as a huge surprise. And because we've paid so little attention to mitigating risk, assuming that the worst case will never materialize, we suffer financial blows we might have avoided. "Life is good," as the saying goes. "Yeah," I say, "except when it sucks!"

Look at that smirk on your face. "Here comes Little Miss Sunshine talking about life sucking," you're saying. "Don't bust my vibe, Schlesinger!"

Yeah, yeah, yeah—I've heard it all before, usually expressed far more colorfully by my clients and listeners ("Buzzkill," "Debbie Downer," "Patty the Pessimist"). As I've explained to them, my perception of risk—which I would argue is balanced, not pessimistic—has been informed by my years of working on Wall Street as a trader. Many people see traders as happy-go-lucky risk-takers, but in truth we were trained to look not at the upside, but at the potential risk we would run in making a given trade. And you sure do pay attention to that downside when your own money, and not that of some massive bank, is at risk. In particular, we were taught to take seriously even those negative outcomes whose probability of occurring was very low.

Picture a curve with a big fat bell at the center, tailing off on either side. Those tails represent low-probability, extreme out-comes, both positive and negative. Most likely, modestly positive or negative outcomes represented in the middle of the curve will come to pass. But don't fool yourself into thinking that the low-probability but catastrophic outcomes on the negative tail can't happen. Sometimes a once-in-a-generation flood will devastate your neighborhood, or the stock or housing market will crash, or the sure-thing bonus won't materialize. What will you do then? Doesn't it make sense to take small, relatively inexpensive steps to prepare for the bad stuff?

I know it's hard to think about potential downsides. It upsets our carefully laid plans, or our sense of what's "fair" in life. I'm also not saying you should live every moment cowering in fear of the unthinkable happening—obviously that's a recipe for misery. But you should at least factor the downside into your plans when contemplating a real estate purchase. Don't drop every last bit of cash you have into building your dream home. You might need some of that cash. Don't stretch your finances to buy a second home, reasoning you'll "rent it out" if you have to. What if nobody wants to rent it? Don't buy a house planning to keep it for a few years, on the assumption that the market will hold up. It might not. And be careful not to buy a house assuming that you will be entitled to tax deductions forever. As many homeowners found out in 2018, laws can change, and your once-beloved tax benefits can disappear in the blink of an eye!

My Bulgarian friend likes to tell a joke about an optimist and a pessimist who encounter one another on the street. "Oh, my God," the pessimist says. "Things can't get any worse." The optimist shakes his head. "No, things *can* get worse."

I just love that joke. I told it on Fox Business Network in the summer of 2008 when the market was sliding, and commentators were blathering on about how stock prices were about to stabilize and the worst would soon be over. A healthy dose of Eastern European cynicism was just what the doctor ordered. Guess what? We need some of that cynicism now! The next time you think of purchasing real estate, remember the one about the Bulgarian Optimist. And act cautiously.

BEING A LANDLORD IS FUN AND OTHER HALF-TRUTHS

A professional opera singer in the Midwest once called my radio show with a tale of real estate obsession. A couple of years back, she'd met the man of her dreams, gotten married, and had her first child. Buying a house seemed like the thing to do.

Not if you're in the arts, it isn't! Musicians, opera singers, ballet dancers—they tend to move around a lot during their careers. And Joy was no exception. Months after she and her husband purchased their small condo, she got the call: an opportunity to be part of the storied Metropolitan Opera in New York City. Fortunately, Joy managed to sell her newly purchased home for about what she had paid for it, and placed the proceeds in the bank. But she still took a hit that she wouldn't have if she had been renting, in the form of $10,000 in closing costs.

I spoke with Joy at about the time she arrived in New York. She couldn't wait to start her prestigious new job. But guess what else she couldn't wait to do? Buy a place in New York. "Whoa, hold on," I said, "didn't you just make that mistake? Why not rent a while and see how your new job goes?"

Joy told me she was now in her "dream job." She couldn't imagine ever leaving.

"Well, what if they fire you?" I asked. I know, Little Miss Sunshine.

She acknowledged this could happen, but she didn't care. She had hundreds of thousands of dollars of cash left over from the sale of her condo just sitting in the bank. It was killing her that she was forking over $5,000 a month to rent a crappy Manhattan apartment when she could just as easily be buying.

"Yeah," I said, "but how much would you have to spend on a place in New York that you liked?"

"About $2 million," she said.

"Isn't $5,000 a month better than $2 million?"

She halfheartedly agreed that it was. I continued needling Joy like this, and she eventually gave in, agreeing to give it a year in New York before trying to buy a place.

Real estate has such a pull on us. It's like that no-good boyfriend or girlfriend we had in college. Even after being cheated on or dumped or talked about behind our backs, we can't help but go back for more. Optimism bias plays a role here, but it's not the whole story. In the United States, people are conned from an early age into believing in the "joys" of owning a home, and into thinking that real estate is the "cornerstone of our financial futures." We encounter people who've made millions flipping houses, amassing vacation rentals, or buying properties in distressed areas that subsequently became trendy and upscale. We're also battered by endless amounts of real estate porn on outlets like HGTV, as well as by special sections of newspapers like *The New York Times* and *The Wall Street Journal.*

Our obsession with ownership dates from the 1950s and 1960s, when the federal government tried to convince World War II veterans to buy homes. Policymakers believed—as many still do—that people would build more stable lives and contribute more to their communities and to the economy if they owned their own homes. Renters trash their properties, they claimed, while owners invest in improving them. Renters traipse around from city to city, while owners put down roots and feel a stake in their communities. On the strength of such assumptions, the government extended low-interest loans to veterans so that they could buy homes, giving rise to the modern mortgage industry.

The huge demand for homes by the Greatest Generation and then their offspring, the Boomers, pushed prices higher for decades, allowing everyday people to accumulate equity, and reinforcing beliefs about ownership's benefits. A mythology around home ownership and "the American dream" took root, one that the financial crisis and real estate bubble have shaken, but not destroyed. Today, the government still offers attractive tax deductions on mortgage interest payments (though a bit less generous after the 2017 tax reform), and our commander in chief happens to be none other than, yes, a real estate mogul.

Is home ownership better for society? That's a subject for another book, but let me just say, I have my doubts. Every month, we plow vast amounts of money into mortgages, as well as upkeep, reasoning that we're building equity and saving for our future. When the mortgage term is up and the home is paid off, we'll have all that equity to fund our retirements. Yeah, but what if when you retire housing prices are 20 percent lower than what you anticipated? What then? Because we've been putting our money into real estate in recent decades, we've put less of it into retirement savings accounts, where we can better monitor and manage the risk. The Economic Policy Institute has reported that middle-aged couples (aged fifty-six to sixty-one) have accumulated average retirement savings of just $163,577.[1] As Baby Boomers age, we'll have to figure out as a society how to support a generation of people who have little or no retirement savings, inadequate equity in their homes, and in the absence of pensions, only Social Security to fall back on—all because we've emphasized home ownership so much.

You'd think that smart people everywhere would see past the myth and take a more measured approach to home ownership. But we don't—the myth is entrenched, among people at all ends of the social spectrum. It also reaches down into our everyday lives, giving rise to a number of related beliefs that influence the brightest among us to invest in real estate even when we shouldn't.

"Oh, Jill," clients have said to me, "instead of investing the extra half-million I have in a balanced portfolio, I'm going to buy an investment property and rent it out." Yeah, great idea (note the sarcasm dripping from my voice). We buy into this notion that anyone can become a landlord, building up little real estate empires of our own, and it'll be great fun! Some of my clients and friends have found it fun, but many others have found it a colossal headache (midnight phone calls, asshole tenants), and far less profitable than they had imagined.

A friend of mine in Rhode Island bought a home with four rental units. She didn't have trouble attracting tenants, since the property was located right near Brown University. But the college students who rented a unit from her trashed the place. One time, they threw such a massive party that one of the police officers on the scene exclaimed, "This place looks like that frat house scene from *Animal House*!" My friend's cleaning service refused to clean the house because it was so disgusting.

And then there was the hassle. Every couple of months or so, my friend would get a call in the middle of the night from a tenant complaining that a toilet wasn't working, or from a neighbor complaining that her tenants were leaving their trash all over the place. Within a few years, this supposedly "good investment" turned into a fiasco. On a cash flow basis, my friend was making money, but when you factored in the time she was putting into the property and the stress it was causing her, it wasn't worth it. One day, she walked into my office, threw up her hands, and said, "I surrender. I can't do this anymore!" Shortly afterward, she sold. She might have hired a company to manage the property for her, but that would have cost her, and the numbers didn't work. Owning a rental property wasn't nearly as attractive as other investment options she might have chosen.

If you're handy and enjoy dealing with people and solving their problems, being a landlord might make for an attractive business prospect. But for many smart people, it's awful. Likewise, many smart people fall prey to another real estate misconception, the notion that owning your home is some kind of nirvana as compared with renting. "Ah," people think, "I can finally relax now that I own my own place. I can make it just the way I like it." It's true that owning a home gives you a sense of psychological security that renting usually doesn't. But many smart people—especially those who complain about "throwing all of their money out the window" as renters—underestimate the headaches that come with home ownership. Appliances break. Basements flood. Roofs leak. A hundred other things go wrong that aren't covered on your homeowner's insurance policy. It's on you, the owner, to fix it yourself, or to hire someone else to do it. Maintenance and renovation experts on my radio show have told me that the typical homeowners should expect to pay 1 to 3 percent of the purchase price *every single year* in upkeep. Talk about money out the window.

One night while in the process of writing this book, I came home to my apartment, which I own, hungry and eager to make dinner for myself. When I turned on the stove to bake the lasagna, the pilot light wouldn't catch. I got it fixed—$425 later (serves me right for trying to cook in the first place).

This kind of thing happens all the time. And it's not only older homes like mine that cause problems. One woman I know bought a brand-new home only to find that fixtures and appliances inside the home were breaking. The builders had apparently cut corners, leaving her to foot the bill for repairs. "You know that TV show *This Old House*," she said. "I'm starting a new one called *This Crappy New House*." At least she had a sense of humor. If you're going to own a piece of property instead of renting, factor in the unexpected costs and hassles that will keep you laughing, or more likely, wringing your hands in frustration.

Another real estate myth that stymies smart people is the notion that it's easy to "time" the market and make money. Shelley and her boyfriend, Claude, came out of the dot-com boom with solid jobs, earning about $150,000 between them. They wanted to move out of their rental in Denver and buy a house, but by 2005 had saved up only half of their desired 20 percent down payment. Still, they were growing antsy to buy. Interest rates had fallen from above 8 percent for a thirty-year fixed-rate mortgage to below 6 percent, and home prices had risen. They feared that if they didn't buy now, they'd "miss" the low interest rates. Further, prices would rise and their "dream home" would become unaffordable. I tried to calm them, advising them to be conservative when shopping for a house. If they waited and put down 20 percent, their monthly payments would be lower, allowing them to save more every month and giving them more security. They didn't listen. "Each day we wait," they told me, "the house we want slips a little farther out of our grasp."

In mid-2005, they plunked down 10 percent on a $350,000 house they loved, taking on a thirty-year mortgage with an interest rate of 5.875 percent. By 2007, the value of their home had risen to $400,000, and they were happy as could be. But then the market tanked, sending the value of their home below $300,000. At the same time, interest rates plunged below 5 percent. Shelley and Claude thought they had been smart buying into a hot market, but they would have been far better off waiting a few more years. In 2012, Claude lost his job, and because the couple lacked an emergency fund to tap into, they were forced to sell their home, locking in the loss of their down payment.

It's foolish to try to time the financial markets—a topic I'll cover in lucky Chapter 13. But people get burned trying to time the real estate market, too. Nobody really knows if prices or interest rates will rise or fall in the short term, or by how much. I know it's hard to do, but you must drown out market conditions and take into account other considerations when deciding to purchase real estate. Determine if you can reasonably afford the house you're eager to buy, and go from there.

REMEMBER THE BIG THREE

How exactly should you determine what you can afford? You might have heard somewhere that your total housing expenses should account for 30 percent of your income, give or take. For some, that rule might serve as a useful yardstick, but depending on where you live, it might not. If you make $200,000 and live in Nebraska, where real estate prices are below the national average, you would be an idiot to spend $75,000 on housing; it simply isn't necessary to spend that much. If you earned that same $200,000, lived in a high-cost area, and knew with reasonable certainty that your income would rise (for instance, you're an associate at a law firm and in two years you're up for partner), then you would be safe going a bit past the 30 percent threshold, and you very well might need to.

The 30 percent rule is about as useful as the rule in nutritional science that a healthy adult should consume 2,000 calories a day. For many people, that might be a good rough estimate, but factor in your own circumstances. A tall marathon runner putting in forty miles a week might need 4,000 calories a day—and then some. A sedentary gal topping out at all of five foot one might need only 1,500. Take the 30 percent rule as a starting point, and adapt it thoughtfully to your circumstances.

Before you even think of applying the 30 percent rule, go back to Chapter 2 and revisit my Big Three. Have you paid off your consumer debt, including those nasty student loans described in Chapter 4? Are you maxing out your retirement contributions? Do you have an emergency account large enough to cover six to twelve months of expenses? If you answered no to any of these questions, then be very cautious about proceeding with a home purchase, even if your total housing costs will fall to under 30 percent of your income.

Keep in mind, there are situations in which you might indeed want to buy a home instead of rent even while grappling with these basics of financial security. In some markets, for instance, purchasing a home might be considerably cheaper than renting, because the rental stock is so low. Run the numbers. If renting is significantly more affordable, choose that as an option while you continue to pay down debt and save for the future.

Let me give you a feel for what a responsible analysis looks like when you're thinking of buying a home. Jerome and Sandy, a married couple, lived in a rent-stabilized apartment in New York City. If you've ever come within a thousand miles of the city, then you know that $1,200 for a three-bedroom pad overlooking Central Park is ridiculously cheap. By the time Jerome was ready to retire at age seventy, their rent had increased somewhat, to $1,800 a month—still an incredible deal. At around the time Jerome was ready to retire, he and Sandy had the opportunity to purchase the apartment outright for a price below market value (their building was turning into a co-op; I'll spare you the details, but just know that many see getting an insider deal on a New York City co-op as a golden ticket). Jerome and Sandy were thinking of buying the apartment, using some portion of their $1 million in retirement savings as the down payment, instead of continuing to rent. They came to me wondering how much of their savings they should use as a down payment.

"I have an easy answer," I said. "I know exactly what that number is."

"Well, what is it?"

"Zero."

"Zero? Why? Shouldn't we buy it?"

"Absolutely not."

If they had $5 million in retirement savings, then buying the apartment might have been a good idea. But it was much cheaper to rent the place at $1,800 a month than to buy. Just the cost of maintaining the apartment and paying property taxes on it would run them about $2,500 a month. If the rent increased by 25 percent over the next decade, owning would still be the more expensive option. Meanwhile, owning would cut into their retirement savings, which they would probably need eventually, and would also leave them without enough of a cushion in case of an unforeseen crisis. It's true that buying their apartment might have allowed them to net a big gain if they ever sold. But maybe it wouldn't, and in the meantime, they were opening themselves up to quite a bit of unnecessary risk.

"Well, if we buy it," Jerome and Sandy said, "at least we'll have an asset to pass on to our kids."

"You already do have an asset," I replied. "It's called a million dollars that you're going to leave alone and do nothing with!"

They looked at one another, and then back at me. I had a point. They decided to pass up this supposedly lucrative opportunity. They would keep renting.

BEHOLD, THE HEROIC (AND HAPPY) AMERICAN RENTER

Given how persistent the "great American dream" myth is, I can't end this chapter without making at least some effort to romanticize renting. We need a new American dream, people! Or at least a modified one. With that goal in mind, here's a story for you from my own social circle.

A close friend of mine, Gus, got divorced in his late fifties after twenty-five years of marriage. He and his wife had owned real estate, and had made a fair amount of money thanks to purchases they'd made that were lucky and smart—lucky because they always occurred at the right time to take advantage of market trends, smart because Gus and his wife had always bought dilapidated properties and improved them. While negotiating the divorce settlement, Gus said to his wife, "You keep the house. I'll keep my retirement plan. We'll move on." And so it was. All of our friends assumed that Gus would buy a new place for himself. He had plenty of savings that he could use for a down payment, and he earned an ample income. Imagine our surprise when he said, "I'm not buying anything. I'm renting! I want to live near my kids, but I don't want to tie myself down to that neighborhood. I want as much opportunity as I can get."

Five years have passed since the divorce, and Gus is one of the happiest renters I've ever met. "It's so great," he tells me. "I pay the money. Someone comes and fixes stuff. I don't have to worry about anything. I can move if I want to, or I can stay where I am." Friends occasionally question his decision, pointing out that he can't deduct his mortgage payments from his taxes. "What," he says, "you think I'm going to buy a piece of real estate because of the tax deduction? I've never done that before."

Way to go, Gus.

I know so many people who write rent checks each month instead of mortgage checks—and love it. From their perspective, renting is freedom. It's opportunity. A young couple might rent, and when an exciting job offer comes in from several states away, they can go for it. A middle-aged couple interested in downsizing might rent while their home is on the market instead of buying a new home right away. When their home doesn't sell, no problem—they can move back in, avoiding the potentially ruinous circumstance of having to carry two mortgages. An older couple might forgo an opportunity to buy a second home on the beach, and rent an even nicer one instead. When one of them has a health crisis and they really need the cash, they'll have it!

My own mother, a longtime real estate agent, developed a love of renting later in life. A couple of years after my father died, a builder knocked on her door and offered her a pile of cash for her house. She knew selling was the right thing to do, but wasn't sure where she would go next. Her first impulse was to sink most of the sale's proceeds into a comfortable new place for herself. My sister and I encouraged her to rent for a few years, then buy, if she still wanted to. What was her rush? Why not take time to see what she really wanted? A few years later, she's thrilled that she followed our advice. Not only does she love her new apartment, but she also cherishes the freedom and flexibility that come with having money in the bank. Unless you have a trust fund or a rich aunt with no kids that I don't know about, you might, too.

You Take On Too Much Risk

Many of the stories I have told so far involve dumb things that came to fruition, so to speak, during extreme events, like the dot-com boom and bust of the late '90s and early 2000s, or the financial crisis and Great Recession of 2008–2009. The dumb thing is always dumb, but periods of chaos can amplify its prevalence and impact. Few stories I could tell better illustrate this "crisis magnification" effect than that of Rodney, a friend of a friend who worked for many years as a trader at the now-defunct Lehman Brothers. Rodney made a great living—in 2007, he was up to $1.8 million in total compensation. Over the years, he had saved $2 million in cash, and he had also accumulated a crapload of Lehman Brothers stock—I'm talking $20 million. He didn't want to sell any of the stock, feeling that it "had always been the best investment for me."

One day, his wife, who didn't work in the financial services industry, asked him about the stock. "Honey," she said, "isn't that a lot of our money tied up in one place? Shouldn't you just sell some?"

Rodney agreed that his wife was right, and as one of his New Year's resolutions in 2008, he promised to sell the stock. But instead of doing it right away, he entered an order to sell the Lehman stock once its price, which Rodney assumed would be higher than it currently was, reached a certain limit price (this is called a "limit order"). He chose $70 a share—seemingly reasonable, since the stock was trading in the mid-$60s. By the end of February, the stock had sunk to $50 and Rodney had to admit that he likely would not see $70 for a while. He reduced the limit price again, to just above $50. When it reached that new price, he figured he'd sell a chunk to satisfy his wife's request.

In March, Lehman Brothers' stock sank into the $30s, but Rodney told himself not to panic, that the company was worth more than $30 per share. When the stock recovered into the $40s, Rodney felt confident that his limit of $50 was in the bag—it was just a matter of time. Again, the stock failed to hit the preset limit, so he lowered the limit price once again. And again. And again. On September 15, 2008, Lehman Brothers filed for bankruptcy, and the stock became worthless. Rodney lost his job and his entire $20 million stake. Luckily for him, he still had the $2 million in savings, but he and his wife had to sell their house. Whereas previously the family didn't have to worry about money, now they did.

Rodney, like so many other smart people, made the mistake of taking on excessive risk. It's a stunningly easy mistake to make, and also a potentially devastating one. As I've mentioned, my father worked as an options trader on the floor of the American Stock Exchange when I was growing up. He liked taking risks, and because he was an independent trader, he could make whatever bets he wanted. That unconstrained risk-taking proved to be his undoing. In the early 1980s, before the bull market in stocks began, my father loved executing a strategy called "short vol," which stands for short volatility. This was a gamble based not on whether a stock would rise or fall, but whether its price would linger within a certain range.

Here's how it works: If XYZ stock has been kind of boring

lately, maybe trading between $9 and $10 for the past six months, a trader would use financial products called "derivatives" or "options" to wager that over the next three or six months, the stock would not drop below $7 or rise above $12. At a time when markets were really not doing too much, this bet was seen as a no-brainer—"free money."

My father made a short vol bet on an energy company called Marathon Oil. What he didn't foresee was that the company, which had become a takeover target by Mobil Corporation for $85 per share in late 1981, would see another, much larger bid by U.S. Steel. Dad had bet that the stock would stay around $85 per share, but when the better bid came in from U.S. Steel, it jumped to $125! The company's shareholders were delighted. In a single day, my father lost his entire trading account—$300,000, which today would be worth just under $800,000. He had no choice but to close up shop and look for a job. If you can believe it, he ended up landing a position at the firm that managed the options for Marathon. After borrowing money from family members, which he repaid in full, he kept our family solvent.

Don't stake your financial future on the success or failure of a single crazy gambit, however lucrative it might seem. It's not prudent to shoulder such risks, nor is it necessary. The best path to take when investing is a middle one, whereby you set reasonable financial goals, accept only as much risk as is necessary to reach your goals, and stick with the plan through both up and down markets. I call it the "defensive driving" theory of investing. Over time, following a "passive" approach such as this will allow you to move ever closer toward your goals, without falling prey to mental processes that distort our perception of risk and leave us vulnerable to poor decision-making. Later in life, when you've achieved your goals, you'll be able to enjoy some hard-won financial freedom rather than continuing to work your butt off after taking one risky bet too many. If you follow the simple steps I'll lay out later in this chapter, you might even find yourself enjoying something more valuable than money: true happiness.

NEVER TAKE INVESTMENT ADVICE FROM A CAVEMAN

Some of you might not be terribly moved by the stories of people like Rodney or my father. "Jill," you say, "give me a little credit here. What they did was out-and-out stupid and irresponsible. I might make mistakes, but I'm not about to do something *that* dumb."

Don't be so sure. Taking on excessive risk quite often has little to do with how smart you are, or how responsible. It has everything to do with how your mind processes risk. Although we might think we perceive risk in a clear, rational way, we actually harbor a number of built-in cognitive biases that warp our perception of probability and cause us to make poor financial decisions. As Dan Egan, director of behavioral finance and investments at Betterment, told me in an interview, human beings "don't pay attention to the future as much as we should, or we pay attention to the wrong things—those that are bright and colorful and sexy rather than the dull and boring things that are actually more effective."[1] We aren't even conscious of these tendencies of ours, which make them all the more dangerous.

As Egan related, our brains evolved over tens of thousands of years in conditions very different from those of modern life. In particular, because most cavemen lived to be thirty or forty, not seventy or eighty, our brains didn't evolve to comprehend phenomena that unfolded over longer time horizons. What did a caveman know about compound interest, or the concept of compounding in general (for instance, the idea that if you exercise each day, the effects can accumulate over a long period)? Not much, which is why these concepts can still feel somewhat counterintuitive or unnatural for us, and why many of us do better with short-term tasks than with long-term, strategic planning.

Consider, for instance, what cognitive scientists call "recency bias." Focused as they are on short time horizons, our reptilian brains incline us to pay attention to events that transpired recently in relation to risk, and to assume that these trends will always hold. This blinds us to the possibility of a change in the existing pattern, and it causes us to make irrational moves that don't reflect the amount of actual risk.

Recency bias is everywhere today, if you know where to look. You see it, for instance, in how people make preventative health care decisions. Between 2009 and 2016, only about 40 percent of American adults got flu shots, even though doctors recommended them and they were cheap and widely available. There were many reasons for this, including persistent myths that vaccines caused autism or that they gave people the flu themselves. But another reason was the "age-old fallacy that something like this [i.e., getting the flu] could never happen to [me]."[2] Many people said to themselves, "I feel fine. Why should I get a flu shot?"[3] Yes, you feel fine now, and you've felt fine over the past few weeks, but what about a few months from now? Recency bias was skewing people's sense of the risk, preventing them from taking action, and leaving them more vulnerable.

Many cognitive biases rear their ugly heads in investing—"loss aversion" (our tendency to fear losses more than we relish gains), for instance, or "anchoring bias" (our tendency to peg our decision-making too closely to certain pieces of information).[4] But in my experience, recency bias is one of the most dangerous blind spots out there. Clients of mine described in previous chapters saw the housing market rise over a period of years, and assumed it always would. They assumed they didn't need various kinds of insurance, because they had always been healthy up to that point. But nothing in life stays the same indefinitely. The ancient Egyptians, the Mayans, the Romans—all seemed invincible in their day, and all saw their civilizations crumble. To make sound financial decisions, we must peer beyond recent time horizons and consider different future scenarios. We must take the concept of risk more seriously than we often do.

Let's say your company updated its 401(k) plan, and you now must choose a new mutual fund. You review your options and the performance of various funds. Mutual fund "A," which was invested in aggressive growth stocks, reported a 2 percent loss in the previous fiscal year. Mutual fund "B," another aggressive growth portfolio, boasted a 6 percent gain. Which one will you choose? Most likely, the fund that posted the gain. Why would you want to be in that crappy fund as opposed to the thing that went up? Because you're human, that's why. You assume that because these funds performed as they did in the recent past, they'll continue to do so in the future.

But recent performance is no guarantee of future performance. Don't believe me? Take a closer look at that big, fat prospectus your fund company has sent you. There is usually a disclaimer that says, "Past performance does not guarantee future returns." The fund companies are forced to put that in writing by regulators, but nearly all investors blow past the warning and do what they always do—buy last year's winners, usually at their own peril. Here's a great recent example: In 2016, natural gas was the top-performing investment asset, up 57.6 percent for the year. "Wow," you might have said, "I want to be in that!" Big mistake. In 2017, natural gas was the third *worst* asset to own, down 21 percent.

Likewise, my father's big investment flop stemmed not from ignorance, but from unchecked recency bias. During the late 1970s, when the stock market was stagnant, my father had made some serious cash betting that stock prices of specific companies would remain muted. He perceived he was taking a fairly measured risk betting similarly on Marathon Oil. In fact, his intense focus on recent performance blinded him to a fundamental reality of the stock market, which is that a company's price can always move up or down in unexpected ways for any number of reasons. Wars break out. Natural disasters happen. Company executives make erroneous revenue projections. In Rodney's case, too, we find recency bias at work. Because his company stock had held its value or increased in recent years, he assumed it always would.[5] So he failed to sell it and diversify his holdings, when even his wife, who wasn't well-versed in finance, thought he should do so.

Stories like Rodney's and my father's are only half of the picture when it comes to recency bias. This blind spot in our thinking can swing both ways, leading to both excessive risk-taking *and* excessive fearfulness. Between 2012 and 2018, the S&P 500 rose an impressive 100 percent. And yet, as *The Wall Street Journal* reported in 2018, "Nearly $1 trillion [was] pulled from retail-investor mutual funds that target U.S. stocks" during that same six-year period. "No one is excited," one analyst was quoted as saying. "This is not like 1999 and 2000, where you went to a bar and CNBC was on TV."[6] Now, why was that? Do you think it might have had something to do with the fact that many Americans lost their shirts during the financial crisis? Um, *yeah*! Many individual investors had a bad experience, and on a conscious or unconscious level, they feared that the future would hold more of the same. It was a classic case of recency bias.

In all likelihood, of course, many of these investors weren't hobbled just by recency bias, but also by the trauma that their losses inflicted. I've known many people who never again feel comfortable taking reasonable risks after sustaining big losses. One woman inherited three million dollars during the mid-1990s when her husband died. She took up day trading, and did well for herself, turning that sum into $5 million by the mid-2000s. When the market fell in 2008, she lost $1.5 million. Horrified, she pulled all of her money out of the stock market and kept it permanently stashed in cash and low-risk bonds. Although she made some small returns, she missed out on the 250 percent return she might have seen over the past decade. My father, too, was so scarred by his experience losing his trading account that for the rest of his life, he became an overly cautious investor—to both his detriment and that of his heirs. (I know: "Boo-hoo, poor us!")

The two faces of recency bias help explain why a passive investment approach such as the one that I'm advocating—where you hatch a plan up front about how to allocate your investments, and then ride out the plan through up and down markets—will usually yield better returns than actively managing your investments. When you manage actively, you tend to react emotionally to your investment's recent performance. If your investment is down, you get scared, and you're more inclined to pull your money out and put it in cash until prices go back up. If it's up, you want to invest even more in it.

This is the very *opposite* of what you should be doing. If you pull your money out of a declining investment and then wait for it to go back up, you're missing out on a portion of its increasing value. In effect, you're selling low and buying high. If you pour money into an investment that's already high, you're more vulnerable to a subsequent price decline if the price is already near its peak. All of those small moves, based on fear and greed and influenced by a focus on what just happened, take their toll. As research has found, active investors trying to match the performance of the S&P 500 lag it by 2.8 percent per year over a twenty-year period.[7] The smartest investing is *passive* investing.

NO MORE KEEPING UP WITH THE JONESES

As important and dangerous as they are, cognitive biases aren't the only reasons smart people often become their own worst enemies when it comes to investing. Many of us simply don't understand our tolerance to risk as well as we should. We tell ourselves we can handle much more risk than we really can—usually, of course, when the markets are riding high. And so, when the opportunity arises, we take on excessive risk, with little holding us back. We learn the hard way that maybe we can't tolerate that much risk after all.

Clients of mine, a married couple, were each retired teachers in their late sixties during the mid-2000s. They had nice pensions, which combined with Social Security totally covered their needs. They also were lucky enough to have a bunch of money stashed away for retirement. Against my advice, they plunged all of this money into the stock market.

"Why take so much risk?" I asked them. "It makes no sense!"

"Well," they said, "we don't need this money, so we thought we'd just invest it for our kids."

Okay, fine, I thought. If they were investing for their children, and they could handle losing some or all of that money in the short or even intermediate term, then perhaps that made sense. But then the market tanked, and what did these clients do? They cut and ran, losing more than they would have if they'd been assuming a more moderate amount of risk all along. Left on our own, most of us are probably like this couple. We overestimate our ability to sustain risk, letting emotions influence our decision-making.

People also take on too much risk because they're overcome by feelings of jealousy and inadequacy. We tend to measure our own self-worth according to what others have, and some of us make risky investment moves in a foolish attempt to measure up, with little thought to our own goals and risk tolerance.

Linda, a paramedic I knew, is a case in point. Her brother was a big success as a furniture designer, and she had always felt self-conscious and insecure about her relative lack of stature and wealth. One day, her brother told her about an opportunity to invest in a couple of antique chairs by a famous designer. If she bought in now and sold the chairs in a year or two, she would make a killing. In her mind, this investment represented her big chance to even out the playing field between her and her brother and to become a "success" in the eyes of their family. I cautioned her to make sure that the furniture she was buying was authentic, and that the price was attractive. Linda said she would, and wound up taking out a home equity loan against the small single-family home she owned in order to invest in the furniture. The furniture turned out to be fake. Linda lost almost all of her investment.

We all harbor feelings of jealousy and inadequacy relative to others. When I ran my own investment firm, I took a relatively small salary in order to grow my business. At a time when colleagues of mine were bringing home $1 million to $2 million, I was making a fraction of that. Do you think my ego took a hit when my mom told me that an old classmate of mine who had taken remedial math in high school had just bought a $6 million home? I'd be lying if I said it didn't. But I never acted on those feelings, sinking my money into some risky scheme in order to get rich quick.

If you want to build toward a healthy financial future, try to ignore external factors. Just because your best friend made $100,000 in Bitcoin doesn't mean you have to take your small nest egg and go all in on the next hot virtual currency to come along. Just because your wealthy sister is putting her money into some obscure biotech stock doesn't mean that's a good investment for you. The secret to sound investing is to know yourself well and to play your own game. Let's take a quick look at exactly what that means.

JILL'S FIVE STEPS TO INVESTING SUCCESS

We can survive recency bias and other distortions by creating a regulating mechanism for ourselves that helps us compensate. Dan

Egan compares it to glasses: Our eyes don't focus properly, so instead of squinting, we create those funny little contraptions that rest on our noses to help us see. Likewise, we need a whole array of funny little contraptions for our financial affairs. My version of "glasses" for investing is a simple, five-step system that allows you to minimize how many direct investment decisions you need to make. The fewer decisions, the less opportunity for your internal biases to wreak havoc. As the market rises and falls, you don't need to worry. Just sit back and let the system you've put in place handle it. Pretty cool, right? Here's what you should do:

Step #1: Mind the Big Three

Have you paid down your debt, amassed an emergency fund large enough to cover six to twelve months of expenses, and maxed out your retirement contributions. No? Then what are you doing reading this chapter? You shouldn't even be *thinking* about investing unless you've tackled the Big Three.

Step #2: Create a Financial Plan

Once you've handled the Big Three, what now? Should you figure out a way to allocate your assets? No. First you need to craft a broader financial plan that encompasses your financial goals, other sources of income you will have in the future, and your tolerance for risk. Your investments should serve this larger plan, not the other way around.

Drafting a financial plan requires serious thought. When do you plan to retire? What kind of Social Security benefit can you expect? Will you have an inheritance? Will you be able to draw on other sources of income? What would you like to be able to afford in the future, besides a comfortable retirement? Do you hope to care for an aging parent? Do you plan to help pay for your children's college education? Do you expect to buy or rent a second home (after the last chapter, I hope the answer is "Rent!").

Once you've answered these questions, calculate the rate of return you'll need on your investments to reach your goals. If you jump online and plug your numbers into a retirement calculator (which I advise you to do), you might find that you have to make some ungodly return on your investment—10 percent, say, or even 12 percent—in order to have enough money later in life. If that's the case, you will need another plan. Some people might believe that 10 percent returns are possible if they take on enough risk, but that's not the case. Over the long term, a risky portfolio probably won't get you that kind of payoff, since the wild swings will likely freak you out and you'll bail. Even if you do invest at an opportune time, you won't get out before a downturn. Are you up for that, considering your age and the number of years remaining before you'll need to tap into your savings?

Conversely, if you run the numbers, you might find that you don't have to take much risk at all to reach your goals. In that case, you might stick to a "boring" portfolio, which doesn't fluctuate too much on either the upside or the downside.

If you haven't taken a risk assessment questionnaire (they're available all over the Web), then what are you waiting for? Or maybe you should remind yourself of exactly how you felt in September 2008, when it looked like markets were melting down toward zero. Did you agonize over those losses? Did you lose sleep? Did you either check your account obsessively or suffer from the Ostrich Effect, where you never wanted to see the bad news?

If your initial goals required too much risk, then throw those goals out the window and settle on some more realistic ones. Maybe you won't retire at age fifty-eight, but rather at sixty-four. Maybe you'll only provide a state college education for your kids. Maybe you'll content yourself with $8,000 a month during retirement, not the $10,000 a month you currently spend. Think it through, perhaps with the aid of a trusted financial planner. Reconciling yourself to reality now will save you untold sleepless nights in the future.

Step #3: Allocate Your Assets

Once you've framed reasonable goals and calculated the rate of return you'll need to achieve them, you have to invest your money in a way that will deliver that return with a minimum of risk. You'll want to diversify your investments, dividing them among the five basic investment classes: stocks, bonds, real estate, commodities, and cash. Want more risk? Go heavier on the percentage of your portfolio you allocate to stocks or commodities. Want less risk? Emphasize bonds and cash. Whatever the case, settle on an allocation formula that reflects your risk tolerance, one that you can stick with both in good times and in bad. The point of asset allocation is that over the long term, when one part of your portfolio zigs, another part zags. Sure, there will be years when multiple asset classes zig or zag (2008 and 2015 come to mind), but the strategy works beautifully over an extended time horizon. Research and common sense both show that a thoughtful and honest asset allocation plan, along with periodic rebalancing, can help investors navigate extreme periods of market movement and avoid acting precipitously.

Step #4: Stick to the Plan!

Every year, one of the asset classes in which you're invested will look crappier than the others. You'll be tempted to shift money from the poorly performing assets to the better ones. Don't do it! Have faith in your plan, knowing that the overall asset mix will yield the best long-term results. The market might change, but you're the same old person—don't forget that! And don't stress out about whether your allocation is too conservative or too risky. What's really going to determine how much wealth you accumulate over your lifetime isn't whether your stock/bond allocation is 70/30 or 60/40 or 50/50. It's whether you saved consistently and refrained from making the big mistakes chronicled in this book.

Once you've come up with your plan, the best approach, I find, is to largely forget about it and focus on other parts of your life. Don't obsess! If you ask me at any given time how my investment accounts are doing, I can't give you the numbers. That's because I only check on a quarterly basis. I've allocated my stocks to reflect my risk tolerance (in my case, it's 50/50 stocks and bonds, and I'm in it for the long term, so I don't need to know on a weekly or monthly basis how I'm doing. This is passive investing at its best!

I do need to rebalance my portfolio periodically (at least annually, although I prefer quarterly) so as to keep my allocations in line with my plan. If stocks did well one quarter, I have to put some of those gains back into the other four categories in order to maintain my desired ratios. Or if I receive new awards of company stock every year, as some people do, I have to sell a portion of that stock to keep to my predetermined allocation. Then again, I could sign up for auto-rebalancing, which many financial companies offer, and which I highly recommend, forgoing even that bit of regular maintenance.

Step #5: Every Three Years, Revisit Your Allocation

Have you experienced any big life changes? As important as it is to stick with the plan, circumstances sometimes arise that do require you to take on more or less risk. Let's say your parents die unexpectedly and you inherit five million dollars. Now you don't need the million dollars you've socked away to pay for your kids' education. You can take more risk with it. On the other hand, perhaps your spouse passes away, leaving you as a single parent. You decide to quit your job to take care of the kids, relying on your savings and the money you'll get from your spouse's life insurance. Whereas previously you had allocated 75 percent of your investments to riskier stocks, now you can't afford to lose some or all of your nest egg, so you lower that allocation to 40 percent, or even 30.

In these kinds of situations, you're changing the plan not because one asset or another seems like a more attractive investment in the moment, but because your life has fundamentally changed, and with it, your financial needs and risk tolerance. When your portfolio takes a hit, or a "sure thing" investment appears on your doorstep, that little "recency bias" voice in your head might try to talk you into changing your risk profile. Ask yourself: Has anything really changed in my life that would require a change? If not, take a deep breath and go back to Step #4.

THE SIXTH STEP

Yes, there is a sixth step to my "defensive driving" approach to investing, and it's the best one of all: strolling off into the sunset. You've thought about your life and goals. You've run the numbers. You've crafted a plan that you can live with in good times and bad. You've stuck with the plan. Now, after all that hard work, you can sit back and enjoy. No, you probably haven't become a zillionaire. No sailing around the Caribbean in a hundred-foot yacht for you.

But you haven't gone bankrupt, either, nor must you become a greeter at the neighborhood big-box store. In addition, there's a special kind of satisfaction that comes with tuning out the noise, taking time to know yourself and your dreams, and staying true to your values, principles, and personality in order to make them a reality. You not only have your retirement nest egg and the peace of mind that this brings, you have the happiness that comes with feeling rooted and solid and strong in your life.

For all of his flaws, my father knew happiness like that. After losing his trading account and taking a job at a firm, he realized that he needed to work with partners who would hold back his urge to take excessive risks. So, he wound up joining another specialist firm, eventually becoming a partner. He repaid all the money he'd borrowed, crafted a financial plan for himself, and stuck to it. Although the plan was overly conservative, it allowed him to retire in his early sixties.

Dad could have worked longer in order to amass more wealth, but he decided not to. "You know what?" he said to me once. "I don't want to work this hard and drop dead staring at a stock screen." Spending time with family and enjoying a well-rounded life mattered to him more than another digit added onto his net worth. He never felt jealous of his wealthier friends or family members, nor did he alter his overly conservative investment strategy to keep up with them. He knew what he was about, and he respected his limits. When he died at age seventy-six, he was calm, happy, and at peace. He had taken risks in the service of greed, but he had learned from his mistakes, and had come to serve as an example to others.

Do you need to learn about excessive risk-taking the hard way? Or will you commit right now to a more disciplined approach, adopting a system that will help you overcome your emotions and cognitive biases? Will you live your life working toward a higher goal you set for yourself, or will you drive yourself crazy perpetually chasing money for its own sake?

Only you know the answer to that. Choose wisely.

You Fail to Protect Your Identity

We're not done with my father just yet. One day, a few years before his death, when he was seventy-three years old, he called to say that he had "screwed up" and thought he "had an identity theft problem." Apparently, the Internal Revenue Service had contacted his accountant, informing him that the agency thought my father had fallen victim to identity theft. Identity theft was not yet part of the national dialogue, but the IRS had developed and deployed software to flag returns that differed from those filed previously. For fifty years, my father had never received a tax refund, nor had he filed his tax return on time—he always went on extension. But that year, the IRS received a tax return soon after tax season opened in February, one that claimed my father was owed a $30,000 federal tax refund. Suspicious, to say the least.

From what we could tell, the IRS was right—someone was trying to scam the agency by pretending to be my father. Most likely, my father, who used computers but wasn't especially tech-savvy, had unwittingly clicked on a link in an email he'd received and divulged personal information, most notably his Social Security number. He didn't realize how vulnerable he was to this kind of fraud. As he discovered, all thieves needed to do, once they obtained his Social Security number, was file a return and either change the address or change the instructions for electronic funds transfer, and Uncle Sam would pay them any tax refund money that was due. Then, when he filed his *real* return, the IRS would say, "Oh, Albie, there must have been some kind of screwup, because we have already received a return from you." (That is, of course, if the IRS talked like a human being.)

Such fraud happens all the time, costing billions of dollars in losses each year. Fortunately, individual filers aren't responsible for these losses—the government eats it. But since we taxpayers fund the government, that means we collectively pay for this fraud in the form of higher taxes.

Since the mammoth 2017 data breach at Equifax, identity theft has been in the news, with experts decrying consumers' vulnerability to a wide range of scams and frauds. Should we believe all the hype?

Absolutely.

Most people—including most smart people—ignore identity theft. They fail to take basic steps that might prevent it, such as changing passwords frequently or checking their credit. In one recent study, 81 percent of participants above the age of thirty reported reusing passwords. Among younger participants, such carelessness was even more rampant, with 87 percent of people reporting reusing.[1] Another study found that in the months after the Equifax breach, half of respondents hadn't bothered to check their credit reports to confirm that their identities hadn't been stolen. Almost half of respondents aged eighteen through thirty-seven were either unaware or only vaguely aware of the Equifax breach. (P.S.: Hackers stole personal data on 146 million Americans, including driver's license numbers and Social Security numbers—possibly *yours*.)[2] Still another study found that 40 percent of respondents used unsecured Wi-Fi networks when logging on, and

35 percent carelessly clicked on links they found on social media sites.[3]

On the brighter side, 52 percent of Americans, according to the Pew Research Center, "report that they use two-step authentication on at least some of their online accounts."[4] But wait: That means almost 50 percent *don't* use two-step authentication. And that, in turn, means I should probably explain what two-step authentication is. While single-factor authentication requires your username and one password, two-step adds another credential to the process, like a code that is sent to your mobile phone, which you then input on the site in order to gain access. Two-factor authentication adds about sixty seconds to your log-in process, which evidently is far too long for most people!

Our lack of patience, combined with a lackadaisical attitude, leaves us open to considerable stress and inconvenience, if not actual financial losses. Trust me, you don't want to have your identity stolen. Reordering your affairs can be a real pain, taking months of effort and requiring the services of attorneys and other experts. Adam Levin, a former director of the New Jersey Division of Consumer Affairs, immersed himself in the world of identity theft and wrote a book on the topic called *Swiped*. In it, he told the story of a woman whose identity was stolen by a person who then committed crimes in her name. "Every time she left her home," Levin writes, the woman "had to worry about something as banal as a traffic stop, because it opened the possibility that her driver's license would be run through a law enforcement database, her 'record' would be discovered, and a call to arrest her would be made." Identity theft cost this woman tens of thousands of dollars, and it made her life an "unmitigated hell." As she explained, "Every day of my life for seven years, I'm on the phone with my fraud specialist trying to figure this thing out."[5]

Are you scared yet? You'd better be! In the face of hacks like the Equifax breach, you have to assume that your personal information is already out there on the Dark Web. For those not familiar with the concept, dark websites are sites that people can access only through special encrypted browsers. Criminals can use them to commit all sorts of misdeeds—like buy drugs, malware, and even your personal data—undetected by law enforcement. The good news is that you can take steps to make it harder for thieves to do serious damage. Would you be dumb enough to leave your car parked in New York City with the windows down and your Gucci handbag in plain view? No way! You'd at least lock it up and put your handbag in the trunk (although my mother would tell you that you are a moron for doing that, too). You can do the same with identity theft. Take it seriously, exercising a baseline level of care and vigilance. Let thieves pick on less conscientious targets first!

SMART PEOPLE GET HACKED, TOO

I suspect that most of you readers will put down my book, go back to whatever you were doing, and forget all about the dire threats you face due to identity theft. Many of you might think you're too smart for identity theft to happen to you. You know to keep your passwords straight, not to give out your Social Security number, and not to click on emails that are obviously spam or phishing. With such safeguards in place, you feel "safe" in online spaces.

You're not safe. As experts will tell you, digital technology is porous from top to bottom. I thought I was pretty safe, too, and then I interviewed cybersecurity expert Kevin Mitnick for my podcast.[6] Known as "the world's most famous hacker," the dude's a bona fide cyberthief who served five years in federal prison, including eight months in solitary confinement. Today, companies pay him and his team to hack their networks in order to expose vulnerabilities. Off-air, to demonstrate what thieves can do, Mitnick asked me for two pieces of information: my name and my address.

He went online and in less than five minutes obtained my Social Security number and several other pieces of very personal information. It doesn't matter how intelligent you are. Nobody's information is safe any longer.

If you think intelligence protects you from identity theft, then I have a joke for you: How many PhDs does it take to protect yourself against identity theft? The answer is more than two. My friend Jason, who has a PhD from an Ivy League university, emailed an invoice for $4,500 to his client, another PhD who worked as a professor at a well-respected business school in another country. His invoice contained wiring instructions for his client to use. Jason waited for payment, and thought it strange when the wire transfer didn't arrive. He sent his client a couple of reminder emails, but received no response. Finally, several weeks later, Jason and his client connected on a previously scheduled Skype call. "I wired you $4,500," Jason's client said. She read aloud the wiring instructions she'd used.

"That's not my bank account," my friend said.

Further investigation revealed that Jason's client's university email had been hacked. The hackers had intercepted Jason's original email with the correct wiring instructions and prevented his client from receiving it. They had then sent his client a new email, ostensibly from him, with substitute wiring instructions inserted. They intercepted all of Jason's follow-up emails, again blocking his client from reading them. She had no idea that he was writing her, and thus no idea for weeks that she'd been conned. (Most likely, the hackers had been scanning emails for words like "invoice" or "wiring instructions.")

As Jason and his client learned, it is *never* a good idea to send wiring instructions or any other sensitive information via email. Since the hackers had his bank account number, Jason had to close his account and open another. His client lost her money—her bank refused to reimburse her. Since then, Jason has become far more careful about his email usage. "Whenever I'm writing anything, I operate on the assumption that a scammer will potentially read it," he said. "I'm sending fewer emails and making more phone calls these days. I never used to think much about identity theft. Now, I obsess over it."

There are a number of other reasons smart people underestimate the risk posed by identity theft. As behavioral economist Dan Egan told me, our limited attention spans figure prominently in how we make financial decisions. Many people don't change bank accounts very frequently, even though some banks offer cash incentives for new accounts, because they want to minimize the number of accounts they have to oversee. Something similar holds true when it comes to identity theft. "We know, in some sort of cold, perfect, rational sense, [that] we should have a different password for everything, and [that] we should have two-factor authentication for everything, but we don't have the memory for it."[7]

Egan observes that identity theft is also a relatively intangible threat, and so more readily ignored. We're far more afraid of airplane crashes than we are of car accidents, or of the Zika virus than we are of heart disease, even though car accidents and heart attacks afflict many more people. Identity theft seems similar to heart disease or car accidents in that we don't register it as an acute catastrophe. Thieves might steal one bit of personal information from you via email, they might obtain others by scanning your social media sites, and they might obtain still others by purchasing them from thieves who hacked into a company you patronize. Only when they compile all of this data do they have the capacity to wreak havoc on your life. If you come to learn that a key piece of information such as your Social Security number was stolen, it might be months or years before you suffer negative consequences, if you suffer any at all. Many of us might be aware of identity threat as a problem, but we don't *feel* it directly—until we do. It's no surprise that many of us are more likely to lock our car doors than we are to set up two-factor authentication.

Some of us might also fail to take action because we aren't aware of the array of potential scams to which we might fall victim. "I had never heard of a scam like this," Jason told me, "and had no idea I was risking anything by sending wiring instructions via email." Would you have ever thought that infants could be vulnerable to identity theft? I didn't, until a caller to my radio show told me that his two-year-old son had his identity stolen. He didn't quite know how it happened—it might have been a bad keystroke, or a slip of his tongue in the course of his daily interactions. But somehow, a thief obtained his son's Social Security number and began opening up credit card accounts in his name. This caller didn't suffer any financial losses, but he did have to spend more than a year working with the Internal Revenue Service, the Federal Trade Commission, and the police to get the matter resolved. Even now, his son's information is still out there. The caller had arranged for a freeze to be put on his son's credit and had taken additional precautionary measures, but his son remained vulnerable to other potential scams.

There are dozens of common scams, and of course they are constantly evolving in line with new technologies and changes in common behaviors. That charitable organization that calls you pleading for a donation as well as for some of your personal information? It could be a scam. That email you got from the IRS informing you that you're entitled to a refund, and just need to enter your personal information to get it? That's definitely a scam—the IRS will never contact you electronically, only by snail mail. That dating website user you're chatting with who seems too good to be true? That could be a scam.[8] Just when you think you understand your main points of vulnerability, new ones pop up—on email, on social media, on websites you might come across during your daily surfing.

In many cases, we fail to protect ourselves because we don't even understand how companies use our data, and hence the ways in which our personal information might be vulnerable. In the wake of the Equifax breach, not one but two famous network anchors asked me to explain the breach and what it meant for them. "But I never gave information to Equifax," one of them said.

"I know," I replied, "but every time you took out a loan or signed a credit card agreement, you agreed to all that fine print, which authorizes the company to run your credit with credit reporting agencies, including Equifax. That's how they got your information."

Here was an extremely smart and well-respected individual whom millions of Americans relied on to convey the day's most important issues. And he didn't know basic facts about credit reporting! Lacking that knowledge, he would have been less inclined to guard his information vigilantly. Many smart people who are preoccupied with their own lives simply don't care to pay attention to the handling of their data. "I don't know how all that stuff works," they say. "I'll just assume the big companies have me covered." The big companies *don't* have you covered. Not even close. You need to cover yourself, to the extent you can.

Finally, I suspect that many of us are simply lazy when it comes to protecting ourselves from technology. We love the convenience that social media, smartphones, and other communication technologies afford, but we're just not into dealing with the hassles that this technology also foists upon us. Who wants to read the small print in that lengthy disclosure form or contract your mobile provider, dating app, or online meals program sends you regarding the handling of your data? Who wants to spend time fussing over passwords? Who wants to think about information you're divulging when writing an email or text? Who wants to think about whether you're using end-to-end encryption or not, or whether you're using a secure server or not? We just want to live our lives and forget about all this crap. And yet, we can't.

BE WILDLY SKEPTICAL

At this point in the chapter, I'm going to stop trying to convince you to get your act together and tell you what you should actually do to protect your identity. I want you to close your eyes and imagine me in my home office, holding my nose as I type into the keyboard. I *know* the measures I'm about to recommend are a) boring; b) unoriginal;[9] and c) a pain in the ass. I know you really, really, really have better things to do. And I know that many of you will follow my advice and *still* wind up getting scammed. Nevertheless, my ten-point plan (juiced up to be as entertaining as possible) will help you to at least reduce your chances of falling victim.

Here's what you should do *starting now* to help prevent identity theft:

1. *Guard your personal information like your life depended on it:* Give out your Social Security number? Maybe, but always ask whether it is necessary in order to complete the transaction. If the company you're dealing with doesn't require it, don't give it. And never give it to a total stranger.
2. *Be less social on social media:* Your friends don't care if you just left for a ten-day jaunt to Machu Picchu, or if you love the new $10,000 home entertainment system that just got delivered. But thieves care. They're scouring social media, monitoring when you're away from home, and compiling profiles on you to sell to others or to use themselves in an upcoming scam. As Adam Levin says, "Facebook and other social media sites can be an identity thief's El Dorado."[10]

3. *Warn the young'uns (and the old'uns):* Children give up a lot of information on social media, and thieves know it. Warn them about the dangers. Your elderly parents and grandparents are likewise easy targets. Alert them to common scams involving technology, and remind them that when they become Facebook friends with their grandchildren, they, too, need to be careful not to overshare. One easy hint: Never ever put your year of birth out there, and don't assume that social media instant or direct messages are secure.

4. *Ditch the 12345678:* You need stronger passwords than that. And you should be changing them every month. I know, this sucks, but there is a reason your company is making you do this, too! If it helps, get yourself a password generator.

5. *Two-factor it, baby:* Passwords aren't enough. When possible, protect your accounts with two-factor authorization. It's like having a double dead bolt on your front door. It's like wearing two condoms instead of one. Yikes, you get the idea.

6. *Whip out the credit card:* If you get scammed on your debit card, you might have to eat the loss. Credit card companies usually do the eatin'.

7. *Fortify the WiFi:* The next time you find yourself in an airport terminal logging into a public WiFi system in order to check your bank balance or pay your bills, know that you're being absolutely ridiculous. Two words: secured networks only. I know, that was three words.

8. *Read before paying:* I'm asking you to do the unthinkable and spend three minutes actually perusing your credit card statement before you click "Pay full balance" on the website. It's so easy to do—and even easier to forget to do. But how else are you going to know your account has been compromised? Here's another way: Have your financial institution notify you if a payment over a fixed amount has been authorized. Most institutions offer this service.

9. *Go in for your twelve-month checkup:* What does getting a physical exam have to do with identity theft? Nothing—I'm talking about checking on your credit scores once a year, just to make sure Dmitri in Vladivostok didn't take out a car loan in your name to buy his new Buick. Best of all, it's free on annualcreditreport.com.

10. *Look, listen, and learn:* Stay abreast of the latest scams and frauds. Aside from just keeping an eye out as you get your daily news fix, you could set up a Google news alert on the topic. And be sure to consult the IRS's "Dirty Dozen," its annual list of tax scams.

The overall theme here is to be wildly skeptical. Not neurotic. Not paranoid. Not I'm-so-terrified-I-can't-sleep-and-need-a-whiskey (although if you want to reward yourself with an amber-colored adult beverage for changing your password, that's fine with me). These ten steps are easy behaviors to adopt. They take hardly any time—certainly far less time than you would spend cleaning up the mess once you've been scammed. You just need to do them.

What if your data has already been compromised? Don't panic. You can take real steps to protect yourself in an hour or less. Contact either Experian, Equifax, or TransUnion and request that they attach a "fraud alert" to your report. Calling only one of these three big credit bureaus does the trick, since federal law compels each to contact the other two. There is one more credit reporting company—Innovis—that you should contact separately.[11] Taking these steps will make it harder, although not impossible, for a bad dude to take out a mortgage or a credit card in your name. You'll need to update the alert every few months. If you've already been defrauded, report it to the Federal Trade Commission and file a police report.

After the Equifax fiasco, I have become a huge fan of freezing credit. You'll have to contact each of the three big credit reporting agencies to do this, but it prevents anyone from taking out credit in your name. If you later wish to obtain credit, you must formally ask to have the freeze removed. That can take a few days, so factor it in if you plan to shop for a house or car or take on new credit cards. That lag time is a bit of a drag, but most people could stand to wait a few days before establishing credit anyway. If you're buying a house, you could use that time to contemplate whether you really should buy instead of rent (wink, wink—see Chapter 5).

TAKE YOUR SAP SWEATSHIRT AND BURN IT!

When I was growing up outside of New York City during the 1970s, our neighborhood was plagued by a crime wave. We got hit by burglaries and vandalism, but in the city itself, there were muggings, assaults—the full-on *Law and Order* stuff. My dad was concerned. "Okay," he said, "we're locking the front door"—something we hadn't been doing, believe it or not. My sister and I hated this idea. We were running in and out of the house a thousand times a day, and a lock on the front door amounted to a serious buzzkill. My dad was firm: We were getting a lock. Now we had to carry keys with us wherever we went. We hated it, but that was reality, and we soon got used to it.

We're in a similar position today with identity theft. Until technology catches up, we need to part with just a bit of the convenience we love in order to protect ourselves. And we can't just lock our front doors when it comes to our identities. We also have to lock our back doors, our side doors, and the sliders heading out to our patios. Heck, might as well lock the gate around the pool while we're at it. And put the damn alarm on. Yes, all of this vigilance really is necessary. Thieves might obtain your information by hacking into the website of a big company you do business with, but they're more likely to get it because you, Mr. or Ms. Dumb-Ass, were shopping online on an unsecured wireless network.

Speaking of dumb-asses, I once had a friend who would say that she should get a sweatshirt printed up with the letters "SAP" emblazoned on it. "Why?" I asked her. "What does SAP stand for?"

"It doesn't stand for anything," she replied. "I'm a sap. I will fall for the scam every single time."

Don't be that person wearing the SAP sweatshirt. Protect your information. A great deal of your informational security lies outside of your control, but you should at least take the basic steps to protect yourself. Otherwise, you're asking for trouble.

While we're at it, there are many other garments you shouldn't wear (who knew I was writing a style book?). Don't be the person wearing the "I ruined my retirement by blowing too much of my nest egg early on" T-shirt. That's yet another big mistake smart people make. They expend all this time and effort saving for retirement, only to blow it by indulging in luxuries they hoped they could enjoy, but that in truth they can ill afford, like fancy travel or overly expensive housing. That's a cardinal sin in my world, one that can potentially leave you with slim options when you're in your eighties or nineties. In the next chapter, we'll explore why.

You Indulge Yourself Too Much During Your Early Retirement Years

When you first cracked open this book of "dumb things," you might have thought that somewhere along the line I was going to wag my finger and goad you into saving more for retirement. If there's a dumb thing smart people do, failing to save enough for retirement has got to be it, right?

Nope.

You're a smart person, so I'm going to *assume* you're rockin' your retirement savings. You know to max out your employer-sponsored 401(k), 403(b), or 457 retirement plan. You might even be contributing to what we planner types call a "backdoor Roth IRA" (probably the sexiest term ever invented in financial planning),* and racking up a decent amount of non-retirement savings. Further, your having read Chapter 4, I am absolutely cer-

---

* A "backdoor Roth" is a way for wealthier earners to contribute to a Roth IRA. As of 2018, you can contribute to a Roth IRA only if you earn less than $135,000 as an individual or $199,000 as a married couple. But there is a neat way to get around that rule: You can make a *nondeductible* IRA contribution (and thus receive no tax benefit), and once it's there you could convert the IRA into a Roth IRA. This little trick, what we planner types call a "backdoor IRA," is totally legit, if a little complicated to explain. There are some thorny rules on conversions if you have other deductible IRA accounts open, so before you do anything, be sure to investigate your situation thoroughly with an adviser or CPA.

tain that you're prioritizing retirement over contributing to your children's college expenses, even if it means forgoing that fancy-schmancy private college for a high-quality but less prestigious public institution.

While you might be the world's best saver, what I'm *not* going to assume is that you know how to *spend* all that hard-earned money once you reach retirement. A woman whom I'll call Gloria was retired, divorced, and in her mid-sixties. She had $2 million in assets, as well as a very nice oceanfront home that was worth about $1.2 million. Earlier in life, Gloria had lived a fairly upscale lifestyle—dinners in nice restaurants, expensive cars, and travel to exotic locations. Gloria's planner told her that she would have to cut back a bit in retirement, because although $2 million sounded like a lot (and it went even farther back then), she needed to make sure that it lasted for at least a couple of decades into the future. Factoring in what she would receive from Social Security each month, and running through her costs and other revenue streams, her planner, Joe, calculated that she could safely draw $60,000 each year, but no more.

Gloria promised to stay on budget, but it soon became clear that she couldn't shake her upscale habits. When she needed a new car, she opted for a $75,000 Mercedes rather than a Honda Accord that might have cost only half as much. When Joe questioned the decision, Gloria said, "Oh, puh-leeze. I could never drive a Honda!" Likewise, in an attempt to downsize, Gloria sold her house and rented an apartment, choosing a spacious three-bedroom number as opposed to a cheaper one-bedroom option that Joe said would conform better to her income expectations. "Gloria, you can't afford this!" he exclaimed, to which Gloria said, "Don't be such a buzzkill. I have three kids. I need the extra room so that they can visit me." Joe showed her the numbers—at her present rate of spending, she would run out of money in her seventies. But she didn't want to hear it. "Who knows if I'm going to be alive in ten or fifteen years? I want to live now. If I run into trouble later, then we can talk about cutting back."

Year after year, Joe urged her to tamp down her spending. Year after year, she declined to do so. By her mid-seventies, about a decade after beginning to work with her planner, she ran out of money and had only Social Security on which to draw. She was forced to move into a cheaper and very small apartment rental in a neighborhood in which she had never pictured herself living. Worse still, she had to ask her kids for money in order to help pay her monthly bills, since her Social Security payments didn't cover them. Hardly the picture of a desirable retirement.

Another couple I know, Nate and Leslie, had likewise amassed $2 million in retirement savings by the time they reached their early sixties, and another $500,000 in non-retirement assets. Determined to retire early from their jobs as a physician (Nate) and a teacher (Leslie), they planned to draw $100,000 each year from their savings during the decades ahead. That, combined with Social Security, would allow them to maintain the lifestyle to which they had grown accustomed. After performing a simple analysis (described more fully below), I told them that their plan seemed reasonable enough. But what Nate and Leslie hadn't disclosed was their desire to travel. Two years after we first spoke, I connected with them again to find that they had taken several big (and expensive) trips to locations like India, Australia, and Africa. "We're young," they explained. "We have to do this kind of thing while we still can." Fair enough, but they also had to be able to afford it.

When we ran through their numbers again, it turned out that Nate and Leslie had blown through all but $50,000 of their non-retirement savings. Further, the stock market was down, so their $2 million in retirement savings was now worth $1.8 million. Going forward, Nate and Leslie would be able to safely draw only $65,000 a year from their retirement account if they wanted their money to last through their lifetimes. Shocked, the two were forced to scale back their lives dramatically—no more golf club membership, one car instead of two, and no more than the occasional dinner out. Not the retirement of which dreams are made.

As essential as it is to plan and save during your working life, you really do have to devote just as much energy to thinking through how you will spend your retirement savings. If you indulge yourself too much during those early years of retirement, you won't leave yourself enough to support yourself years or decades later. I know you're itching to make the most of the years when you're still healthy and able to enjoy life to the fullest. You've worked so hard for so long—now is the time to enjoy it. And not to be morbid, but you probably know of friends or relatives who died earlier than expected, before they had a chance to enjoy their "golden years." So by all means, please, enjoy yourself. Live for today. You do deserve it. But be reasonable. A decade later, maybe two, you'll be glad you were.

WHY YOU MIGHT NOT BE "FINE"

Invariably, the tendency to indulge too much early on in retirement amounts to a failure in long-term planning. So many smart people are surprisingly ignorant of exactly how much we'll need when we grow old. We might put money into our 401(k) plans through our jobs, but most of us don't sit down and review the numbers methodically. Who really wants to think about growing old and—eeeek—dying? So, the years pass by, and when we get to retirement, we wing it. We look at our retirement accounts and see some sizable figure—$1 million, $2 million, $3 million, or more—and we say, "Eh, that's a big chunk of change. I can splurge on myself right now while I'm still feeling great, and I'll be fine." My response: Not necessarily.

Let's say that by diligently contributing to your 401(k) and taking advantage of a company match, you're on track to amass

$2 million of retirement savings. To many people, that still sounds like a lot, especially compared with how little many Americans save (according to one report, by their late fifties the typical family has socked away only about $160,000 for retirement).[1] Here's a reality check. Guess how much of that $2 million you get to draw every year once you hit retirement age? Only about $60,000 to $65,000, if you want the money to last. Oh, and you have to pay taxes on that, because it's coming from a retirement account and Uncle Sam has not yet taken his share. So that $2 million nest egg really translates into about $45,000 in annual income when used responsibly.

Some financial planners disagree, arguing that people should peg their withdrawals each year to their investments earnings. But in my experience, that approach doesn't work very well, because people need a consistent guidepost in order to plan. I would argue that as a rough estimate, a responsible plan allows you to withdraw only 3 to 3.5 percent each year in retirement. So, let's say you need $15,000 a month in retirement income based on your current monthly expenses. (And have you taken the time to figure those out? Track your money for six months, and you will have the answer.) You and your spouse might expect to draw a combined $5,000 per month of income from Social Security. To have $15,000 each month to spend, you'll need to save enough money to generate $10,000 a month, or $120,000 a year, after taxes. Without adjusting for factors like inflation, you'll need to save roughly $4 million by the time you retire—twice as much as you have. Crazy, right? When it comes to retirement, a million bucks ain't what it used to be. And if you factor in inflation, the numbers look even worse!

"Jill," you might say, "come on—I might spend $120,000 a year on expenses now, but in retirement I won't need nearly that much. I'll have a smaller house once the kids are gone, I won't need to pay as much for child care and other big expenses, and"—you say this with a twinkle in your eye—"I won't be contributing to retirement then either, right?"

All of that is true, and decades ago, a financial planner might have agreed with you, advising you to budget less for retirement than you spend earlier in life; if your annual expenses ran at a $100,000 clip, maybe you would budget only for $80,000 a year in retirement. But these days, most advisers assume that your expenses will be more or less the same later as they are now. Even if you're not spending as much on housing and you no longer need to allot money each month for retirement savings, health care expenses have been rising, with no end in sight, so you need to factor that in. According to one estimate, "An average retired couple age 65 in 2018 may need approximately $280,000 saved (after tax) to cover health care expenses in retirement,"[2] not including the cost of long-term care. As you can see, your retirement needs are no joke. They require serious thought—quite possibly more than you're giving them. You can't just assume you'll have enough.

"But Jill," you protest, "I'm serious—I really will downsize, and my expenses will be going *way* down, more than enough to compensate for any new costs I might have." Listen, I hope that's true, but if I had a dollar for every time people told me that they were going to downsize and then failed to significantly lower their expenses, I'd be a rich woman. Listen closely to Aunt Jill: It's very difficult to downsize unless you're willing to radically transform your lifestyle by moving to a locale with a much lower cost of living (especially a locale with no state income tax).* If you sell your $1 million house and buy a $600,000 condo in an attractive senior community nearby, you might think you'll come out ahead. But what about the capital gains tax you might owe? When you sell a primary residence that you have lived in for two of the past five

---

* Which states have no state income tax, you ask? Well, Florida, of course. And if you don't like the idea of living in the Sunshine State, you can choose from among Alaska, Nevada, South Dakota, Texas, Washington State, and Wyoming.

years, the IRS allows you to exclude $250,000 of gain ($500,000 if you are married). Many people who purchased their properties at lower prices will face a tax bill. And what about that monthly condo fee? What about the costs of furnishing your new place? What about the extra amenities you might want to enjoy (and have to pay for)? What about the costs of moving and paying property taxes in your new locale? When you add it all up, you might not be saving nearly as much by "downsizing" as you presume.

Clients tend to tune out when financial planners throw these kinds of complicating questions at them. Look—you're tuning out right now! Why is that? After years of having these kinds of conversations with people, and after reading numerous articles and books about research in neuroscience and behavioral finance, I suspect that these kinds of conversations trigger fear in our sad, old, reptilian brains. Numbers and future financial needs during retirement seem so overwhelming that we often shut down.

Add to that the concrete and depressing news that you might not be able to afford the retirement you think you want (not to mention, deserve!) and *POOF:* Your rational brain short-circuits, and your prehistoric amygdala takes over. You go into "fight or flight" mode, and stop listening to what your adviser—or your friendly aunt Jill—is saying. In essence, you can't process it. As a result, you might ignore the sound advice and take that monthlong safari in Kenya a year or two after you retire, even though you can't really afford it.

On a deeper level, many people also tune out and make poor spending choices when they retire because they feel overwhelmed, depressed, or just plain out of sorts. For the bulk of our working lives, retirement seems like an abstraction, something that will happen someday but not now. We think about what it might be like, but we don't really *think* about it. All of a sudden, it's upon us—a major life change akin to getting married or having kids.

For decades, we got up and went to work. Now we don't. For decades, we had colleagues supporting and annoying us. Now we don't. For decades, we had goals and a sense of forward motion in our lives. Now we don't. For decades, we might have had illusions of living forever. Now we don't. Add to all this, we're surrounded by experts telling us what to do and not do to get the most out of our "golden years." And our kids are giving us advice. And we're thinking about the example set by our own parents. So much information! Oh, and did I mention the ghastly specter of death staring us in the face? All of this is enough to cause any of us to freak, tune out the actual numbers, ignore the voice of reason, and make poor spending decisions. "The hell with it," we say, "I'm going to live for now." So, we do—only to regret it later.

AVOIDING THE RETIREMENT FREAK-OUT

Is this chapter depressing enough for you? Let's turn it around. It's true that if you're retired and in your late sixties or mid-seventies and you've already made poor spending decisions, there isn't much you can do. Unless you win the lottery, which gives pretty crappy odds, you're going to have to dramatically adjust your lifestyle or risk running out of money. On the other hand, if you're still ten years or more away from retirement, there are many things you can do to prepare yourself financially and mentally so that you make sound spending decisions once retirement arrives. And by "many things," I mean five key actions that you can take in advance to reduce your chances of suffering a painful—and impoverishing—retirement freak-out.

Action #1: Have This Five-Minute Conversation

Force yourself to sit down and crunch the numbers. I recommend holding a simple five-minute conversation with yourself about your plans. I have these conversations all the time with callers on my radio show and podcast. Probably half the calls I field are about retirement, and in a good number of those cases, people have only the roughest sense of how much they'll need and what decisions they'll have to make now in order to amass enough savings. I could tell them to consult one of the zillions of retirement calculators out there provided by financial institutions, but people seldom follow up—they don't want to take the time sitting there at their computer. So, my five-minute conversation is a good substitute. Are you ready? Pretend you're a caller on my show:

JILL: *Let's first calculate how much you anticipate needing on a monthly basis. What bills will you have to pay? Add up your expenses for your basic needs—housing, food, utilities, insurance, health care, and so on. What do you come up with?*

YOU:

JILL: *Okay, nice. Now what do you anticipate wanting to spend on a monthly basis for fun? Consider costs like dining out at those froufrou restaurants that put, like, three peas on your plate; travel (divided across twelve months); ill-advised benders at the nearby casino with your buddies; day trips to the spa with your besties; any and all tickets to Bruce Springsteen concerts; and the monthly payment on that new Ducati or silly sailboat that you plan to buy (when, of course, you should rent) to make yourself feel younger— that sort of thing.*

YOU:

JILL: *Now add in monthly expenses related to ongoing obligations you have toward others. Are you planning on paying a certain amount to help out with your parents' care? Will you be helping your adult child with his or her car loan or paying for the grandkids' camps?*

YOU:

JILL: *Okay, now add up all the expenses we've tallied so far. What do you have as a grand total?*

YOU:

JILL: *Nice work—and we've only been at this for, what, two minutes nineteen seconds? Now, let's go on to calculate your anticipated income during retirement. Will you receive a pension?*

YOU:

JILL: *If you are receiving a pension, you're one lucky devil, because the vast majority of us are receiving bupkes. How about Social Security? Do you know what your benefit will be? How about your spouse's benefit?*

YOU:

JILL: *What? You don't know? Just hop on to SSA.gov and you'll see your tax dollars hard at work, because the website is awesome. Presume that you will work until your full retirement age (FRA), which is probably sixty-five to sixty-seven years old. (Quit your whining—I can hear it all the way from here!)*

YOU: I'm not whining!

JILL: *Oh, sorry, that must have been my two incredibly cute Norwich Terriers asking for a snack. Tell me, will you have any income from real estate during your retirement? Are you a trust fund baby who'll get some juicy distributions?*

YOU:

JILL: *Okay, now that we have all of this information jotted down, we get to the fun part. Take your total anticipated monthly needs, subtract you future income, and—presto!—you have that magic number you'll need to fund. So, what is it?*

YOU:

JILL: *Now that you have this number, calculate how much total retirement savings you'll need, assuming you'll be able to draw only 3 or 3.5 percent of your savings each year to apply to your monthly expenses. What do you come up with?*

YOU:

JILL: *See? That wasn't so bad.*

YOU: You're right, Jill, that was awesome. I'm so glad I finally made myself do this! I feel like an entirely new person. I can't wait to read the rest of this book and buy it for everyone I know!

Okay, let's not get too excited here. Just realize that it wasn't *that* hard to get a reasonably precise picture of your retirement needs. And now that you've done it, you can assess whether you've contributed adequately and will be in a position to maintain the lifestyle you desire. If not, then you still have time to make choices that will increase your income during retirement. If you're fortunate enough to have more than the current retirement plan limit, then get busy! You may want to consider funding a Roth IRA, or if you make too much for a Roth, put those dollars into a non-deductible IRA and then convert it to one of those sexy backdoor Roths. Or just sock that money away in a plain old non-retirement investment account and buy a diversified portfolio of index funds. You might want to find ways to cut back on expenses, such as selling your house and renting a place instead, or giving up one of your cars. What you do is up to you, but now is the time to crank on your savings plan, so that you can afford to indulge yourself more lavishly when you retire.

After working through the above exercise, some readers—especially younger ones—might question whether I was right to include anticipated Social Security income. Won't Social Security be bankrupt inside of a decade or two? After all, these skeptics might argue, the giant Social Security trust fund that we all pay into now has to support all of those retiring baby boomers. Relatively few people in the prime of their careers are paying into it. Over time, the program will become insolvent. In fact, according to the Trustees of the Social Security and Medicare Trusts, by 2034 enough funds will remain for people to receive about 77 percent of the benefits they've been promised, assuming nothing is done.[3] And given the dysfunction in Washington, nothing will be done.

I actually don't believe in that dire scenario. Originally, Social Security was supposed to be part of a "three-legged stool" of retirement income for people, alongside a company pension and savings. Over time, pensions have largely disappeared, and other costs like health care have soared, leaving millions of people to rely on Social Security as their sole retirement lifeline. On that basis alone, the program won't simply go away—the people who depend on it and their family members will use their votes to punish politicians who are content to let the social safety net collapse. What will more likely happen is that Social Security will become a bit less generous. People might have to work longer before becoming eligible for benefits. Or we might have to pay slightly more in FICA taxes to fund the system. Or the amount of income subject to FICA taxes might rise. Through a combination of measures such as these, the system will live on. I feel very comfortable advising you to factor it into your retirement planning.

Action #2: Rethink Your Retirement Age

If after running the numbers you're not too pleased with what you uncovered, don't worry, there's another way to brighten your retirement picture besides saving more, and that's working longer. One mistake that Nate and Leslie made was that they retired when they were only in their early sixties. If Nate and Leslie had put off retirement by a few years, they could have amassed some extra "fun money" to fund extravagant vacations during their first few years of postwork freedom, and they would still probably be young and healthy enough to enjoy travel once they retired.

Some people might not be in a position to work longer, while others might get nauseous at the very thought of clocking in a minute longer than absolutely necessary. For the rest of us, working longer is something we should consider, not least because it: a) provides more time to contribute to your retirement plan; b) prevents us from dipping into our nest eggs; and c) can increase our Social Security monthly retirement benefit. According to one recent study, "delaying retirement by 3–6 months has the same impact on the retirement standard of living as saving an additional one-percentage point of labor earnings for 30 years."[4]

A lot of that impact has to do with Social Security, which makes up a significant portion of most Americans' retirement income. Go to SSA.gov, and you can obtain an estimate of what you'll receive if you retire at ages sixty-two, sixty-seven, and seventy. As you'll see, your benefits rise enormously if you retire later. While you can certainly access the system at sixty-two, doing so will *permanently* reduce your benefits by as much as 25 percent, and if your non-working spouse is claiming based on your record, his or her benefits will also be reduced for life.

Conversely, each month you work beyond your full retirement age will mean extra money. If you delay retirement until seventy, your Social Security benefits will increase by 8 percent each year. That's a RISK-FREE increase in return! One friend of mine in his late forties who made about $250,000 a year found that he would receive only $1,923 a month if he retired at sixty-two, but $2,933 a month if he waited until sixty-seven. If he could stay on the job until he was seventy, he'd receive a whopping $3,714.

Retiring later can also help inoculate you against the kind of early-retirement existential funk that might result in your making irrational spending choices. Many people aren't quite sure what they'll do during retirement. If that's you, then why not continue to work until you figure that out? Think of retirement as another "job." You wouldn't quit one job until you already had another one lined up, would you?

One wealthy Wall Street executive I know went into a deep depression after retiring at age sixty-three because he had no clue what he was going to do. He had no special hobbies he wanted to pursue, no social cause he wanted to dedicate himself to, no second career he wanted to embark on—nothing. His wife was at her wit's end. Every day, he got up and moped around the house, driving her nuts. Finally, he went back to work at a law firm, not because he wanted to practice law, but because he needed something to do. I suppose he was satisfied enough, but he wasn't truly happy. To me, that's a sad story. Assuming that it had been possible to continue at his old job, he would have been far better off doing so for a few more years while his retirement plans crystallized. Of course, retirement plans don't just "crystallize." You have to work at it. Which brings me to my next point.

Action #3: Dream About Retirement More

So many people don't know what they'll do during retirement because they don't spend enough time thinking it through in advance. They might harbor vague notions of playing more golf, spending more time with their grandchildren, or traveling more, but they haven't ruminated on the specifics, assessing the pros and cons of various courses of action. That's a mistake. If you're in your mid-fifties, now is the time to imagine your post-retirement activities and lifestyle as fully as possible. Ask yourself:

- Do you have any old goals or ambitions you never got around to that you might wish to pursue? What are they? How might you pursue them now? Could you enroll in university courses? Could you start a second career, maybe as a consultant who can impart wisdom to young professionals in your field? Or perhaps you'd like to take a stab at the "Great American Novel"?

- How about physical activities? Are there any you'd like to take more seriously? How would you do that? Would you join a gym or country club? Would you move to a sunnier climate? Would you travel to faraway places for yoga retreats or to go mountain-biking?

- Do you imagine yourself pursuing a certain lifestyle, such as living on the beach? If so, would you move to a new city? Sell your house and rent? Are you planning to move closer to your kids? If so, how will you create a life of your own that is independent of theirs?

- Retirement is a great time to give back. Which social or civic activities might you like to pursue? What organizations might you join? How much time each week would you envision volunteering? Many retirees find great joy teaching or coaching young people—everything from helping out with the girls' basketball team to serving as an adjunct lecturer at a local community college. Do any opportunities of that sort appeal to you?

- Would you like to get more involved politically? Would you become a donor and help out with fund-raising? Would you run for local political office?

- Would you like to spend more time taking care of your elderly parents, your young grandchildren, or other family members in need of care? How much time each week? Would you have to move? Even if you don't have to serve as the primary caretaker, be sure to factor in some amount of time weekly to address the needs of your aging parents (see Chapter 10).

The more precisely you can frame your retirement plans, the more grounded you'll be when you do retire, and the less prone you'll be to a freak-out and the ill-advised spending that comes with it. Dreaming about your retirement also makes sense because it allows you to take proactive steps to make the transition to your new activities. A friend of mine, "Casey," knew she wanted to devote her early retirement years to becoming more involved in social issues that mattered to her. Thinking about it more, she decided she wanted to contribute to environmental causes, especially those focused on clean water (she grew up in a small town that was near a river). She also realized that she wanted to make a difference by serving on a philanthropic board on a volunteer basis. But she had never served on a board. How would she make that happen?

Because Casey still had years to go before she retired, she was able to research various organizations that might be a good fit for her and to begin to cultivate relationships. She started volunteering and making small donations. A few years later, she reached out to the development director at one organization she volunteered at and asked if she could learn more about the organization's mission and board development plans. "I just want you to know," she said, "if an opportunity arises, I'd be very interested in participating." Thanks to such outreach, Casey will likely be able to slip right into a board seat when she retires, rather than spending months or years making the transition. She won't suffer through long days not knowing what to do with herself but instead will be busy, focused, and happy from the start.

Action #4: Embrace the Gray

I'm not talking about loving your gray hair. I'm saying you should look for creative solutions that flirt with the boundaries of retirement. One reason people fall into retirement funks and wind up spending too much early on is they become ensnared in black-and-white thinking. We tend to draw a bright red line between "work" and "retirement," regarding the two as completely distinct from one another. Under that schema, "work" denotes the period of your life when you have an income, "retirement" the period when you no longer draw a salary.

Look a bit closer, and you find that there are shades or gradations of retirement. If you're a doctor, lawyer, or other professional and no longer can stomach the idea of putting in full-time hours, could you take on a younger partner and work part-time? If you're a professor, could you continue to teach a course or two per semester as an adjunct? If you work for a company or nonprofit, could you stay on board part-time or as a consultant? Many organizations are willing to consider more creative arrangements—they benefit from your experience, and they don't need to provide you with health or retirement benefits any longer. You get to stay engaged with your work and draw a partial paycheck, which in turn allows you to improve your quality of life either now or in the future. You still have the time you want to take your grandkids to their soccer games, take those once-in-a-lifetime trips, and so on.

One friend of mine, a television producer, elected to take a buyout when she was in her early sixties, but she didn't feel ready to retire. So, she started asking around for freelance production assignments. The first year, she earned about $40,000 a year from that work—much less than her previous $140,000-a-year salary, but still pretty good. The second year she took in $60,000, and the third year $80,000. She and her husband didn't need this money to support them during retirement, but it dramatically improved their quality of life, allowing them to pay for extras like travel and to gift some money to their grandchildren's 529 plans. When she didn't feel like working, she could decline to take on assignments offered to her. She didn't receive any health insurance benefits, but that was okay—she received her insurance through her husband's job (he wasn't ready to retire just yet). What a fantastic way to ease into retirement, and to give yourself the means to indulge yourself a bit.

You can also find a middle ground when it comes to the other side of your financial equation—your spending. I totally understand why Nate and Leslie would want to travel to India or Australia while they were still hale and hearty. But did they have to take three such trips within a two-year period? Perhaps they could have satisfied their travel bug with one big trip. Or taken one expensive trip and two lesser trips to exciting places closer to home. Or traveled on the cheap, flying last-minute, choosing budget accommodations, and renting their own house out on Airbnb (there's nothing like a good "travel hack").

If you're like Gloria and enjoy the look and feel of a Mercedes, maybe you could buy one that's "previously enjoyed." Or maybe you decide that you don't drive all that much, and you could go without a car, walking more and relying on Uber. At all times when you're tempted to splurge on a purchase, ask yourself: Do you *really* need or want it? Gloria might have thought she "needed" a three-bedroom apartment so that her kids and grandkids could stay with her, but how often would they really wind up visiting? If they planned only occasional visits, maybe it would have been cheaper (and frankly, more enjoyable for the kids) if she chose the less expensive one-bedroom but offered to help them out with the costs of staying in a nearby hotel during their visits. Likewise, do you really need that golf membership you use once a month? Could you sign up for a cheaper, "house" membership at the club instead? Now that you have more time to cook, do you really need to go out for dinner several times a week? Now that you're not dressing up for work every day, do you really need to spend as much on your wardrobe?

Action #5: Hire a Financial Planner

In Chapter 2, I advised you to seek out (and pay for) professional help when you're confronted with a financial situation that you haven't seen before and truly can't handle yourself. If any situation meets that criterion for most people, it's retirement. Die-hard DIYers call my radio show all the time when they're about to retire. Although they know how to put money into their retirement account, they lack a strategy for taking it out. How much money can they afford to spend? Are they in good enough shape financially to do what they want to do? In what order should they spend down their assets? Can they afford to make charitable contributions or gifts to their grandchildren?

If you're unsure how to handle questions like these, it might be worth spending a few bucks to obtain real advice from a professional. Retirement really is a huge life change. You're in uncharted territory, and it's okay to admit you need a little help. But please, heed another piece of advice from Chapter 2: Make sure the planner you consult is a fiduciary! And for God's sake, if you're going to hire a planner, be sure to actually *listen* to him or her. Don't make the mistake that the free-spending Gloria did.

THE RETIREMENT PROBLEM THAT WASN'T

A man named Rory once called in to my radio show with questions about his retirement picture. Hailing from the great state of North Carolina, Rory was sixty-seven years old and had recently retired. His wife, who had also recently retired, was a year younger. As Rory told me, he had been taking a closer look at his assets to "get a better picture" of what he and his wife had. He wondered if they were really in good shape, and wanted my advice. Could he weather a financial downturn if and when it occurred?

My first move was to delve into the numbers, running Rory through a version of the "Five-Minute Conversation" outlined here. As he told me, his total annual retirement income from Social Security, pensions, and real estate was about $100,000, enough to cover his and his wife's basic needs. Of that money, $75,000 came to him automatically through his Social Security and pensions, and he would draw on his retirement assets for the other $25,000.

So, I asked him, how much did he have in the way of retirement assets? His answer: $2 million, plus another $1 million in non-retirement savings. Not too shabby. In addition, Rory and his wife owned their home outright—no mortgage.

I had great news for Rory: He was in fantastic shape. Not only was he spending within his means, but he would be in excellent shape to weather a financial downturn. With his $2 million in retirement savings, he could draw down about $60,000 a year if he wanted to. But because he had a pension and Social Security, he needed only $25,000 a year after taxes. Amazing! His non-retirement savings gave him an extra cushion if he wanted to splurge on a fancy vacation, and it also allowed for more security in the event of a downturn. At their present rate of spending, Rory and his wife would have enough money to last them into their eighties, nineties, and beyond. All Rory would have to do was make sure not to take any undue risks in how he invested his money (see Chapter 6). He and his wife had done the hard work of saving, and now they were taking care to live within their means. Good for them!

You can embark on retirement in a smart way, too. Drown out that little devil perched on your shoulder that says, without much reflection, "Oh, I can afford it" and "You only live once." Sure, you do only live once, but that "once" might turn out to be longer than you think. Plan ahead. Know what you can afford to spend. And take some time to really think about what you'd like to spend it on.

Of course, it would be a mistake to limit such thoughtfulness to retirement. As any shrink or spiritual guru will tell you, the more self-aware and reflective you can be throughout your life, the better. A financial guru—me—will tell you that, too. A good example has to do with your kids. Many of us make the mistake of allowing money to play a bigger role in our parenting than it should. Without realizing it, we saddle our kids with our own money issues, spewing our emotional shit onto them and in the process giving them baggage of their own to deal with. If you want to avoid years of therapy bills for your kids, you must think more carefully about how you communicate with them about financial matters. Please do yourself and your kids a favor, and turn the page!

You Saddle Your Kids with Your Own Money Issues

Fernando, my friend Maria's father, immigrated to this country from Portugal during the 1940s, settling in Fall River, Massachusetts. Although he spoke no English, he managed to find work as a janitor at a small textile company, supplementing his modest salary by taking on handyman jobs on the weekends. A couple of years later, he got married and started a family. During the 1950s, when his kids were still small, he was promoted at the textile firm on the strength of his ability to fix everything and anything. Soon he became head of plant operations, propelling the family squarely into the middle class.

Despite making the equivalent in today's dollars of $100,000 a year in salary, Fernando could never shrug off the scrappy immigrant spirit that had helped him gain a foothold. He continued to work weekends during the 1950s and '60s, saving every penny. He refused to take family vacations, even though the family could well afford them, and he refused to give his kids weekly allowances. Maria and her siblings received all the basics growing up—a roof over their heads, food to eat, school supplies. But their father constantly reminded them of how much things cost, put intense pressure on them to cut back on spending, and made them feel guilty for wanting the nonessentials that their peers took for granted. "I had to work for every single thing I had," he said to his kids, "so you have to, too. Do you know how much it cost me to put that food on the table? Do you know how hard I have to work?"

Maria's father probably thought he was helping his kids by instilling solid values around money. Instead, his constant harping was breeding neuroses. It's kind of like when parents focus too much on their kids' weight—they want their kids to develop healthy habits, but all too often, their kids wind up resenting them, or worse, developing eating disorders.

When I first met Maria, she was in her thirties and already had an unhealthy relationship with money. She had been treated so stringently by her father—never given what she wanted, always made to feel guilty—that she overcompensated with her own kids, refusing to say no at all to them. During the 1980s, Maria and her husband, Abe, lived in Chicago and made a combined $200,000 a year. Although that income provided for an upper-middle-class lifestyle, the family didn't have a great deal of disposable income. The cost of living in Chicago was high, and Maria's son Kenny had a learning disability, so the family had to pay to send him to a private school. Still, Maria insisted that she and Abe give their kids every luxury—new clothes, spending money, expensive trips, summer camps. "I just didn't want my kids to experience what I had to go through growing up," Maria said.

When their kids went to college, Maria's indulgence of them continued. She insisted on paying for expensive private school tuitions—no loans or work for *her* kids. Later, she bought her kids cars, paid for insurance on these cars, helped pay their apartment rents, and slipped them money for their other bills when they were short. Whatever her kids asked for, they got—even if Maria and Abe couldn't afford it. So, how did they pay for these gifts? After reading Chapter 4, you know: They skimped on their retirement savings. Both were lucky enough to have pensions, which they expected would fund a good chunk of retirement. As for the rest of what they would need, they would "figure it out."

Maria and Abe did largely "figure it out," but her tendency to spoil her kids took a steep emotional toll. Whereas her father's behavior had prompted her to become excessively independent, afraid to ask for anything because her father would likely say no and make her feel guilty, today her children, all in their forties, have the opposite problem: They are overly dependent on her. One of her kids, for instance, couldn't fathom how to purchase a home on his $300,000 salary without Mom and Dad's help. Another relied on Maria and Abe to send his kids to summer camp. Don't get me wrong: The children are wonderful people who have done well for themselves. Still, whenever they have problems, and especially financial problems, they come running to Mommy. They never learned how to discipline themselves around money, and as a result they lack resourcefulness and self-confidence.

Maria continues to indulge her kids by paying for luxuries they can't afford. In so doing, she has made her and Abe's retirement less comfortable. Although the two of them are now in their seventies and are well provided for in retirement, Maria feels pressure to keep working part-time. Abe, meanwhile, feels cheated. "We worked our butts off so that we could enjoy these last couple of decades," he said, "and now she is consumed by this need to work, robbing us of what should be a great time in our lives." More important, Maria's behavior has prevented her kids from coming into their own as adults—all because she never managed to come to grips with her issues around money, and because her father had never managed to come to grips with his.

How you behave around money with your kids matters. I am not a parent myself (which of course, makes me an expert!), but I frequently encounter smart people who emphasize financial matters too much in their parenting, saddling their kids with their own money issues. Some people, like Maria's dad, do it by counting pennies and making money part of even the smallest decisions. They lecture their kids about thrift, needle them, and cajole them. Others, like Maria, do it by spoiling their kids and failing to set reasonable limits around money. Still others fixate on what those around them have, constantly seeking to "keep up with the Joneses," expressing resentment when they don't, and pressuring their kids to succeed financially. In a variety of ways, parents grant money an unhealthy prominence in the household. They might think they're being good parents, but in truth they're spawning anxiety, insecurity, self-doubt, and other negative emotions in their children.

As a parent, strive to strike a balance here. You want to instruct your kids about money so that they understand how it works and can take responsibility, but you don't want to do it so much or so intensely that your kids treat money in unbalanced ways. At all times, you want to maintain a healthy relationship with money yourself (Chapter 3), so that you can pass positive attitudes, behaviors, and values on to your kids. Money is a loaded topic, and when it's handled poorly, the effects can ricochet in subtle ways down the generations, leading to chronically poor decision-making, not to mention damaged relationships and emotional turmoil. Reflect on how you talk about money at home, and how you actually spend it. Make sure the messages you're sending through your behavior and spoken words are the right ones.

"MONEY EMOTIONS"

When I say that many smart people saddle their kids with their own money issues, what I really mean is that in their interactions with their children, parents imbue money with too much *emotion*. In his interview with me, Dr. Jim Grubman, whom we met in Chapter 3, described emotional decision-making as one of the biggest mistakes people make around money—a view borne out throughout this book.

But even when we're not making specific decisions such as how to invest or whether to buy or rent a home, our emotions inflect how we talk about and treat money. If we feel permanently anxious about money, as Maria's dad did, we might treat it as something precious, to be hoarded and not enjoyed, day in and day out, in big and little ways. If we resent how paltry our income is compared with others', we might complain about our finances, fixate on others' possessions, and obsess about getting that next raise or closing the next big deal. One way or another, our emotions peek through, profoundly affecting our ever-observant kids. If they don't come away traumatized per se, they learn to cultivate emotions around money themselves, rather than handling it coolly and rationally. No surprise when they make their own emotion-laden decisions around money as adults—and pay the price.

Two clients of mine, Alex and Andrea, were lawyers who settled in the Bay Area during the early 1990s. Andrea worked as a corporate attorney at a big law firm serving big tech companies, while Alex worked as in-house counsel at the private office of a wealthy family. Together, they earned $700,000 annually—a fantastic income by most people's standards. But Andrea and Alex weren't satisfied. There they were, they said, killing themselves for $700,000, while their "asshole" clients were megamillionaires, all because these clients had happened to come on board early as employees at large tech companies and then were lucky enough to cash out when these companies went public. Where was the justice?

Night after night, Andrea and Alex came home and bitched about how hard they worked and how little they made, in relative terms. Their son, Steven, heard all this and understood that

a) money was all that mattered; b) if you didn't make a lot of it, you didn't "succeed"; and c) if you didn't succeed, you weren't worth very much as a person. Before Steven had even graduated from high school, he and his parents had hatched an elaborate strategy to turn him into a multimillionaire. He would study finance in college, land a job at an investment bank or consulting firm, move up the ranks, get an MBA, go back to his finance job, and eventually leave to work at a start-up, where he, too, would be showered with IPO cash. Following this path, he would make "real money."

At first, Steven's life unfolded according to plan. He enrolled in an elite college and did well there. Upon graduation, he landed a plum job at a prestigious global investment bank. He showed up at work eager to work hard and succeed, but almost immediately, he was miserable. He hated his hyper-competitive type-A colleagues. He hated his overbearing bosses. He hated that he was working a hundred hours a week to "pay his dues." He hated that he wasn't giving back to society in some way. His friends pointed out that he would have to work at this job for only a few years before going off for his MBA, but that didn't help. He saw no future in investment banking, and couldn't stand the thought of continuing with it just for the sake of getting rich. He dreamed of somehow putting his finance background to work helping others, but he didn't know how. He was also terrified of disappointing his parents. They had made it known that they expected him to establish a career in finance and make "real money." Anything other than that would seem unworthy in their eyes.

For a few years, Steven soldiered on, despising his job but hoping that it would get better. Eventually, he couldn't stand it any longer. Without clearing it with his parents, he quit his job and enrolled in classes to become a Certified Financial Planner. He knew it wasn't the most glamorous or remunerative option in the world of finance. In fact, when his friends heard that he was ditching the elite investment banking world to become a planner, they warned that people would regard him as "one rung above a used car salesman." But that was okay with Steven. He had tried the more prestigious route and found that it didn't work for him. He didn't need to "keep up with the Joneses" the way his parents had. Instead, he saw financial planning as a way to help people and make a difference in their lives. He could still work as a money guy, but he could feel passionate about what he was doing, enjoy a more relaxed lifestyle, and earn a respectable but not outrageous living.

Years later, Steven still works as a financial planner. When he hears about former coworkers who have scored big bucks in their careers, he feels the occasional pang of regret—Steven is human, after all. On the whole, though, he loves his career and is happy with his life. The jealousy and resentment his parents showed toward their wealthier clients and friends led him initially to make a poor career choice, costing him several years of misery until he straightened his life out.

As Steven anticipated, his parents weren't happy with his decision to leave investment banking. They thought he was wasting his life and would never be happy unless he became filthy rich. Steven in turn resented them for putting so much pressure on him, and he felt alienated from them because his attitudes and goals seemed so different from theirs. Why couldn't they let him pursue happiness on his own terms? It would be many years before Andrea and Alex could forge a healthy, satisfying relationship with their adult son— all because their own emotions around money had gone unchecked.

In Andrea and Alex's case, the "money emotions" in question were jealousy, resentment, and perhaps a bit of anger, but a range of other emotions can also cause damage, chief among them anxiety. When my friend Chester was growing up during the 1980s, his mother stayed at home with the kids and his father had a high-pressure job as a trial attorney in private practice. Because his father specialized in a certain form of litigation, he would take on only a few big cases a year. If he won those cases, he could earn $500,000 or more (about $1,200,000 in today's dollars). If he lost them, he might make a fraction of that, or lose money for the year.

Given these circumstances, and the fact that he was the family's sole earner, his father worried obsessively about money. He criticized Chester's mother for spending too freely, and made "No" his default answer when fielding even small requests from his children. On several occasions when he had lost big cases, the family had to dramatically slash its expenditures for months in order to stay afloat. "Those times were scary," Chester recalls. "Overall, we lived an upper-middle-class lifestyle, but there was a constant element of uncertainty. My dad's anxiety was ever-present, and it sort of bled onto the rest of us. We became worried, too—probably far more than was healthy or productive. We never knew when the bottom might fall out."

As an adult, Chester struggled with generalized anxiety, and he worried in particular about money, just as his father had. Chester initially embarked on a career his father deemed "safe," attending graduate school to become a professor. He hated it, but pressed on to get his PhD. In his early thirties, after considerable angst, he worked up the courage to transition to a more satisfying career, as a graphic designer. Still, his anxiety continued to haunt him. In running his own freelance design business, he tended to make fear-based decisions about such things as which clients to take on, how to negotiate with them, and how to handle the occasional difficulties or disagreements that arose. As a result, he often accepted reduced fees, took on less attractive and less profitable clients, and made other unnecessary compromises—hating himself afterward for doing so.

Although he made a nice living and was building up a great reputation for himself, fears about scarcity haunted him—the fantasy that his clients would abandon him if he made the slightest mistake, and that like his father he had little protection against financial insecurity. Only after years of struggle (and years of working with a good therapist) did he manage to overcome these feelings, feel more confident, and maximize his potential as a professional.

In exposing his kids to his own anxiety around money, Chester's father committed a big parenting no-no. "There is one thing that, depending on the age of the child, parents should be careful about," Dr. Jim Grubman told me, and that is "conveying too much anxiety and having kids injected with a lot of anxiety in a way that they can't really handle or understand." Kids get scared when they see you upset or anxious around money—more than you probably realize. That memory becomes imprinted in their brains, potentially traumatizing them. It's far better, Dr. Grubman said, to "[keep] the focus on learning" when it comes to finances, and to sustain a "nonemotional way of understanding money."

Parents should also understand how their own generalized anxiety affects their behavior around their kids. You'll recall Dr. Grubman's story from Chapter 3 of a wealthy woman who refused to give money to her kids because of a range of worries she had. Her children didn't understand the reasons behind her lack of generosity, and they perceived it as manipulative. Another scenario, especially in wealthier families, involves parents who bestow too much on their children because they feel anxious about their welfare and can't bear to see them struggle. These parents throw money at problems to prevent their kids from suffering major (or even minor) setbacks. Dr. Grubman calls this "snowplow" parenting: Rather than hovering over their kids to protect them as "helicopter" parents do, these parents stay in front of them, clearing the way so that the going is smooth. Do that too much, of course, and your children never learn how to solve problems for themselves.

They become victims of your own need to "medicate" your anxiety through the dispensing of money.

I was lucky as a child: Although my father had his ups and downs as a trader (including a pretty big down, as we've seen), he wasn't an especially anxious person, nor did he express anxiety about money around my sister and me. For years, he would return home at the end of each day and speak matter-of-factly about whether he'd made or lost money. He presented his financial performance like a sports score—up or down, win or lose. There was never much emotion of any kind attached to it. Moreover, my father was always clear about what we could or couldn't afford as a family, again without conveying emotions like fear, anger, resentment, or jealousy. The lesson I took away from all this was a healthy one: Sometimes you succeed with money, sometimes you don't. When you don't succeed, you might have to work hard to deal with the consequences, but you can do it. My dad didn't get everything right—not as a parent, and not as a manager of his own money. But he did model calmness and balance around financial affairs that positioned my sister and me to deal with money more rationally as adults. For that, I will always be grateful.

SIX PARENTING TIPS TO LIVE BY

If you think you might be making too much ado about money around your kids, don't worry: You can't change the past, but it's not too late to mend your ways. The key, as I've emphasized elsewhere in this book, is self-awareness. Scrutinize your issues around money, and consider how those issues express themselves in your behavior. What common sayings or expressions do you have when it comes to money? What rituals do you sustain around money (for example, monthly bill paying or shopping)? Do you and your spouse argue about money a lot? Think, too, about the financial lessons you learned from your parents. Are you replicating their behaviors? Are you reacting to what they did by doing the opposite?

The more self-aware you can be, the more you can shape your behavior around your kids to communicate positive messages. You can't fight against your tendency to anxiously and unnecessarily scrimp and save, for instance, if you don't know you have that tendency.

Beyond the general exhortation to "know thyself," you should also know some communication basics. As I've found in counseling clients and callers to my radio show, fostering healthy attitudes is as much about what you do as a parent as what you *don't* do. Here are some tips to keep in the back of your mind when interacting with your kids around money:

1. Communicate Transparently

Many parents I meet don't communicate enough about money with their kids. They leave the family finances shrouded in mystery. Do that too much, and your kids won't understand the rationales behind your money decisions ("No, you can't buy that sweater," or "No, you can only have $10 a week allowance, not $20"). They'll come to regard you as a dictator operating on the basis of whim and caprice, not reason and wisdom. They also won't understand much about the world of money—because you haven't taken these valuable opportunities to instruct and inform them. My father was completely transparent about our family's finances, sometimes to the consternation of my mother. He had no problem telling us how much he made. While you don't want to go too far into the details (your children might not know what to tell others outside the family and what to keep secret), you should try to give your children a general sense of your financial circumstances, in age-appropriate language they can understand. And be sure to emphasize, like my father did, that money isn't that important—other parts of life matter more.

You should also feel free to discuss the financial mistakes you've made in your life, including those covered in this book. I learned a lot from talking with my father about his mistakes with risk-taking. When you admit your mistakes in front of your kids, it humanizes you and allows them to understand you better. By explaining your mistakes as well as their consequences, you can inspire your kids to behave differently in their own lives. Of course, you'll want to treat yourself compassionately when having these kinds of conversations. Don't say "I was the biggest asshole in the world for taking on too much credit card debt right out of college." The more you can avoid negative emotions and offer a calm and balanced assessment of the mistakes you've made, the better.

2. Keep Your Money Problems to Yourself

Don't regard transparency as a license to unload your money problems on your kids. Are you tossing and turning at night because your small business isn't doing as well this year as you had hoped and you've fallen behind on your bills? Do you worry about how to pay for college even as you care for your own ailing parents? While it's probably okay to tell your kids about these situations in general terms, and while you'll want to make them aware of any big changes that will affect their lives, don't complain at length and repeatedly about these problems. Keep your emotions to yourself, and if you slip up, try to make a quick recovery. Your kids aren't your shrink, and they're certainly not your financial planner. If you find yourself unduly burdened by money problems, get help. And do it quickly, *before* your parenting becomes compromised. As hard as it is, you need to set aside your own problems and be there for your kids. Otherwise, you risk fostering anxiety and self-doubt that, as we've seen, will come back to bite you.

3. Get Them Jobs

One of the best ways to teach your kids healthy attitudes and habits around money is to encourage them to work. When I was growing up, I was constantly working crappy minimum-wage jobs, even though my family was privileged. I raked leaves, shoveled snow, performed secretarial tasks at a real estate office, and served as a referee for athletic leagues, where I delighted in tossing hyper-aggressive and verbally abusive parents out of gyms. When I wanted something my parents considered a luxury, I usually had to pay for at least part of it myself. All of this working taught me life lessons, such as how to handle those ranting and raving parents, and how hard it can be to be the low woman on the clerical totem pole. My childhood jobs also shaped how I thought about money. I knew not to waste it, because I understood what it took to make it. And I had an appreciation for how hard my parents had to work to keep our family financially secure.

4. Be Careful When Helping Out Your Kids

Just because your kids are working doesn't mean they should pay for everything. Let Maria's story be a cautionary tale about the risks of being too strict around money. At the same time, be sure that any help you give your kids still allows them to take responsibility for their own financial well-being. This is especially important as your kids grow older and leave the house. If you're paying your kids' expenses in college, pay them monthly. That way, your kids can get in the habit of managing their bills for themselves, just as they'll do once they've graduated and are living on their own. If you wish to help your kids out with their student loans, consider repaying all or a portion of the loan, and then having them continue to make payments to you for a period of time. If you have a so-called boomerang kid who is moving back in with you after college, don't let him or her free-ride off you. Expect your son or daughter to contribute to the family finances, whether by paying rent, helping with groceries or bills, or performing cleaning or other chores. If your child is unemployed, make looking for a job a condition of living with you. To make sure everyone understands the arrangement, it's a good idea to jot it down on paper.[1]

5. Cultivate Financial Literacy

As your kids grow up, explain the basics of money to them. As research has shown, kids start to form money habits by age seven, so it's imperative to start early.[2] When your children are between the ages of three and five, begin identifying coins and their value. Discuss how something that is free, like playing with a friend, is different from an item that costs money, like an ice cream cone. Also introduce the concept of work and the idea that one sometimes has to wait a bit before obtaining a desired item.

I never received an allowance, and the jury is out on whether or not it really matters. If you decide that you will provide allowances to your kids, start when they're six. Most experts agree that you shouldn't base an allowance on the performance of household chores, but rather on what you already spend on small, discretionary items your child likes but doesn't need (toys, treats, and so on). Make it clear that the amount you're giving replaces what you otherwise would have spent on such items. Encourage your kids to save 10 percent of their allowance by opening a savings account for them and explaining the concept of earning interest. To reinforce the savings habit, you might offer a "matching plan" for your child's savings: For every dollar your child saves, you'll put in twenty-five cents. Once your kids get into their teens, start to explain the concept of debt. In high school, talk about the cost of college, and about whether or how much the family plans to contribute toward it.[3]

When your kids enter college and begin transitioning into adulthood, teach them the basics of how to manage their money, including how to create realistic budgets for themselves. Arrange for them to obtain secured credit cards (a card that you secure with cash collateral, and that unlike debit cards allows you to build a credit history). Also, encourage your child to check his or her credit report periodically—preferably at the beginning of each academic year. Shop for a checking or savings account with your child, teach him or her how to balance the account, and stress how important it is to check it regularly. Have your child get in the habit of setting aside a small portion of his or her earnings from any part-time jobs, and teach him or her some of the basics of identity theft protection described in Chapter 7.[4]

6. Nurture Feelings of Appreciation

One of my friends who works on Wall Street came home one day dejected and angry about her annual bonus. Be prepared to hate her, because her bonus was—are you ready for this?—$1 million! She was upset because she learned that her equally qualified male peers earned $2 million bonuses. (We should all have such problems, right?) I would be upset, too, if I felt I was being unfairly treated. Equality is important. But at the same time, think of the message you're sending your kids when you bitch and moan about a $1 million bonus. If you don't seem grateful after receiving such a mammoth bonus, don't expect them to feel grateful if the generosity you show toward them isn't what they feel they deserve.

As human beings, we'll all feel jealous and resentful of others at times. That's okay. To raise kids with healthy attitudes about money, try to put the spotlight as much as possible on all your family has, not what your family lacks in comparison to others. If your family can provide for everyone's needs, celebrate that. And don't forget to discuss the deeper meaning you derive from your work, above and beyond your paycheck.

MONEY–THAT *OTHER* TRICKY CONVERSATION

In some ways, talking about money with your kids is similar to talking about sex. Both are charged topics, and as a result, many parents want to avoid them. They know they should talk about these topics at least a little bit—how else will their kids stay safe and healthy? But they don't know what to say to help their kids, or out of anxiety they might talk about it too much or too little, or in the wrong ways.

The best approach when it comes to money (don't get me started about sex) is to discuss it in a *thoughtful,* measured, balanced way. Help your kids understand the basics, but don't disclose too much, don't allow your emotions to dictate what you say, and don't give money an outsized presence in the household so that it pops up in every conversation and influences every family decision. Control your speech and behavior around money, understanding tendencies of yours that might not be the healthiest, and correcting for them. Again, make sure to communicate in what you say and do that money isn't everything—that it's the means to an end, not the end itself.

Parenting around money isn't hard (says the mother of two spoiled Norwich Terriers), but it does require some extra care and attention. My friend Bonnie doesn't come from a wealthy background, but her husband had the good fortune to become a billionaire—yup, "billion" with a b. Their kids aren't snotty or entitled, they don't waste money, and they're not ignorant about the world. That's because all along, Bonnie consciously considered how to handle money issues around her kids in healthy ways. She didn't offer many details about what their father made. She didn't give them everything they wanted. She made them perform chores around the house, and she talked to them from a young age about the purpose of money and what was truly important in life. Most of all, she wove the concept of gratitude into conversations about money. And that's how her kids grew up—grateful for what they had, and not judging others for what they didn't.

As I tell people, the happiest clients I've had weren't the wealthiest. They were those who worked hard with an eye not toward accumulating wealth, but toward living meaningful, well-balanced lives. You can help your kids become happier by putting aside your issues and behaving mindfully around money. Start as early as possible—like, how about *now*?

You Don't Plan for the Care of Your Aging Parents

By this point in the book, a few of you might be thinking, "Yeah, I've got most of these dumb mistakes in check. I've rented instead of buying, I'm spending my retirement nest egg wisely, I'm forgoing financial products I don't understand, I've got a responsible financial adviser, and on and on. I'm pretty much all set!"

Yeah, but have you figured out how you're going to take care of Mom and Dad when they get old?

We don't like to think about our parents aging, any more than we like to think about ourselves dying or our homes getting pummelled by Hurricane Irma. And we don't know how to broach the subject with our parents. How can we possibly have an honest conversation with them when what we're considering saying goes a little bit like this: *"Hey, Mom and Dad, we need to talk. . . . You're definitely losing a step. Mom, you've told me the exact same thing three times in the space of a five-minute conversation. And Dad, seeing as you clipped that fire hydrant last week and nearly got yourself killed, you really shouldn't be driving at night, especially after draining your gin and tonic. The idea of both of you getting old like Nana and Poppy is freaking me out. I can't bear the idea of you moving in with me because I know there will be blood. So, what should we do about this?"*

Because talking about aging is so difficult, we fail to discuss our parents' needs and desires, we fail to research what those needs and desires might cost, and most of all, *we fail to come up with a plan for the future.* Before we know it, the future arrives, and we suffer unnecessary financial pain—not to mention the avoidable emotional pain our whole family might suffer—because we're scrambling to figure out solutions.

A woman I know, "Gina," never got around to talking about her parents' needs as they aged. When they reached their late seventies and began to slow down, she asked them to move in with her so she could take care of them. (Yes, she'll be going to "Daughter Heaven," though I'm guessing she'll be very lonely, because most of us can't bear the thought of Mom and Dad as roomies.) If all of her siblings had sat down years earlier and hashed out a plan, perhaps the parents would have taken her up on her offer. But the parents declined, saying they were already building a new house for themselves with everything on one floor.

Without having consulted a financial professional or anyone in the family, they had put a down payment on some land and, just like that, the idea was in motion. The purchase had been an impulse move all the way: Her parents had driven by an empty lot, fallen in love with the land, and decided then and there to buy and build. By the time the house was complete, they were stuck—the real estate market in their area was weak and they couldn't sell their existing house. They couldn't afford to maintain two houses, so they had to sell the new one and try to "age in place" in the old one as best they could. A colossal waste of time and money.

A couple of years later, Gina's father had a stroke and had to enter a nursing home. A couple of years after that, her parents had blown through their savings, and Gina and her siblings had to chip in to help out their mother. If the family had planned for the future and arrived at a reasonable game plan that included either downsizing or having the parents move in with one of the kids, they would have avoided this situation.

Poor planning can cost you tens or even hundreds of thousands of dollars in unanticipated costs for your aging parents. If you haven't bothered to figure out how much care costs these days, you might be shocked. According to the Genworth 2017 Cost of Care Survey, assisted living residents pay a median cost of $3,750 a month, while private nursing home care costs $8,121 a month. If you need a home health aide, you're talking $21.50 an hour, or tens of thousands a year, not covered by health insurance. And these are median numbers—your actual costs might be higher.

Also, Genworth found that these costs were rising. Between 2016 and 2017 alone, they rose 4.5 percent, on average, far outpacing inflation.[1] This is to say nothing of additional costs like the travel expenses you'll accrue if your parents live in a faraway city, or the costs of health care expenses that insurance doesn't reimburse. Need to hire someone local to keep track of your elderly parents' affairs? Pay up!

Planning in advance, you might be able to provide for these costs. If you don't plan, you'll still feel pressured to foot the bill—you love your parents, after all. But that might mean sacrificing your own needs and those of your kids. Far better to set realistic expectations earlier on, and to prepare to fund those expectations well in advance.

Planning is especially important for members of the "sandwich generation," the 47 percent of adults who have both aging parents and kids to care for and support.[2] As a parent, the last thing you want is to find yourself overwhelmed both financially and emotionally when Grandma or Grandpops experiences a health setback and needs help. Who's going to take Grandma or Grandpops to medical appointments if you've got to pick up your kids every afternoon from soccer practice? You need to think about this stuff!

Even if you're not a sandwicher, planning is simply the smart thing to do. You plan for retirement decades in advance (I hope). You sock away money for college when your kids are still small (please tell me you do). Why not overcome your discomfort, huddle together with your family members, and create a care plan for your parents as well?

PLANNING ROCKS!

Skeptics out there—the cocky ones who think they've got all of their dumb mistakes in check—might counter that planning for aging doesn't make much of a difference, given the astronomical costs of care. No matter how carefully you plan, you'll probably still wind up paying more than you would like, and also worrying more than you would like—that's just a fact. So instead of putting yourself through a series of painful family conversations, why not save yourself the trouble and let it ride?

I agree that no amount of planning can free us entirely from the burdens of caring for aging parents. When we study and analyze our options, we might find them to be few and unattractive. But planning still helps, because it allows us to gain at least a semblance of control over an inherently chaotic and unpredictable situation. You might not like your options, but if you plan, you at least understand them well in advance, you can adjust emotionally to them, and you can attack them proactively.

One couple who contacted my radio show, Barb and Dennis, quit their jobs, sold their home, and moved in with Barb's elderly parents in order to care for them. A few years later, Barb's parents died within months of each other. Barb and Dennis split the inheritance, including proceeds from the sale of her parents' home, with Barb's two siblings. That left Barb and Dennis with about $550,000 in total assets, but no place to live. They had to pay in full for a new house (without jobs, they couldn't qualify for a mortgage, and Barb didn't want to rent). As a result, they had only about $300,000 in liquid assets, not enough to fund a comfortable retirement.

If Barb and Dennis had sat down with her siblings and parents to plan, they might not have chosen to move in with Barb's parents. Instead, they might have had their parents move into their home. Either Barb or Dennis could have kept working, arranging if they needed to for an aide or a nurse to come in and assist the other in caring for Barb's parents. Now, because they didn't plan, Barb and Dennis would either have to settle for a bare-bones retirement or one of them would have to go back to work for four or five more years—both poor options, in their eyes. Even if advance planning had not allowed them to avoid this outcome, they still would at least have known what they were in for, and thus avoided an unpleasant retirement surprise. Remember back in Chapter 3 how painful people in that scientific experiment found uncertainty? Barb and Dennis would have bypassed that pain.

Considering Gina's situation more closely, we find that planning might have made a significant difference. If Gina had taken the initiative and triggered a family conversation about aging, she and her siblings might have influenced their parents to think more carefully about selling their existing house and building a new one. To Gina's parents, building a new home had seemed like a prudent move. This new home, they reasoned, would be smaller and built for aging, and when the sale of their old home and the construction of their new home were both complete, they would bank some profit—about $150,000, as they calculated it. With this money, they could help fund their care. They didn't want to burden their kids financially or emotionally with their future health needs, and they felt that they had found a way ahead that was in the family's best interests.

During planning conversations, Gina and her siblings might have shaken their parents out of this thinking, questioning whether they wouldn't be better off moving near one of them. If their parents wanted to stay in Arizona, Gina and her siblings might have proposed adapting their existing house as a more economical option. If the parents were bent on selling, Gina and her siblings might have convinced them to look at renting instead of buying. Or they might have pushed their parents to consult a financial planner, who would have alerted them to these and other options.

Of course, the debacle with the new home wasn't the reason Gina and her siblings wound up supporting their mom financially in old age. That owed to the exorbitant cost of nursing care. Here again, planning might have helped. Gina's parents might have investigated whether they could afford long-term care insurance (LTCI), which would have paid for a portion or all of the nursing care at home. These policies are quite expensive, and fewer reputable companies provide them than did so years ago, so perhaps that might not have been an attractive option.* In that case, Gina and her siblings might have decided to do what they did: let their parents spend down their assets on a nursing home, and afterward pay for the expenses of the parent who was not receiving nursing care, sharing it among themselves. But if they had settled on that scenario years in advance, each of the siblings would have had years to plan and save, and each could have made other financial decisions in his or her life accordingly. As it stood, the siblings had to make painful choices when confronted all of a sudden with their mother's need, in some cases sacrificing their emergency funds or kid's college savings to pay their share. Planning would have stood them on more solid financial ground.

Planning can also help with the substantial emotional and relationship costs of caring for an aging parent. I've helped to care for aging parents, and I can tell you, it's really frigging hard. Most of

---

* If you are considering LTCI, be sure to work with a fiduciary adviser to determine which policy is most appropriate for you or whether other insurance products might provide some coverage.

the time, the task of caring for parents falls unequally on the siblings—often the female sibling who lives closest to the parents bears the worst of it. In the absence of planning, and a care plan to which everyone agrees, the unequal burdens can lead to all manner of tension and resentment.

In one family I know with seven adult children (yes, seven!), the two daughters who lived closest to the parents handled most of the caregiving. As time passed, they felt as if their out-of-town brothers and sisters were taking advantage of them. Of course, neither had complained years earlier when their parents provided both of them with endless amounts of free child care for their kids—a perk their faraway siblings didn't enjoy. "Hey," one of the brothers told me, "my sisters *chose* to live in the neighborhood where we grew up. Nobody forced them. I'm sick of my sisters playing the martyr, when they put themselves in the situation."

It's hard to talk with your siblings about your parents' future care, especially if you and your siblings don't get along. The best approach, if you can manage it, is to set aside your squeamishness and attack the problem directly. "Bro," you might say, "I know we're not close, but we're family and we care about Mom and Dad. What would be the way you think you could help out, even from a distance? Can you commit to visiting a certain number of times a year, or would you prefer to help in some other way?" Not speaking forthrightly and letting your siblings do the same robs you of the possibility of making progress on this issue and maybe working out a solution. Resentments might still arise, but they probably won't fester as much.

At its best, planning can bring parents and children closer together, allowing everyone to enjoy the parents' waning years to the fullest. My friend Stacey grew up in Virginia and moved to Providence, Rhode Island, after college. Her brother moved out to Utah, and her parents stayed in Virginia. When her parents were in their seventies and still in reasonably good health, Staccy urged them to move closer to her; it would be less of a stretch for them than moving all the way out to Utah, and Stacey didn't want to leave Rhode Island to move near her parents. Her parents were reluctant. "Honey," her mom said, "they are going to take me out of this house feetfirst. . . . I am *not* moving." Her dad chimed in, "Move to New England? It's cold, and they talk funny."

I've lived in New England—he had a point. Still, Stacey was undeterred by the pushback. One day, not long after her dad took a tumble down the stairs, she casually planted a seed by saying "Dad, the house is tough to navigate with my fifty-year-old knees. I don't know how you and mom are going to manage." The next month, when her parents came to visit, Stacey gently asked if she could drive them an hour to Cape Cod to see a new 55+ community that was being built. Her parents agreed, and wound up loving it—the place looked like a resort, with every amenity they could think of, including a state-of-the-art gym, a beautiful movie theater, and card rooms galore, all of which supported a vibrant social scene. Over the next two years, Stacey, her husband, and her parents continued to talk, and after her father took a couple more spills in the old house, they wound up putting a game plan together for her parents to move.

First, her parents rented an apartment in the 55+ community for the summer to confirm that they liked it and to spend time with Stacey and her husband. They also visited in the dead of winter to see if they could handle the region's harsh weather. Stacey knew that the plan was working when her father said, "Well, you can't play golf in January up here. On the other hand, you can't play it at home, either, and there's no way I'm moving to Florida!" and her mother added, "I think the snow is kind of pretty." At around this time, some of the parents' close friends fell ill, prompting their realization that they needed to think realistically about the next phase of their lives. They saw that this community would allow them to make new friends and remain engaged with the world while putting them close to family in case their health declined.

Her parents purchased a condo, and within months felt happy and settled. They loved being near their daughter, and didn't miss their old community as much as they had expected. They were better off financially as well. Because they had planned their move in advance, they were able to time strategically when to put their existing home on the market, rather than rushing it to market and settling for a reduced price because they felt pressured to sell. They sold their primary residence for $750,000 and purchased the new place for $600,000. The extra $150,000 went toward moving and decorating costs and also funded their "Virginia account"—money to pay for travel back and forth to visit old friends.

The move also felt easier emotionally because it took place slowly, in a stepwise way. As with most life transitions, a more methodical pace can make an adjustment less painful. "I never would have predicted that walking away from my home of forty years would be possible," Stacey's mom said. "But in the end, we saw the move up north as an exciting next chapter in our lives." As for Stacey, she felt much less anxious having her parents close by, where she could personally check in on them and monitor their well-being. No longer did she have to fly down to Virginia every time one of her parents had a health issue. If she hadn't prodded her parents to think more seriously about their aging plan and moving closer to her, they wouldn't have done it.

When you were little, your parents expanded your horizons, pushing you in ways that helped you grow. Now it's time to return the favor. Help your parents understand their situation more completely, including options for aging that they might not have considered. Doing so will save everyone trouble, and who knows: It might allow you to deepen your relationship with your parents.

THE FOUR AGING FOIBLES

In case I still haven't convinced you to get off your duff and plan, let me be more specific. There are a number of financial mistakes that I've seen aging parents repeatedly make. We could blame parents for failing to plan appropriately, but I put a good part of the blame on adult kids for shirking their responsibilities. If you've failed to prod your parents into collaborating with you to craft an aging plan, don't get pissed at your parents for screwing up—they need your help! The following mistakes, so easy to avoid, have an emotional impact and cost families big money. If they don't scare you into taking action, nothing will!

Aging Foible #1: Your Parents Put Their House in Your Name

When your parents go into a nursing home and Medicaid foots the bill, the government allows them to keep their house if it's worth up to a preset limit ($500,000 in some states, more in others). If the price exceeds the magic threshold, your parents either have to sell the home or arrange to pay Medicaid the difference between its value and the threshold number. Many older people don't understand this rule—they think Medicaid will automatically take their home from them if it's worth more than the threshold amount. So, what do they do? They arrange to transfer the title to the home to one of their children. Pretty smart—except that it's not.

What aging parents don't realize, beyond the fact that they might be able to keep their homes, is that transferring the title saddles their child with a hefty potential tax liability. If the parent purchased a house decades earlier for $100,000, and it's now worth $650,000, the child upon receipt of this gift now also inherits the parents' original cost basis of $100,000. This means that when they sell the property, they will have to pay long-term capital gains tax on the difference between the current price and the low cost basis that represents what the parents paid for it. In other words, the child must pay long-term capital gains tax on $550,000. At a 20 percent tax rate (or 23.8 if you are in the top bracket), that amounts to a bill of $110,000!

To make matters worse, some parents transfer the title without even telling their child beforehand. Nice little tax surprise, right? If the parent had died and the child had inherited the property, he would be entitled to a step-up in cost basis, meaning that he would be taxed as if he had bought the property for its present value of $650,000 and then later sold it for the same amount. Total tax due: zero. If your parents are thinking of putting their house in your name, interceding and preventing the transfer would itself make a planning conversation well worth it.

Aging Foible #2: Your Parents Don't Have Enough Liquid Assets

A couple I know, Tom and Chrissy, had $5 million in assets, consisting of a $1 million house, a $3 million vacation property, and $1 million in cash and investments. Chrissy didn't pay much attention to financial planning, since Tom always assured her he was taking care of it. "Don't worry," he would say, "everything's fine." The couple's three children never challenged this assertion. And for years into their retirement, everything did seem fine—until Tom passed away. At that point, Chrissy and the adult children found themselves in a quandary. Chrissy was only sixty-nine years old, at the beginning of her retirement. With $1 million in liquid assets to draw on in addition to Social Security, she would have enough to live on, but not enough to maintain both properties. To set her future on firmer ground, she would need to sell the vacation property.

The children were heartbroken: This property had been in the family for decades; they had been counting on raising their own kids there. But Chrissy had no choice. "I can't put my welfare over the next twenty years at risk," she said to the kids. "If you'd like to pool your money and buy it from me, we can do that, but otherwise, I'm cutting it loose." Chrissy sold the vacation property, netting $2.3 million after taxes and fees.

If the kids had helped their parents plan for their care as they aged, they might have spotted this problem years earlier and figured out a way for the family to keep the home. If that had proven impossible, they would have had time to reconcile themselves to losing the vacation home—it wouldn't have come as such a shock. Under Tom's watch, he and Chrissy had managed to accumulate $5 million in retirement assets—a fantastic accomplishment. But he hadn't paid sufficient attention to the need for liquidity as he and his wife aged.

Aging Foible #3: Your Parents Give You Too Much Money

This mistake is related to the previous one. Let's say parents have six kids, and they've entered retirement with $5 million in assets, $3 million of which is in real estate and $2 million of which is in liquid assets—savings accounts, IRAs, and so on. The parents decide to give each kid $15,000 per year as they age, or $90,000 total per year. That doesn't sound like a lot compared with $5 million. But the parents are actually bestowing that money out of their $2 million in liquid assets. They can't take their living room or backyard swimming pool to the grocery store to pay with, right? So, every year, they're giving away 4.5 percent of their liquid assets—considerably more than the 3 percent or so that people can safely withdraw during retirement. Add to this the fact that they're probably also drawing on those liquid assets to pay at least a portion of their living expenses.

The risk—which all too often comes to fruition—is that parents will run out of money during retirement. When that happens, seniors are often forced to sell their homes or call upon their kids for financial help (See Chapter 8). What a terrible situation—and one that's totally avoidable with proper planning. Your parents might not have nearly as much money to spend during retirement as they think they do. As an adult child, you need to explore this issue with them as part of your overall discussion about their care.

Aging Foible #4: Your Parents Retire Too Early

Many parents don't fully understand how much more comfortable their retirement might be if they waited a few more years. According to a National Bureau of Economic Research report, people can bump up their standard of living by one-third if they work four years longer. If they work eight years longer, their standard of living rises by 74 percent.[3] That's huge! In planning conversations with your parents, you can broach the question of whether they've really analyzed their retirement numbers (again, please see Chapter 8). Do they have the monthly income that they need? You can also check to make sure your parents aren't running through their money too quickly early on in their retirement, leaving them less to draw on later.

If you don't talk with your parents about their plans for aging, you'll never know if they're making sound decisions. You're going to have these conversations anyway if a mistake is made and your family needs to handle the consequences. Why not have them now, when you can actually prevent financial sorrows? Isn't it worth a bit of awkwardness or discomfort to avoid losing the family vacation home? I think so!

GETTING THE CARE PLAN RIGHT

Now that I've convinced you to schedule a face-to-face with your parents and siblings, here are some suggestions for how to handle these conversations:

- *Start the conversation early:* I think of retirement as composed of three phases. During the first phase, when your parents are between sixty-five and seventy-five, they tend to be active and are perhaps still working. Between seventy-five and eighty-five, they're slowing down somewhat but are probably still quite active. After age eighty-five, your parents will usually require more care because of declining health. I advise that people start having conversations about aging when their parents are about seventy years old. That way, you have enough time to plan for stages II and III, and you can do so while your parents' minds are still sharp.

- *Take baby steps:* If you or your parents find it hard to think about the reality of aging, go slowly. You don't have to figure everything out at once, nor do your parents have to destroy their present lives overnight to prepare for aging. My friend Stacey nudged her parents to think more about aging and to involve her in the deliberations. When they began exploring their options, they did so at a reasonable pace and with a minimum amount of risk, renting first instead of buying. Of course, you can only go slowly if you start the conversation *early.*

- *Don't dictate solutions:* As I've suggested, you can help your family so much simply by making your parents and siblings aware of issues or options they might not have considered. If your parents hold strong opinions, listen closely to them, and do the best that you can to accommodate their desires. When my grandparents were growing older, my father sat down with them to help them plan. My grandmother insisted that she and my grandfather age in place in their existing three-bedroom home in Florida rather than move to a smaller place, and eventually, a nursing home. My father suggested other options, like having his parents move up to New York to live near our family, but my grandmother was adamant: She wanted to stay in their home.

Running the numbers, my father concluded that my grandmother's plan was financially practicable. Also, given its layout, my grandparents' house was suitable for aging in place with just a few adjustments. Since the plan generally made sense, my father saw no reason to force my grandparents to leave their home. And so they didn't.

- *Cover the financial basics:* Proper planning includes a financial plan for your parents' retirement, covering topics like what will happen to their home or other real estate they might own, whether they have a will in place (see Chapter 12), and what financial contributions you and your siblings will make toward their care. Will one of you be moving in with your parents to care for them? Will one of you renovate a section of your home so your parents can move in with you? Should you consider whether your parents need long-term care insurance? If they have less than $500,000 in assets, they don't have to worry about it, because they will probably qualify for government assistance (Medicaid) once they spend down their assets. If they have more than $2 million in assets, they also don't need the insurance, as they'll probably have enough to "self-insure" or fund the care they need, though less money will remain to pass on to you and/or your siblings upon their deaths. People who fall in the middle, possessing between $500,000 and $2 million in assets, are at risk, especially if they are married. They should consider buying at least some baseline insurance when they're in their fifties—say, enough to cover half the annual cost of a nursing home.

- *Work out a care schedule with your siblings:* Who will care for your parents in case of sickness? Discuss this with your siblings, taking into account what each person can realistically contribute given his or her financial and family circumstances. Be sure to consider emotions, too. One friend of mine is wealthy but can't stand her mother. She and her siblings have agreed that she'll pay a bigger chunk of the bill for Mom's care, but she won't have to do any of the day-to-day caregiving. In another family, four adult children live near their elderly parents, and they all get along with the parents and one another. Each child has committed to spend one day a week with the parents. Whatever arrangement you decide upon, be equitable in your treatment of each family member. If one sibling shoulders a disproportionate amount of the care burden, quitting a job or making some other financial sacrifice, you might wish to offer him or her a bigger chunk of your parents' estate as compensation.

- *Get organized:* Once you've devised a care schedule, put it down on paper to ensure that everyone understands and agrees to it. If you and your siblings will be coordinating care for your parents, give everyone access to the schedule, and have someone manage the process on an ongoing basis. If you can't handle the care requirements, hire nurses, home aides, or other caretakers to fill the gaps.

- *Be creative:* In some cases, it might be clear which sibling should take care of the parents, where the parents should live, and so on. Other times, you might have to do some creative problem-solving. One friend of mine, an investment banker living in New York, wasn't sure where her parents would live as they aged. She didn't have the time to care for them, her brother lived off in Georgia, and her parents lived far away in Ohio. Her brother came up with an ingenious solution: Their parents could sell their house and come to live with his family. He would take the proceeds of the house sale and use them to find housing for their parents and to care for them, keeping any unused money for himself at the time of their death. My friend enthusiastically agreed. She loved knowing that her parents would be well taken care of, and that she wouldn't have to shoulder the day-to-day burden. She didn't care that she wouldn't receive any money from the sale of their house. Her parents loved that they would live close to her brother's family and be able to spend time with their grandchildren. Because her brother was compensated financially, he didn't feel that he was shouldering an unfair burden.

- *If necessary, bring in a third-party mediator:* Nothing will stir up old tensions and resentments like crafting a care plan. If you've had difficulties with your siblings or parents in the past, or you've reached a dead end in your negotiations and just can't agree, bring in a third party, whether a financial planner, attorney, family wealth counselor, clergyperson, or even just a trusted family friend. Whomever you choose, make sure all parties regard this person as truly impartial. I can't emphasize enough how important it is to come up with some kind of arrangement that everyone can live with. I've seen siblings sue one another after a parent's death, accusing one another of frivolously spending down the parents' retirement money on the pretext of obtaining care. Guess who wins in a situation like that? The attorneys! Don't let that happen in your family. Have the hard conversations now, and get the outside help you need to reach common ground.

As difficult as aging is, there are many possible arrangements that will allow siblings to ensure appropriate care for their parents, without putting unnecessary burdens on themselves. Some clients of mine moved into their parents' home to care for them, with the understanding that they would receive the home in the will when their parents passed away. My grandfather married a woman thirty-five years younger who received a chunk of his estate but also provided care for him during his final years. Unorthodox? Perhaps. But it worked (third time's a charm for Poppy!). My mother received less of an inheritance, but she was spared much of the hard work of caring for my grandfather. (Lest you think that we Schlesingers are saintly, we lament to this day the fact that Poppy left his third wife a beautiful New York City apartment with—wait for it—a dedicated parking spot in the building's garage!)

Think hard about your parents and their needs, as well as your and your siblings' capacity to care for them. Then start a dialogue, recognizing that the process might require months or even years to bear fruit. I know it's tough. I know you really don't want to. But someone has to buck up and serve as the convener and instigator. Why not you? Make a good-faith effort and see what happens. If the conversation leads nowhere, and it very well might, don't berate yourself over it. Feel proud that you tried. By doing so, you served your family's best interests, as well as your own.

MAKING THE BEST OF IT

Stacey, the friend of mine who convinced her parents to move up to a 55+ community near her home, had hoped she would enjoy having her parents nearby for years to come. But sadly, it was not to be. Several months after their move, Stacey's father fell ill with an infection. He was hospitalized and released, but afterward he never regained his health. For several weeks, he was in and out of the hospital. About eight months after the move, he died of cardiac arrest at the age of seventy-nine.

As traumatic as this event was for Stacey and her mother, it could have been worse. Imagine how hard it would have been on Stacey to try to oversee her father's care from hundreds of miles away, or to care for her mother from that great distance once he was gone. Reflecting on her father's death, Stacey feels heartbroken that he was not able to enjoy his new home and lifestyle for very long, but she takes comfort in knowing that her mother was provided for. Because Stacey's parents had been planning for and executing stages II and III of their retirement plan for years, Stacey's mom was in the best possible position to go on with life without her husband by her side. She had her daughter nearby and new friends to help her through the mourning process.

Life isn't all sunshine and jelly beans. If you can make your parents' aging just a bit more tolerable for them and for you by planning for it, then you've accomplished a lot. You might have to endure some unpleasant conversations, but hey, you're an adult, right? You can handle it.

While we're at it, we might as well acknowledge some other unpleasant tasks we'll have to shoulder to ensure our family's financial and emotional well-being. It's not fun to contemplate the many horrible things that might happen to us in life, including property damage, disability, and death. And yet, we must entertain these possibilities if we are to take steps to protect against them. So many smart people don't force themselves to think about unpleasant "what if" scenarios, and so they don't get the insurance coverage they need. When disaster strikes, as it sometimes does, they or their family members are left to bear the brunt. You've bucked up once in this chapter and taken responsibility for your family members. In the next chapter, I'll ask you to buck up again, this time taking responsibility for *yourself.*

You Buy the Wrong Kinds of Insurance, or None at All

magine what it would be like to slap a big, fat "Closed" sign on your office door, buy a picturesque shack on a remote patch of beach, and live out your days in relaxing, sun-drenched bliss. Amazing, right? That's what my friend Danny, a tenured professor in his mid-sixties, decided to do after his beloved wife of several decades passed away. He retired from his university job, sold the family home, and plunked down $300,000 in cash for a two-bedroom house on the beach in the Florida Keys. Not across the street from the beach. Not around the block. Right smack on the beach. Awakening each morning to the sound of crashing surf, he set about healing his wounds and making a new life for himself.

Danny's new house had a certain Hemingwayesque allure to it, but truth be told, it wasn't much to look at. You know those dilapidated places you pass by that prompt you to say "Does anybody actually live there?" That was Danny's. But he didn't care about impressing the neighbors. What he cared about was his lifestyle. Every day in Florida, he reveled in his own, personal million-dollar view. He enjoyed morning jogs along the beach, fishing trips with new friends, regular visits from his children up north, and dinner out on his deck as the sun set over the water. But most of all, Danny enjoyed not having to think about money. He didn't have a ton in the bank after his purchase—just a few hundred thousand dollars—but with his housing now taken care of and his cost of living fairly low (his big extravagance was a new fishing lure every so often), his Social Security check covered the rest of his monthly living expenses. After decades of running the publish-or-perish gauntlet, Danny could finally relax. He was set for life—on his terms.

Or so he thought. In 2017, several years after he bought the property, when Danny was in his early seventies, Hurricane Irma struck. Unlike some of his neighbors, Danny heeded official warnings and left town before the storm hit. But upon his return, he was heartbroken to find that his beach house was a wreck. The structure was still standing, but floodwaters had ruined the interior from top to bottom. Making the house habitable again would cost at least a couple of hundred thousand dollars.

If Danny had carried flood insurance, that expense would have been no problem. But he hadn't. Many people who own homes in federally designated flood zones carry special coverage as a matter of course, participating in the U.S. government's National Flood Insurance Program because their mortgage companies require it. Although private flood insurance options exist, they are usually expensive. Since Danny had paid cash for his house, nobody had told him—much less forced him—to purchase the insurance. Danny hadn't bought it on his own because he had mistakenly assumed that his homeowner's insurance would cover any damage that might occur. Well, that's not exactly true. In reality, he hadn't thought much about insurance at all. Now, as he peered at swaths of green and blue mold cropping up on his living room wall, he desperately wished he had paid more attention.

Before you say to yourself "What an idiot!" you should know that plenty of American coastal dwellers have made this mistake. These aren't dumb people—Danny had a PhD, for goodness' sake.

But in this instance, they've screwed up. Why? Well, there's a couple of reasons. As a consumer product, insurance is painfully, atrociously boring, not to mention thankless. You pay good money now, yet you might never receive a benefit in the future. The only way you do is if something totally awful happens to you. How compelling is that? Not very—we humans don't like to dwell on all the unfortunate eventualities that might befall us. We prefer to think about the good things life holds in store. We also believe these good things are *more likely* to happen to us. So why spend our precious time worrying about insurance, and whether we're protected against every potential calamity?

Another reason we tend to neglect insurance is that although it's easy to buy policies, it's hard to comprehend them. Policy agreements and disclosure statements are notoriously dense—loads of legal jargon rendered in teeny-tiny print. As a 2017 YouGov survey found, almost three-quarters (72 percent) of respondents agreed that "insurance companies use confusing language which is difficult to understand."[1] The pricing of insurance policies is also elusive. When buying a car, you can hop online and learn what the dealer paid for it, and you can use that information to bargain for a better price.

By contrast, insurance products have layer upon layer of fees built into their prices. There's no bargaining, and it's hard to know whether you're getting the lowest price. If the policy you're considering costs less, does it offer inferior coverage? And will you have trouble collecting if you file a claim? Stories abound of consumers fighting with their insurance companies after making legitimate claims. For these reasons, buying insurance is stressful, anxiety-producing, and frankly, a pain in the heinie. We might buy certain kinds of insurance because we have to or we know we need to, but who among us wakes up thinking, "Today is going to be great, because today is the day I am going to make sure that I'm adequately insured!"

If you find yourself about to take a pass on insurance, please pay heed to Danny's experience. Without an insurance check, he couldn't afford to repair his house, because doing so would drain every last cent out of his retirement account. Unable to work at his old job again, he was forced to sell his house for what the raw land was worth and teach a few classes a semester at the local community college. Even with the extra cash and proceeds from the sale of his house, he lacked enough for a down payment on a new home without digging too far into his savings. He had no choice but to find a cheap rental, one located on the Florida mainland, miles from the beach. He wouldn't be out on the street or go hungry, but his golden years wouldn't be nearly as enjoyable or enriching as he had hoped.

You might insist that you'd *never* make Danny's mistake—in our era of global warming, with big weather events constantly in the news, flood insurance is a no-brainer! Maybe so, but this is only one of many insurance blunders smart people routinely make. Earlier in this book, we met a former client of mine who went without disability insurance—and sadly, regretted it. We met others who purchased an expensive whole life insurance policy they didn't need. We saw what can happen when people fail to procure long-term care insurance. All of this is to say nothing about the pervasive problem of underinsurance. Do you know how much life, property, or auto insurance you need right now? Do you *really*?

Let's all hold our noses and get serious about insurance. I'll do my part by promising—pinky swear—that this won't be a boring chapter. Okay, it won't be a *long,* boring chapter. I'll offer some deep thoughts on insurance, and then address the main insurance "danger zones" I've encountered working with clients and fielding calls and emails from radio listeners. With that out of the way, we can all go bungee jumping, swim in shark-infested Florida waters, speed 95 down the Interstate in a rainstorm, host an unsupervised trampoline party at our homes for a class of hyperactive kinder-garteners, or engage in any other high-risk behavior we want. Do we have a deal?

MY X-RATED LOVE AFFAIR WITH INSURANCE

I'll begin this nonboring chapter with a confession. I *love* insur-ance. Truly. That might come as a shock to people in the industry who listen to my radio show or read my blog and hear me criticize insurance companies for their slick marketing and opaque sales techniques. Not long ago, a large global insurance company con-sidered me for a lucrative position as their U.S. spokeswoman. Near the end of a yearlong hiring process, after I'd survived several rounds of interviews, they finally went back and read some of what I'd written over the years. That did it: job offer *withdrawn*.

I really do love insurance—not the way many specific products are packaged and pushed on ill-informed, unsuspecting consum-ers, but the pure concept of insurance. Why? Because life is a risky endeavor. You might feel amazing as you read this, but tomorrow you could contract Ebola and die. Or you could contract Ebola and not die but permanently lose all feeling in your hands and feet, preventing you from ever performing cardiothoracic surgery again. Or a tree could fall on your swank riverfront condo, causing $250,000 in damage. Or a tree could narrowly miss your river-front condo, but your upstairs neighbor could back up his toilet, flood your condo, and ruin your prized art collection. Or your limited-edition Andy Warhol print could be fine, but when the plumber rings the doorbell to ask you a question, he might notice your Warhol, tip off his cousin the convicted art thief, and the next weekend, when you return from visiting your elderly aunt, the print is gone. And on and on.

For most of the infinite number of risks, it's on you to protect yourself. You know it might be dangerous to cross a certain busy street near your home at night (living in New York City's Upper West Side, I am terrified of being hit by the M57 bus), so you mitigate the risk by looking both ways twenty times or avoid the risk altogether by taking a different route home. You know it might be risky to invest in growth stocks, so you allot a portion of your portfolio to less risky bonds. But for some of the biggest risks, you don't have to act on your own to mitigate or avoid the risk. Instead, you can live your life and *pay someone else* to take on the risk for you.

Yes, you might have a neighbor who floods his toilet, but that's okay. If you pay a tiny bit of money today to a group of strangers called an insurance company, those strangers will assume the risk and *pay you money* if your apartment is ever damaged. Yes, you might get stricken with Ebola if you go on safari, but that's okay. If you pay a tiny bit of money today to a group of strangers called an insurance company, those strangers will assume the risk today and *pay your heirs money* if you succumb.

That's, like, the sweetest freaking thing I've ever heard of! The insurance company can afford to assume your risk and still make a reasonable profit because it *pools* your risk together with that of many other people like you. The vast majority of those covered won't experience a disaster at exactly the same time, if at all (unless it's life insurance, because *BREAKING NEWS*—we're all going to die!). If each of these people pays just a little bit to the insurance company, that entity can guarantee that the few unlucky souls who do experience catastrophe at any given time are covered. The *community* of consumers, through the person of the insurance company, is coming together and taking the risk together, protecting you if it materializes. That's incredible!

You know what the best thing of all is about insurance? Most of the time, we really do only have to pay just a little bit of money for it. Long-term care insurance is expensive—it could run you $10,000 a year or more. The vast majority of people don't need it, but the risk you're insuring there is enormous. By contrast, insuring the valuables in your home from theft or fire is cheap—just a few hundred dollars a year, or maybe a thousand. Term life insurance? Cheap—a healthy thirty-five-year-old who needs $1,000,000 of coverage will probably pay around $1,000 a year. Flood insurance? The average government-backed policy, according to Kiplinger, will set you back roughly $700.[2]

If you earn a middle-class income or better, chances are you wouldn't think twice about paying others to handle unpleasant or difficult tasks, like babysitting your cranky kids or cleaning your house. Over a year's time, you might pay hundreds or thousands of dollars for these services. So why would you think twice about paying someone to handle significant risks in your life? Insurance gives you the chance to make the chaos of life just a little bit more controllable. Isn't that worth paying a couple of bucks for?

AVOID THE DANGER ZONES

With my paean to insurance out of the way, let's get into some specific mistakes smart people make around insurance. Be sure to avoid the following five danger zones:

Danger Zone #1: Underestimating Your Life Insurance Needs

Many smart people underestimate their life insurance needs because they don't know how much they spend each month. Insurance calculators readily available online can help you figure out how much insurance you need, but you can't make use of them unless you've bothered to do an expense analysis first. After all, for most people the point of life insurance is precisely to help your family provide for their ongoing expenses in the event of your death. As with retirement, you should plan on your heirs drawing about 3 percent of these assets every year—so $1 million of insurance proceeds will yield about $30,000 of annual income for your loved ones—less if the money is needed for a long period of time, due to inflation. Factor in any other assets your heirs might have at their disposal, as well as anticipated changes in expenses. Would your family want to move to a cheaper home if you died, or remain in the same home? Would your spouse wish to stay at home and not work? Do you want to provide for your kids' college funding and your spouse's retirement?

Many people also underestimate the need to insure the lives of their stay-at-home spouses. Thirty-five-year-old Jason earned $150,000 as the executive producer of a local television station, and his wife stayed home to take care of their three kids. He didn't think he needed to buy life insurance, because his job gave him a policy worth his annual salary. Wrong! As I explained to him, $150,000 wouldn't be nearly enough to help his wife pay the bills if he passed away. We ran the numbers—Jason would need $1 million in death benefits to provide the necessary coverage for his wife and kids. That may sound like a lot, but because Jason was healthy, it cost only about $900 a year.

Jason was also shocked to hear me tell him that Melinda, his wife, needed life insurance as well. Why? Well, if she died, who would look after the kids? Jason would need to hire someone, and that would cost money, too. (Does anyone think Mary Poppins tends to their children on the cheap? That umbrella is expensive!) Failing to consider these kinds of scenarios leads to underinsurance, which in turn leads to needless suffering if the unlikely does in fact happen (which, sadly, it sometimes does).

We agreed to insure Melinda for $800,000, leaving Jason with an annual insurance bill of under $1,500. Not such a huge price to pay to mitigate risk and give you some well-deserved peace of mind.

In working with clients, I've found that some underinsure because they simply can't fathom the idea of catastrophes happening to them. One client of mine, the artistic director of a theater company, was a supercool biker dude—long salt-and-pepper hair, goatee, shades. On beautiful Sunday afternoons when the kids were off doing their thing, he and his wife, a stay-at-home mom, loved to get on his Harley and just *ride*. When I told him that he needed to take out $1 million of coverage for himself, he was on board, but he bristled when I suggested covering his wife, at an added cost of about $500 a year. I explained the whole Mary Poppins thing. "Yeah, Jill, I get that," he said, "but come on, you're a numbers person. What is the chance that she's going to die in the next twenty years? Pretty low, right? So why do I have to pay to insure her?"

The three of us were sitting in my office, which overlooked the parking area. Glancing out the window, I saw their motorcycle parked there. "Let me ask you something," I said. "Did you guys just drive here from your house twenty minutes away?"

"Yeah," he said. "It was a beautiful drive."

"Uh-huh," I said. "Did you wear helmets?"

He smirked at me. "Nope."

"So," I said, "what's the survival rate of people who get into motorcycle accidents and don't wear helmets? Don't emergency room doctors call motorcycles 'donor-cycles'?"

His wife leaned in across the table. "Jill, we're buying the insurance!"

Most people know they should purchase life insurance for themselves, but they fail to think about other kinds of risks. They don't think that their wives might predecease them. Or that the guy fixing their roof might fall off his ladder and sue them. Or that they might become disabled and thus unable to work. The truth is that many kinds of calamities might strike us, and if we can pay modestly to insure ourselves against them, we should.

Danger Zone #2: Buying Permanent Insurance

Once people determine how much life insurance they need, they sometimes go on to make a classic mistake: purchasing the wrong *type* of insurance. As I indicated in Chapter 2, you can buy either "term" or "permanent" life insurance. Term is simple: You purchase insurance for a fixed term or period of time, after which you are again uninsured. You can purchase term for periods of up to thirty years, paying either an increasing premium each year based on your age, or locking in a fixed premium amount for the entire term of the policy. Upon your death, the insurer pays the face value of the policy to your designated beneficiary.

Permanent life insurance has no expiration date, so long as you keep paying enough money to keep it in force. Another important feature of this type of policy is that it combines insurance with a savings component. You pay an annual premium, and a portion of that goes to pay for the insurance, while the other portion is kept in an account for you as savings, with the interest accumulating on a tax-deferred basis. (Psst: I see that you're dozing off. Wake up! Just a few more paragraphs to go on this subject.) Insurers sell three basic kinds of permanent life insurance policies: traditional whole life, universal, and variable universal or adjustable. Whole life policies tend to be the most expensive, because they cover you for your "whole life," providing guaranteed rates of return on the savings component. The insurance company assumes the investment risk and guarantees that the policy will stay in force so long as you make the premium payment.

Universal or variable universal policies are not guaranteed, and are subject to risk based on the return. Consumers assume this investment risk via sub-accounts, which are like mutual fund–type instrument vehicles included within the policy. Universal and variable universal policies offer more flexibility than whole life policies in terms of the investment options, the premiums customers pay, and hence, the benefits their heirs receive upon their death.

Insurance salespeople love to tout the tax benefits of permanent policies, but they often "forget" to tell you that these policies usually cost a lot, with high fees and commissions lopping off up to three percentage points of the annual investment return. In addition, up-front (but hidden) commissions can cost up to 100 percent of the first year's premium. Some analysts estimate that many permanent life policies take years to deliver the returns you would get if you had simply purchased term insurance and invested the difference in index funds.[3] That said, if you opt to buy term and invest the difference, it's imperative that you do just that. Don't buy term and then use the extra money to go on a fabulous trip every year!

The insurance industry wants you to think that you need permanent insurance, but most people don't. Choose term if you need insurance for a specific time window (for instance, you and your spouse are in your early thirties, you have a three-year-old and another on the way, and you don't have much savings that your family can draw on if you die). If you pass away during the term of the policy, your beneficiary will receive a nice little check from the insurance company for the amount of the policy. If you're healthy, term policy premiums won't cost you very much—that is, until you turn fifty or so. After that age, you're considered more of a risk, because you are *old* (hey, look who's talking, right?) and the price of premiums ratchets up year after year. The good news is that your need for insurance likely fades after fifty, for two reasons: Your kids are grown and are with any luck self-sufficient, and you have accumulated wealth in savings and retirement accounts.[4]

If you buy whole life insurance when you really just need term, you might be wasting thousands of dollars. And it's a hard mistake to undo, as it costs money to extract yourself from an insurance policy (more on that later). On the other hand, if you're in your sixties shopping for insurance, term coverage costs so damn much that permanent insurance might be a better option. You should also consider permanent insurance in situations where you need a tax shelter, or where you need coverage beyond a fixed term—for instance, if you're buying insurance in order to help your heirs pay estate taxes upon your death, to fund a small business buy-sell agreement, or to take care of a special-needs child on a permanent basis.

Danger Zone #3: Your Needs Have Changed, but Not Your Insurance

Your insurance needs don't stay the same over time—they change as you do. Did you get married? Did you have another kid? Then you might want to think about upping your life insurance coverage. (Another benefit of term insurance is that if you find you do need permanent coverage, you can always convert to a permanent policy without going through the underwriting process all over again.) Did you put an addition on your house? You might need more homeowner's coverage. Did you make any big purchases, like jewelry or art? Then you might want to insure for that on your homeowner's policy. Did you get divorced? If your ex is a beneficiary on any of your policies, you might want to change that. Did you get a raise, and did your spouse in turn downshift his or her career to spend more time with the kids? Then you might want to make sure that you're each carrying the appropriate amount of insurance to replace lost income if either of you were to pass away.

Many people buy insurance—or don't buy it—and then forget all about it. That's a mistake. You don't have to obsess about insurance all year long, but be sure to take a quick peek at your insurance picture annually to review whether your coverage still matches your needs. Do this just after tax time as part of your annual financial review (see the Appendix). And has it been a while since you shopped for insurance for your auto, home, and/or possessions? Insurance is a competitive business, so you might want to take the opportunity every few years to shop around. Just a few clicks are all it takes.

Danger Zone #4: You're Failing to Take Full Advantage of Your Employee Benefits

Many people have access to amazing coverage through their jobs, and they don't use it. Employers might include in your benefits package a life insurance policy worth some multiple of your annual salary, and they might offer you the opportunity to purchase additional coverage for yourself or your spouse if you choose. If your employer does allow you to buy more coverage, you might want to do it, as the additional coverage could cost you considerably less than if you were to buy it yourself on the private market. Also, if you have a preexisting condition, take note: Some life insurance plans offered through employers don't require that you undergo a physical exam. This could be your ticket to some awesome coverage you might otherwise not be eligible to obtain.

Of course, because workers are changing jobs with increased frequency, be careful not to rely on your company for all of your insurance needs. Your new company might not offer the same coverage, and if you become self-employed, you might not retain any coverage at all.

If you're self-employed, you really should consider purchasing disability insurance, despite the high cost (ditto if you have a job and your employer doesn't provide it). Are you a member of a professional association or a networking group—for instance, a university alumni association? If so, you might be able to access lower group rates through that organization. Or if you're like me, just pay for private individual coverage and pray you never have to make a claim!

Danger Zone #5: You're Surrendering Your Policy Too Soon

My mother bought long-term care insurance at age sixty. For fifteen years, her health held up, and she didn't file any claims. Then, at age seventy-five, she began pestering me (like only a mother can) about whether she should drop the coverage. She had paid all this money over the years, for nothing! Why continue?

"I'll tell you why," I said. "You're entering a period in your life when you might actually experience some health setbacks. As painful as it might feel to you, keep the insurance." Happily, she did.

As a study by Boston College's Center for Retirement Research has reported, "more than one quarter of those who buy long-term care insurance at age 65 will let their policies lapse at some point, forfeiting all benefits."[5] If you're self-employed and you've been paying for disability coverage, you might also feel after a number of years that you want to rid yourself of that coverage. Consider that decision carefully. By age sixty, you're living with an elevated risk of experiencing a disability that prevents you from working, compared with your risk at age fifty. You've amassed a nest egg, but do you know for sure whether you have enough in there to help you survive unforeseen health crises? Remember the story that opened this book. You don't want to be that guy!

You should also take care not to exit a permanent insurance policy too soon. Most insurers discourage people from abandoning their policies, levying a so-called surrender charge. That's right—not only do these policies charge you a big, fat commission to get in, and not only are the ongoing costs more expensive, but you have to pay to get out. Or as the classic-rock band The Eagles would say, "You can check out anytime you like, but you can never leave!" If you've held the policy for fewer than five years, the surrender charge will probably be so gargantuan that it will not make good financial sense to exit. These charges usually decline as time passes, so after five years, exiting and purchasing cheaper term insurance might make more sense.

Jill's Quick Insurance Self-Check

Have you (or your adviser or insurance salesperson) calculated your insurance needs? If so, is term insurance better for you, or do you really need permanent?

If you're married, over age fifty-five, and have a net worth between $500,000 and $2 million, have you considered long-term care insurance?

Does your employer provide you with life, disability, or long-term care insurance? If so, can you purchase additional coverage for you or your spouse?

If you own permanent insurance and want to get out of it, have you held it for at least five years?

Are you reviewing your insurance needs as part of your annual financial review?

Let me say a word here about how to shop for insurance. These days, you can hop online and obtain competing quotes for many kinds of insurance in minutes. If you can get a good insurance salesperson to help you alongside a great fiduciary adviser, all the better. I'm much more protected today because my fiduciary adviser told me he suspected I didn't have enough property coverage. He referred me to an amazing professional who lives and breathes property and casualty insurance, and who alerted me to the fact that my coverage would likely fall short in the event of a disaster. To find a wonderful agent of your own, ask your adviser, CPA, or attorney for a referral. If you happen to have wealthy friends, ask them whom they use. When you find an agent with a great reputation, listen to his or her advice, and don't skimp! There are places in life to skimp, and an extra $500 a year on an insurance policy isn't one of them.

THE GIFT THAT KEEPS ON GIVING

Kelly, a client of mine in her fifties, came into my office one day and told me that she'd been diagnosed with advanced-stage breast cancer. She had only months to live, and was getting her affairs in order, including her family's insurance needs. Would her husband and son have enough to live on when she was gone? She wanted to know.

It was a terrible task, but never in my career had I been so honored to help out a client. "Let's take a look," I said. Her family was in pretty good shape: As a longtime state employee, she had retirement savings as well as a decent pension that her husband would inherit. She also had an insurance policy offered through her job— but as we discovered, the policy had lapsed; it was a term policy that Kelly had to renew every year if she wanted coverage, and she hadn't paid the premium for a couple of years. The policy was cheap—only about $250.

We wondered if Kelly could possibly renew this coverage. It turned out she could: The insurer didn't require a physical exam or disclosure of information about any illnesses Kelly might have had. (By the way, never, *ever* lie when applying for insurance. Don't kinda, sorta bend the truth, either. Just don't do it.) All Kelly had to do was pay the back premium she owed. She did, and as a result, her husband would receive a $250,000 payment upon her death.

Eight months later, Kelly passed away, and her husband received the insurance money. It made all the difference. With Kelly's pension and their family's savings, her husband and son could live as they had while she was alive and manage their bills. And because her husband had that extra $250,000, he was able to take a year off work to spend time with their grieving son. "Without that money," he later told me, "I never could have done it. It was such a gift." For that year, Kelly's husband didn't have to worry about financial matters. He could just focus on his kid's and his own emotional health. Nobody could give their son his mother back, but at least he had his father's close support to rely on.

When we smart people talk about insurance, we tend to think of it as a chore or an annoyance—an opportunity for some overzealous salesperson to rip us off. But insurance is so much more than that. If we clear away all of the crap, we find that insurance is, as Kelly's husband said, a "gift" that we bestow on ourselves and our families. It's a gift for the future, so that at the very worst of times, we have a safety net holding us up. Why not make sure you're adequately insured? Why not spend just a little bit more time understanding your policies and contacting your financial planner, CPA, or attorney for advice and referrals?

There's another gift you can give your loved ones, one that likewise requires only a small investment on your part. It's a gift that you probably seldom think about, but that will save your loved ones a great deal of pain, suffering, and financial loss they would otherwise experience. Any idea what it is? So many smart people don't. Turn the page to find out!

You Don't Have a Will

When I was in junior high school, I was addicted to Agatha Christie novels. I read every Miss Marple mystery, and when the original *Murder on the Orient Express* movie came out in 1974, my whole family headed to the theater to watch our favorite Belgian, Hercule Poirot, solve the mystery. That guy was *awesome*!

A couple of years ago, my friend Eileen embarked on an investigation every bit as arduous, time-consuming, and, in her eyes, high-stakes as the ones Miss Marple and Hercule Poirot handled. Day after day, she made phone calls, followed paper trails, navigated around dead ends, all in the hopes of piecing together a mysterious picture. No, Eileen wasn't trying to catch a murderer. She wasn't a police officer or private investigator. Rather, she was a woman whose husband had died without a will (or "intestate," as my lawyer friends call it) and who had to get his affairs in order so that she could go on with her life.

Eileen's husband, Jim, had passed away while still in his forties. For at least a decade prior, he had been ill, and at one point had received a kidney transplant. Eileen was a social worker, and the couple had a twelve-year-old son. When Jim first fell ill, Eileen asked him if he'd taken care of their affairs in case anything happened to him. "Oh, sure," he said. As his condition deteriorated over the years, she inquired several more times as to whether he had a will, and he always told her not to worry about it, that everything was taken care of.

Upon his death, Eileen searched for the will, but couldn't find it. Because there wasn't one. Eileen called Jim's attorney, and he informed her that he had sent Jim a draft of a will, but Jim had never gotten back to him. This omission represented a tragedy for Eileen, one I witnessed with my own eyes. Can you imagine how hard it must be for a spouse who is grieving to have to (a) process the fact that her husband lied to her, and (b) worry about money? But that's what Eileen had to do. She had to hire an attorney and endure a torturous process stretching out over months before the estate was finally resolved in probate court. During that time, she couldn't access many of Jim's accounts to pay off debts related to his funeral or other outstanding expenses. In the end, Eileen spent tens of thousands of dollars in legal fees that she could have avoided had Jim gotten his act together and put a will in place. And the process took twice as long, making her grieving process that much more difficult.

Of all the off-the-hook *stupid* mistakes you can make with your money, failing to have a will is indisputably the worst. Not only can it result in massive financial losses for your loved ones, depending on the size of the estate, but it can also cause them any number of other hardships. Want to leave open the possibility that the people closest to you *don't* receive any money from your estate, while other, less deserving people do? Want to leave open the possibility that your minor children are improperly cared for after you're gone? Or that your loved ones have to sell heirloom property in order to pay estate taxes or settle other debts? Or that, like

Eileen, they have to undergo terrible stress, anxiety, and hassle? Then by all means, don't get a will. Oh, and while you're at it, don't engage in any other form of end-of-life planning, either.

So many people fail to plan for their own demise. A 2017 survey by caring.com found that fewer than half of adults in the United States—42 percent—"currently have estate planning documents such as a will or living trust."[1] Almost two-thirds of Gen X respondents didn't have these documents, even though this cohort was heading into middle age and many of its members had small children for whom to provide. In fact, the survey found that just 36 percent of respondents with minor children had plans in place in case they died. That's crazy!

If you're noticing an edge in my voice here, it's no accident. The failure to get a will is probably the only mistake I encounter that really pisses me off, for a couple of reasons. First, there's no excuse. It doesn't cost much to have an estate attorney draw up the necessary documents—as little as $500 to $1,000 for a simple will and maybe a few thousand if your situation is more complex. If you're a total cheap-o, you can draw a will up yourself using legal forms available online (although I do not advise this; for God's sake, hire an attorney—and make it a qualified estate attorney, not the guy or gal who managed the closing of your house or handles your traffic tickets). Second, failing to draw up a will and perform proper estate planning is unmistakably selfish on your part—in fact, the height of irresponsibility. If you don't have the right documents and planning strategy in place, you might experience some of the consequences yourself, but your family members will pay the biggest price. You'd hate it if your parent or spouse died without his or her affairs in order and you had to run around like Miss Marple and Hercule Poirot, sorting it out. What a pain! So why in God's name are you putting that crap on *your* loved ones?

Fair warning: The rest of this chapter will be an extended rant intended to guilt you into preparing a will. If you're up for a little tough love, then listen to me, and listen good. Get. A. Damn. Will. Do it! Like, now. Before you get up to go to the bathroom or grab a drink. Before you check Snapchat or look at another precious cat picture on Facebook. And if you don't have a hot young estate attorney in your life yet, call around to your friends or family members to find one. I don't want any excuses. Not this time. Getting a will and planning your estate is that important. You're a bad person if you don't have a will. And I say that with the utmost love and respect.

ANY DAY IS A GOOD DAY TO THINK ABOUT DEATH

Many of us know intellectually that we should draw up a will, but we just can't sit our fannies down with an attorney and get it done. In the care.com survey mentioned above, almost half of respondents who didn't have wills explained their failure by responding that they "just haven't gotten around to it." Oh, I see. You "haven't gotten around to it." You're just *so* busy. You must plan your next trip, and you really *have* to help Junior with those college essays. What, you think you're going to live forever? Are you *that* afraid of your own death? I've had many clients who have asked aging parents to draft a will, only to hear: "What, you want me to die?" or "You're just asking me about this because you want my money!" (I'll help you deal with your intransigent parents later in the chapter, but let's focus on you right now.) Just as we don't want to think about worst-case scenarios of any kind, we don't want to contemplate the reality that one day, we won't be here on planet Earth. But that's the reality. You might as well accept and plan for it.

Another reason smart people don't put their affairs in order is they don't fully understand the need for it. If I had a dollar for every client or radio caller (primarily younger ones) who've told me that they don't need a will because they "don't have any assets," I'd be a rich woman. You know what I tell these people? Yes, it's true that only some responsible adults need wills, but it has nothing to do with how old you are or how much money you have. Rather, there's an easy rule of thumb to follow. If you: a) have a brain, and b) are breathing, then you need a will. Everyone else is hereby excused from this chapter.

I got my first will at the age of twenty-five. It wasn't a big decision—I was getting married, and it seemed like the right thing to do. I was taking on the immense responsibility to another person that marriage entailed, so I figured I might as well have a piece of paper giving that person all my earthly possessions if I kicked off before him, as well as the authority to make medical decisions on my behalf. These days, many a young person is putting off marriage and living with his or her partner for years. In that situation, a will is an especially good idea. If you're living with a boyfriend, girlfriend, or gender-nonconforming friend whom you love, he or she has no legal standing in the event of your death. Wouldn't you want that person to inherit your possessions, so that he or she is taken care of to the extent possible?

Even if you're not married, you and your parents might not agree about how you'd like events to go down during your final hours. You might want to donate your organs, or you might want doctors to pull the plug on you if you have no hope of recovery, and your parents might have different ideas. If you have the proper estate documents in place, the doctors will honor *your* wishes.

Some people I've met who have considerable assets haven't gotten wills because they assume that their spouse will automatically get everything. So what, they say, if the state law dictates the process. It's no big deal . . . and I'll be dead, anyway.

Ask my friend Eileen if it's no big deal. In fact, let's dig a bit deeper into her story. Whenever a person dies, his or her estate has to go through probate court. Some assets pass on to heirs outside of probate court: assets held in trust, life insurance benefits with named beneficiaries, retirement accounts with beneficiaries, or real estate held jointly or in what's called "tenants by the entirety." Most other assets, including most checking and savings accounts, most brokerage accounts, most real estate, and personal possessions must go through probate court before they can be dispensed to heirs. If you have a will in place that specifies who gets what, the probate process is no problem (although it might still take weeks or months to run its course). If you don't have a will in place, settling the estate becomes a monumental pain.

My friend Eileen had to go through stacks of unopened mail that her husband had accumulated—she had no idea what assets he had on their behalf, and in fact her search turned up some pleasant surprises: Her husband had two "secret" bank accounts that he had never shared with her, containing a total of $10,000. That was nice, but not enough to make it worth the painstaking effort. Of course, she also found a few secret credit card accounts too, with total balances of $3,000. I guess she should have expected surprises: Her man lied about having a will, after all. Nor is so-called financial infidelity all that uncommon. According to a creditcards .com survey, "a full 23 percent of respondents in relationships— living together or apart—said they have kept accounts hidden from their partners."[2] Oy. Not good.

Poor Eileen's legal process also became instantly more complicated once it became clear that her husband lacked a will—more papers to file in the court, more court appearances, and as I've said, more legal fees: a total of about $20,000. Still, she got off relatively easy. In some cases, the absence of clarity provided for in a will triggers nasty disputes among potential heirs—I'm talking seemingly endless litigation and six-figure attorney's fees. These conflicts can also result in outcomes that are manifestly unjust.

Consider the following fictional scenario, based on a compilation of real-life situations I've seen. Let's say Charles is forty-eight years old and became a widower seventeen years ago, when his wife had an aneurism and died instantly. Back then, he and his wife had no money and they did not have a will. Busy raising kids and establishing himself in his career, Charles executed a simple will, leaving whatever meager savings he had to his three kids and naming his sister their guardian.

Today, his kids are all in their mid-twenties and self-sufficient. Charles has gone on to build a successful career in advertising, which has allowed him to accumulate a nice nest egg. For the past three years, he has been sharing his $500,000 lakefront condo with his girlfriend, a lovely woman named Diana. His kids hate Diana, a divorcée ten years Charles' junior, because they haven't fully gotten over their mother's death and because they suspect that Diana is only after their father's money. But Charles loves Diana, and she him. She even has grown to love his kids, and hopes that they'll one day warm up to her. She and Charles plan to drive off into the sunset, but because she suffered through a divorce and his kids are so bothered by their relationship, neither is in a hurry to remarry.

One day, Charles goes to the doctor to check out some symptoms he's been experiencing and learns that he has bladder cancer. It's pretty bad—stage III. Over the next two and a half years, Diana quits her job and devotes herself full-time to taking care of him. She's a true angel, ministering to his every need. With Diana by his side, Charles endures multiple rounds of chemotherapy and radiation and learns to live with a urostomy. Over the course of a year or so, he improves—it seems like he's going to beat this thing.

Diana never thinks to ask if Charles has an updated will. Since he has kids to think about and considerable property (about $2 million in assets), she assumes he does. In fact, Charles had never revisited that simple will that he had created right after his wife died. Until now, he had always been healthy and had never thought much about dying. Even now, he doesn't go back to the lawyer to update the will, because his doctor has told him about exciting new treatments, and Charles doesn't even want to contemplate losing his battle. He's determined to think positive. If his condition declines, then he'll revise his will.

Charles never gets that chance. He goes on a business trip to Japan, and when he returns, his body feels different. He goes to the doctor and learns that his cancer is not only back, but raging out of control. Five weeks later, he's dead.

Diana is devastated. After the funeral, she goes home and cries nonstop for a week. One morning, she receives an unpleasant surprise. Charles's eldest son calls her and tells her that she is going to have to vacate the condo where she's living at the end of the month. Since Charles has only that old will, the property automatically goes to the kids. "But you can't do that to me!" she cries. Charles's son mumbles an apology and hangs up.

Diana doesn't understand. For years, she has taken care of Charles. She knew he would have never wanted her to leave his condo. But his children, either out of spite or because they are emotional basket cases, are kicking her out. How could this happen?

Diana finds an attorney who is willing to sue on her behalf to retain control of the property. For four years, Diana and Charles's kids battle it out in court. Although the kids inherit $1 million in retirement assets from Charles (they are named beneficiaries, so Diana can't contest that), they blow through $250,000 fighting off her legal challenge—half of the $500,000 in non-retirement assets Charles left behind. In the end, the kids win. Diana, who devoted so much of herself to caring for Charles, receives nothing. And the kids lose $250,000 of money they might have inherited. All because Charles didn't get his act together and draw up a will.

Scenarios like this unfold every day in this country. We like to think we're immortal, but any of us can eat some bad guacamole

(I mean, *real* bad) or get blindsided by a car going 80. If you don't have a will and related documents in place, you're leaving your loved ones vulnerable. And this is to say nothing of what could happen to your minor children. If you have a will, you can specify that they go to a guardian of your choice, someone whom you know the kids love and who would raise them in ways that accord with your beliefs and values. Without one, the court decides who gets your kids, applying rules that differ state by state. Your kids could go to a loving grandparent who will raise them right, or to a ne'er-do-well aunt or uncle. Do you want to leave your kids to the whim and caprice of a judge? No? Then draft a will! And if you and your spouse have punted on the process because you can't agree on a guardian for your children, assign one provisionally. You can always change your designated guardian once you decide for sure whom you want it to be.

ANY DAY IS A GOOD DAY FOR AN ESTATE PLAN

Please don't neglect the broader process of estate planning, either. In Chapter 10, I told the story of Chrissy, who upon her husband Tom's death had to sell the family's vacation home because Tom hadn't left her enough liquid assets to pay for both that property and their main residence. That's poor estate planning if I've ever heard of it. And it's nothing compared with some of the other stories I've come across.

A relative of mine went to college with the heir to a major real estate fortune. This woman's father built up the family business before passing away in the late 1960s, at which time the woman's mother took over. When her mother passed away in the 1990s, the estate was worth hundreds of millions of dollars and included properties in a number of states. Since the vast majority of that money was in real estate, the estate had liquidity issues: The heirs couldn't pay the tens of millions of dollars of estate taxes owed to

Uncle Sam with the cash on hand. They had no choice but to sell some prime properties—and to do it fast. That might not have posed much of a problem if the real estate market was strong, but it wasn't. The properties they sold garnered low prices, costing the family about $100 million. With proper planning, the family could have moved properties into the kids' names at various times. They could have taken out life insurance policies to create liquidity upon their mother's death. Unfortunately, the family didn't get the competent legal help they needed to put these contingencies in place.

I know you feel *so* sorry for this family for losing $100 million—wouldn't we all like to have such troubles. But you're missing the point. Your heirs, too, could struggle with some very significant tax issues upon your death if you don't plan properly. Recall another common mistake we discussed in Chapter 10: gifting too much money to your kids while you're alive. The more you give them now, the less cash will pass over to them in your estate when you die. If your kids use the gifts you give them now for other purposes, they might not have cash available to pay the estate taxes or to maintain the real estate properties you leave them. They might be forced to sell heirloom properties that everyone thought would remain in the family. And depending on market conditions, those properties might go for fire-sale prices.

Remember how I advised that you prioritize saving for retirement *before* paying for your kids' college? Here again, putting yourself first is the least selfish thing you can do. If you do give gifts of money, don't promise multiple or yearly gifts. Tell your kids you're giving them money now, and that you'll see what you can do later on. And let's not lose sight of the broader point: Plan, plan, plan, making sure to involve qualified attorneys and financial advisers as necessary.

KNOW YOUR ESTATE PLANNING BASICS

Estate planning isn't that hard—you just have to do it. Let's take a quick peek at the process. First, you'll need to put a number of legal documents in place, not just a will. Documents your attorney will want to prepare include the following:[3]

- **Letter of Instruction:** This document specifies how you would like your remains to be disposed of. Do you want a big-time funeral mass, or would you like the service held in a synagogue? Maybe you just want a simple graveside ceremony with family. A letter of instruction helps to address these kinds of issues beforehand. And if you want to be cremated, drop that little ditty in here, too.

- **Power of Attorney:** This document allows an individual to conduct legal or financial business on your behalf—potentially helpful if you are sick and your heirs need to make a mortgage payment, for instance, out of your bank account. Your relatives can't just withdraw the money—the bank won't let them. They need a power of attorney.

- **Health Care Proxy:** In this document, you formally authorize someone to act on your behalf in case you become so impaired that you can no longer make health care decisions for yourself. I like to call this the "Pull the Plug" document, which means you'd better select someone to execute your wishes who won't have a problem pulling the plug, discontinuing treatment, or getting the hospice team in place.

- **Trusts:** Most often, people whose estates exceed $11.2 million (or $22.4 million for married couples) will leave property to their heirs through a trust, since it can allow their heirs to minimize federal estate taxes (the first $11.2 million for an individual or $22.4 million for a married couple—what attorneys call the "exclusion amount"—is not taxed at the federal level). Trusts can also be important for those with minor children or children subject to potential litigation. But individuals with smaller estates should know that some states levy state death taxes at much lower levels. For example, Massachusetts estates worth more than $1 million will pay a tax and "future changes to the federal estate tax law will have no impact on the Massachusetts estate tax."[4] Additionally, a trust can allow heirs to gain access to their inheritance more quickly and easily, because the trust's assets don't have to enter probate.

- **Do-Not-Resuscitate Order:** This isn't, strictly speaking, part of your estate documents, but it's something to keep in mind. Every time you enter a hospital or nursing home, you'll need to sign one of these, stating that you don't want to be put on life support in the event that you can't breathe or pump blood on your own. Be sure that you've thought through carefully whether you want extreme medical intervention to be kept alive. How you feel now might *not* be how you'll feel when you're desperately ill.

When preparing estate documents for you, a qualified estate attorney will pose a range of questions about your assets and how you wish to dispose of them upon your death, as well as other preferences you might have. To make your planning proceed as smoothly and inexpensively as possible, think about these questions *before* meeting with your attorney:

Where, generally speaking, do you want your money to go? Do you wish to donate some or all of your assets to charity? Do you want to leave them to your kids or grandchildren? If you do wish to leave your assets to family members, do you need to protect those assets using a trust or some other means? (For instance, are you concerned that one of your heirs will squander the money, or that he or she will soon divorce and his or her spouse will receive a portion of the inheritance?) If you wish to leave your assets to family members, do you wish to treat them all equally? Are you worried about offending one heir or another? And whom do you wish to make the executor of your will? Where is this person located? (I've found that it's much easier to have an executor who lives in the same state as the deceased.) Is this person equipped to handle administrative tasks? Is he or she organized? Finally, whom do you wish to make the guardian of your minor children? Have you spoken with this person to inform him or her of your plans?

You should also take the opportunity to think more about your death. Do you want a do-not-resuscitate order? Do you have any preferences concerning how you wish for your survivors to dispose of your remains? What do you want your funeral to look like? Cynthia, the wife of a friend of mine, planned her funeral before dying of cancer. Her obituary, read aloud at the proceedings, was one of the most beautiful I've heard. Mourners were asked to donate to a cancer charity, or in lieu of that to just buy themselves something nice—because Cynthia had always liked nice things (every time I wear the earrings that I bought right after she died, I say to myself, "This is for you, Cyn!"). After the funeral, mourners assembled at a special luncheon Cynthia had organized at a beautiful spot overlooking a river. When you walked in, servers offered you vodka and gin martinis on silver trays. Cynthia cared about her loved ones and didn't want her death to burden them unduly. She wanted them to feel joy as well as sadness. What a wonderful final gesture on her part!

Once you've plotted an estate plan, revisit it periodically to gauge whether your feelings have changed and you need to make adjustments. Make sure to compile all of the information and documents your next of kin will need to settle your estate. I've run through the list of these documents and pieces of information on my blog, but for the sake of convenience, here it is again. Get out a big file box, and pile the following inside:

- A master list of all bank accounts.

- A list of all user names and passwords for your financial accounts, social media, email, and so on.

- A list of your automatic bill-paying accounts, complete with name and contact information.

- A list of all safe-deposit boxes you maintain.

- Information pertaining to your 401(k) accounts, IRAs, and Roth IRAs.

- Pension information (if you're one of the lucky few to have a pension).

- Any annuity contracts as well as insurance contracts you have (life, car, home, long-term care, etc.).

- A detailed list of savings bonds (as well as copies of those bonds, if they still exist in physical form).

- Contact information for any brokerage accounts you have.

- Deeds to your properties and cemetery plots.

- Vehicle titles.

- Marriage license (or divorce papers).

- Military discharge information.

- Documents pertaining to any businesses you own or operate.

- Tax returns for the previous three years.

- Contact information (including names, addresses, and Social Security numbers) of anyone named in your legal documents, as well as of the attorneys and CPAs handling your estate.

I know it's a pain to compile all this, but trust me, it will make your descendants' lives *much* easier. When my father died, I knew quite a bit about the process of settling estates, yet I still found it exhausting to bring this process to its conclusion, both because of the emotions I was feeling and because I couldn't easily access all of the information. Your family members might well be suffering and in emotional disarray. If they have to do all of this work themselves, the process of settling your estate might drag out significantly longer.

Sit down with your loved ones to run through your estate plan with them, inform them of where all the documents and information are located, and give them some basic advice as to how to settle an estate with a minimum of stress and effort. They'll want to order at least ten copies of your death certificate, as many financial institutions and government bodies insist on receiving originals, not copies. Also tell them to track all expenses related to your funeral and memorial, as your estate will likely reimburse individuals for these costs. Finally, advise them to contact your estate attorney, financial adviser, and CPA as soon as possible to pursue the legal process of settling your estate. One of these three professionals—usually the financial adviser—will likely spearhead the process.

What if it's not you who needs to plan your aging parents' estate, but them? How do you start the conversation? A few years ago, when estate attorney Virginia Hammerle appeared on my radio show,[5] I asked her what to do when you try and start a conversation and your parents brush it off. She told me you should stand down and not escalate the situation if you encounter resistance. Let some time pass—a few days, a week—and then try again. This might be hard to do, I know, but it's vital to keep cool and stay on point. If your parents have not actually updated their estate plan, you can remind them that tax laws have changed and it may make sense to revisit the old documents with an attorney. If the original attorney is still around, great, but if not, offer to contact another who works in the same office.

If you can't get your parents to agree to plan their estate, try pointing to a friend's or relative's situation as an example to be avoided: "Remember my high school friend Sally? She has had her hands full taking care of her mother's affairs. I guess her parents hadn't updated their wills in, like, forty years!" Hammerle also suggests focusing initially "on an isolated issue, like titling of a bank account or making a beneficiary designation," using that as a springboard to a broader discussion on family finances and estate planning. If you've made multiple attempts and your parents still stubbornly refuse to engage, leave it alone. After all, you still have to get through holidays with them.

MY FATHER'S FINAL GIFT

My father died of an infection after spending several months in and out of the hospital. During his final hospital stay, doctors tried to save him by administering a megadose of antibiotics, but his condition kept worsening. When it became clear that the end was near, my mother, sister, and I made the decision to forgo further medical care. The doctors looking after him had a tougher time coming to terms with the situation than we did. But their views shifted after we posed a direct question: Did they really foresee a scenario whereby his condition would improve significantly? They looked at one another and admitted that they didn't. So, we made the sad decision: It was over.

Although the experience of watching a vibrant man succumb to illness was excruciating, our decision wasn't particularly difficult to make. That's because we knew full well what my father wanted. He had done his estate planning, and had talked about his wishes with us—not just once, but a number of times during the years preceding his death. Earlier in his life, medical issues he'd experienced had alerted him to the reality that he could die at any time, and that he had to assure that his own wishes would be respected and that his heirs would not be unduly burdened by administrative crap. He had signed a Do-Not-Resuscitate order upon entering the hospital, but he had also consistently communicated to us that he didn't want to live in a compromised state. He enjoyed being physically active, and if he ever couldn't perform normal daily activities, he didn't want to live.

For me, knowing his wishes so fully and intimately made all the difference. I could do what was needed in good conscience. If we hadn't known his wishes, we might have stretched out his dying for weeks longer, causing him unnecessary pain. We would have been beholden to the doctors, who in many cases aren't trained to handle end-of-life circumstances very well. We also would have suffered more ourselves, tormenting ourselves with the medical pros and cons, and with trying to decipher "what Daddy would have wanted." We were exhausted and emotionally distraught as it was, but our clarity made the situation just a bit more tolerable. It was my father's last gift, and not an inconsiderable one.

Please get your affairs in order, setting aside this silly idea that you'll live forever. My wonderful friend Mary, who passed away years ago from leukemia, was often asked by friends and family, "Do you ever wonder why you?" Her response: "No. I wonder why *not* me." She's right: Bad things happen to us all the time, and we just have to accept it. We're not special. We're just like everyone else. We don't have to dwell on the dark sides of life, but in my experience, planning your estate actually frees you of a lot of the worries that would otherwise pull at you. Just ask one of my producers at CBS News. She finally drafted a will for herself after two *long* years of nagging on my part. Snapping a picture of the signature page, she texted it to me with the following message: "DONE. DONE. DONE. RELIEVED. THANX!"

The observation that we're not special leads me to the final "dumb thing" that smart people do. Many of us think we're so special—so inordinately intelligent—that we can predict when our investments will gain or lose value. Alas, we can't. As we'll see in the next chapter, we each have a choice as investors: We can come to grips with this reality now, or we can learn the hard way, at great financial cost.

You Try to "Time" the Market

During the 1990s and early 2000s, I worked in Rhode Island as a financial planner and investment adviser. Although I was young, I was already a financial veteran, having worked as an options trader on Wall Street during the late 1980s. With a local radio show and gigs writing for the newspaper, I had become a minor celebrity in the Ocean State. Although Little Rhody is known as the "biggest little state in the union," emphasis on "little," I still found the attention kind of thrilling, especially because it was inconceivable in my hometown of New York City, the center of the financial universe. In Providence, Rhode Island's capital, strangers would approach me in the IGA grocery store as I was squeezing avocados and ask for advice on how to manage their portfolios. When I bumped into the city's notorious mayor, Buddy Cianci, he would ask for advice on which stocks to buy and which to avoid. "Hey, money lady," he'd say, "whaddaya think?"

During the early 2000s in Providence, I basked in the glow of my apparent "brilliance." You see, I had recently come out way ahead as an investor, partially selling out of fast-growing tech stocks at the height of the bubble, just as it burst in 2000. It felt to me like payback, since during the late 1990s I had been called out for being a wimpy, overly risk-averse adviser who had missed the tech boom (my local media platform meant that every opinion that ever left my lips was publicly recorded). Now vindicated, I appeared to some Rhode Islanders as a financial "genius" who had mastered the market and the intricacies of investing.

With the market in the dumps, I now felt certain that I could time a reentry into growth stocks. But it was not to be. In 2002, the stock market started to recover, as markets usually do. If I had really been a "genius," I would have shifted the investments I was managing more fully back into growth stocks around then. Instead, I told myself that I would find *just the right moment* to buy back into the market. That way, I could ride the new bull market in stocks right through the next upward cycle. I waited and waited, mustering tons of data and third-party analysis that confirmed my thesis, convincing myself that the market hadn't yet hit bottom. Throughout 2003, my overall allocation was only about 40 percent stocks, plus 40 percent bonds and 20 percent cash. Too bad: That year, the broader stock market jumped 26 percent, while my portfolio rose by only about 12 percent. My belief that I could discern the exact "right" time to get back into the market fully led me to underweight stocks. As a result, I missed the early stages of a red-hot stock market.

I had egg on my face—big-time. And this being Rhode Island, the locals didn't hesitate to call me out on it. One guy wrote a letter to our local paper publicly eviscerating me.

My mistake has a name: thinking you can "time" the market. Some smart people believe so much in their (or someone else's) financial acumen that they think they can pick that precise moment when a market will fall or when they can maximize their profits on the sale of an individual stock or mutual fund. Sometimes their instincts prove correct, but more often than not, they sell either before or after a market has peaked. And even if they do time the market's drop, they also have to know when to reenter a rising market—an equally tricky proposition. It's hard enough making one perfect decision. But two?

Experts have long cautioned against trying to time the market. As the financial journalist Jane Bryant Quinn observed, "The market timer's *Hall of Fame* is an empty room."[1] In his book *The Devil's Financial Dictionary,* Jason Zweig, the *Wall Street Journal* columnist, defines market timing as: "The attempt to avoid losing money in bear markets. The most common result, however, is to avoid making money in bull markets."[2] Yes, Jason, I know—oh, how I know! The problem is that so many smart people still *don't* know this. In fact, when I pitched this book, one editor asked me, "Do you really need a whole chapter on market timing? Doesn't everyone know it doesn't work?" Um, no, they don't. If we all knew it, we wouldn't keep on doing it.

Repeatedly in this book, we've observed intelligent people trying to predict short-term market movements—and failing. These individuals bought real estate thinking that they'd sell at a certain point, only to see the market drop. They held on to company stock thinking it would keep rising, but lost their shirts when it tanked. My own father, with years of trading experience under his belt, bet that the market could remain stable for a certain period of time, and lost everything when it proved volatile.

Nobody is smarter than the market. *Nobody.* By trying to time the market, you're potentially making investment decisions that are based on emotions, and that are colored by your own individual biases and blind spots. As I've argued throughout this book, our money decisions of all kinds are not nearly as rational as we think. We let our monkey minds get the better of us, we make mistakes, and we lose out—again and again. The same holds true for investing. Chastened by my father's risk-taking and the losses I saw him suffer when I was a child, I'm a conservative investor. And that conservatism prevented me from pulling the trigger and buying back into stocks at the right time.

To invest prudently, stop trying to make the genius purchase or sale. Instead, take the disciplined, "passive" approach to saving and investing that I laid out in Chapter 6. Maintain a diversified portfolio, pegging the allocation between stocks, bonds, commodities, cash, and so on according to your time horizon (when you will need your money) and a realistic assessment of your financial goals and risk tolerance. At least annually, make sure to rebalance your portfolio so that your allocation again reflects the level of risk on which you originally decided. Will you maximize your profits on every single short-term market shift? Probably not. But over the long term, you'll achieve the stable growth you need to achieve your goals, while accepting a level of risk that is comfortable for you.

THE CLASSIC SMART PERSON'S MISTAKE

I have a theory: We smart people persist in timing the market *because* we're so smart. Think about it: If anyone is liable to believe in the power of human intelligence to control and manipulate reality, and in particular to get the better of markets, it's going to be smart people. We've been conditioned all our lives to value intelligence, and to believe in *our own* intelligence. Many of us occupy positions of power or authority, and we are accustomed to having others see us as "smart," in medicine, law, politics, business management, sales, education, or whatever our area of expertise happens to be. So why shouldn't we be able to predict short-term market movements more shrewdly than others?

We also have a hard time extricating ourselves from market timing behavior, in part because we're not even aware we're doing it. In February 2018, the stock market had its worst week in two years, with each major index down more than 5 percent. I received dozens of emails from colleagues at CBS who were freaked out about their retirement accounts, including one who had about half of his $1.5 million retirement account in CBS stock. Four years earlier, when the stock traded at $70 a share, he had promised he would unload his position to restore more balance to his portfolio. Of course, he hadn't. Now the stock was trading at $55, and he still didn't want to sell. "I don't want to lock in a loss," he said. That made no sense: This colleague had originally purchased the stock years earlier when it was trading for only $6. He wasn't locking in a loss—he was locking in a major gain, albeit less of one than he would have realized just weeks earlier. "You have to sell right now," I told him. "Don't delay." He promised me that he would.

A week later, CBS stock had fallen to about $50 a share. Wondering if he had sold, I sent him a quick text, writing, "Presume you got out of at least some of the position."

His response: a sad, frowny emoticon.

When the stock was trading between $40 and $50 a share, this colleague would have been thrilled to imagine that he would be able to sell it at $55. Now, he wouldn't sell. If I turned the question around and asked him if he wished to buy it at this price, he would have refused, saying it's much too expensive—after all, he had bought it when it was only $6. But if it's so expensive, why not sell it in the fifty-dollar range?

When I point out to people that they're timing the market, they often acknowledge that it's a bozo move, but they present all sorts of excuses as to why in *their* situation doing so makes sense. If they're thinking of investing in real estate, they might say "I just haven't found the right property yet," or if they need to sell company stock, they might say "I'll know when to sell, and it just isn't time yet." I especially love people who fool themselves into thinking they're taking principled stands by timing a purchase or sale. A scientist type I know graduated from an elite college at the top of his class (I can't reveal which college, but let's just say it rhymes with Bartmouth). This guy convinced himself that he understands blockchain, the technology behind Bitcoin. He put $1,000 into Bitcoin early, and rode the currency up until his investment was worth $50,000. I begged him to sell at least a portion of it to pay back his student loans. He refused, claiming that he knew *for a fact* that blockchain technology would change the world, and that Bitcoin was going much higher, "which would make my $50K worth $300,000!" Maybe he's right about that, but as of the summer of 2018, the price of Bitcoin had plunged and his investment is worth only $10,000.

If you're waiting to buy or sell until some point in the future, then you're timing the market. Own it! And better yet, stop doing it.

No matter how many cautionary tales like this I recount, smart people I meet brush them off. "But Jill," they say, "I really do know what I'm doing!" As evidence, they point to some great investing success they've had, as if that's a compelling argument. It isn't. As champion poker player Annie Duke told me on my podcast, people commonly regard their successes as evidence of brilliance on their part and their setbacks as bad luck. Poker players have a name for such machinations of logic: "resulting," or conflation of the quality of decisions with their results. To explode this logic for me, Duke asked me how often I've run a red light. "A few times," I said. She asked if I'd ever gotten into an accident or received a ticket as a result. "No, I haven't," I replied. She asked if I thought the decision to run a red light was a good one because the outcome worked out. "Not at all," I said.

"Exactly," she said. So if I keep running red lights presuming that I will suffer no negative consequences, I might be guilty of resulting.[3]

Smart people are guilty of "resulting" all the time when they invest. You might take money you've been saving for a down payment on a house and invest it in a growth fund. When you're ready to buy your house, the market happens to be up, and you get a nice price when you sell out of the growth fund. You're a genius—you made the right decision! No, you didn't. You made a crappy decision, one based on absolutely nothing. It just happened to work out for you. Further, your willingness to bask in the glow of your success will cause you to continue your market timing behavior, exposing you to future moments when luck will turn against you.

In her book *Thinking in Bets,* Duke further observes that smart people generally remain more vulnerable to their biases than the rest of the population. We would presume it's the opposite—that intelligence allows us to think critically about information and decisions. In fact, Duke writes, intelligence makes us more self-righteous, and less self-aware: "The smarter you are, the better you are at constructing a narrative that supports your beliefs, rationalizing and framing the data to fit your argument or point of view. After all, people in the spin room, in a political setting, are generally pretty smart for a reason."[4] Duke cites psychological research that finds that people do a much better job perceiving biases at work in others than they do seeing it in their own thinking. "The surprise is that blind spot bias is greater the smarter you are."

If you've been timing your financial decisions hoping for greater gain, please reconsider your behavior. The very ability that has helped you succeed in life—your intelligence—may now be leading you astray, convincing you that you're acting rationally when in truth you're not. What a wily foe intelligence is!

LAZY INVESTING IS *WISE* INVESTING

Many people, acknowledging that they can't reliably time the market, and perhaps sick of expending so much energy thinking about their damn money, have a ready solution that they regard as eminently wise: Have an expert do it. In some cases, these experts are individuals we know and trust. We'll hear about a friend or relative who has expertise in biotech, for instance, and who is making a fortune picking stocks in that field. "I've got to get a piece of that for myself," we'll say to ourselves, and hand over a chunk of cash to our resident expert. Big mistake. Nobody can time the markets—not you, not other experts in your life.

A friend of mine, Tracy, earned $125,000 a year at her job in sales. Her brother was a technology geek who had made a fortune investing in stocks like Netflix and Facebook. He had recently completed a project for General Electric and was convinced that the company was going to turn around. In the beginning of 2017, when GE was trading just under $30, Tracy told me that she wanted to give her brother her $200,000 nest egg to invest. "Be careful," I told her. "You have a lot to lose."

"But Jill," she said, "he's smart, and he knows what he's doing. He's made $3 million in stocks over the past five years."

Ignoring my counsel, she bought in, thinking GE would skyrocket. Instead, it tanked 45 percent by the end of 2017, distinguishing itself as the Dow Jones's worst performer that year. Early in 2018, I ran into a friend of a friend of a friend, and asked how Tracy and her investment were doing. "Oh, my God," this person said. "She's freaking out! I think she's going to sell it." I don't know if she did, but selling would have locked in a near-$100,000 loss. So much for her expert brother. He was just timing the market, like anyone else.

It's a good rule not to take investment advice from friends, relatives, or colleagues, however well-intentioned they might be. Unless these individuals possess special training or expertise, they probably don't know what they're talking about. While you're at it, try not to blindly trust people you know in *any* situation where significant amounts of money are at stake. I've made costly mistakes by relying excessively on others, whether for personal finance advice or in business matters. Years ago, one such mistake led to regulatory issues for me and my firm that took years to resolve. The lesson I learned was to trust, but verify. You are entitled to ask uncomfortable questions, even of people to whom you feel close. Doing so might test your relationship, but it will save you a lot of money and heartache in the long run.

If your personal contacts aren't the epic investment gurus they might seem to be, neither are professional mutual fund managers. At the end of 2017, Americans owned $11.4 trillion of actively managed funds, and put only $6.7 trillion into passive funds, according to Morningstar.[5] (What are active and passive funds? you ask. In active management, an investment company or mutual fund hires a bunch of analysts who try to find the best assets that can beat an index, like the S&P 500. To do so, they might buy and sell those assets on a daily basis. With a passive approach, the company mimics a particular index by purchasing the stocks that comprise the index. Once in place, purchases and sales occur only if the underlying index changes.)

The active investors continue to believe that a few money managers know how to pick better assets than everyone else and can "beat the market." What do you think these money managers are doing in managing your hard-earned dollars? Sure, they might pick a good company that is undervalued, but quite often they are simply timing the market. Are they any good at it? Almost always, no. Or to be more precise, they're not appreciably better than passive investing via index funds.

According to 2017 data from investment research firm Dalbar, the S&P 500 yielded a twenty-year return of 7.68 percent, significantly better than the 4.79 percent achieved, on average, by equity fund investors. This difference partially reflected the higher fees that active managers typically command.[6] You'll also recall from

Chapter 1 how Warren Buffett famously challenged hedge fund managers to outperform the S&P 500 over ten years, and how the sole manager who took the bet failed to do so. As Buffett has advised, investors large and small should choose index funds over higher-cost managed funds. "When trillions of dollars are managed by Wall Streeters charging high fees," he said in 2017, "it will usually be the managers who reap outsized profits, not the clients."[7] Add in fees and taxes, and actively managed funds become even less attractive.

Of course, such advice is hardly breaking news. In September 2016, I interviewed Charley Ellis, who has been a key voice for five decades in the debate about active versus passive investment management. In his book *The Index Revolution: Why Investors Should Join It Now,* Ellis puts it bluntly: "The stunning reality is that most actively managed mutual funds fail to keep up with index funds."

Ellis's opinions on the issue date back to the 1960s, when he was analyzing individual companies and recommending stocks to clients. Ellis started to sense that markets were factoring the corporate information he was discovering into stock prices ever more quickly, and that his entire profession was in for a rude awakening. In a 1975 article titled "The Loser's Game," published in the *Financial Analysts Journal,* he remarked: "The investment management business (it should be a profession but is not) is built upon a simple and basic belief: Professional money managers can beat the market. That premise appears to be false."[8] That same year, Vanguard came out with the world's first index mutual fund, making passive investing easier and more accessible to everyday consumers.

Today, of course, financial information whizzes around the globe in seconds. Any insight a professional manager might have about a company's balance sheet, management shake-up, or philandering executive is almost immediately reflected in market prices. And that information is not hidden inside a Bloomberg terminal, but available online in public filings with the Securities and Exchange Commission, in chat rooms and message boards, and even on Twitter.

As uninspiring as "passive" investing sounds, it really is the wisest approach. Decide upon your goals and your risk tolerance, craft a plan to allocate your investments accordingly across the different classes or types of investment using the appropriate index funds, and then stick with the plan. On a regular basis (quarterly, semiannually, or annually), rebalance your accounts, or activate "auto-rebalancing" if your retirement plan or financial institution offers it. If you need to rebalance manually, then rotate some of your higher-performing positions into those that lagged in order to maintain your preset allocation.

Consistently rebalancing in this way forces you to sell high and buy low. Yes, you might miss some of the upside when you're selling your stock, but following this formula in a disciplined way allows you to avoid potential disasters you would stumble into by waiting too long to sell. In essence, you're taking out an insurance policy against yourself, agreeing to forgo some of the upside in exchange for protection from your own worst tendencies. Over the long term, you'll do as well as most everyone else, maybe even a bit better, while minimizing some of the risk that can creep into an unbalanced portfolio.

Rebalancing is brilliant when you think about it: Instead of turning to some genius investor to pick when to buy or sell, you decide how often you will rebalance and either do it or have your fund do it automatically. Of course, as investors, we want to believe that *someone* out there has mastered the market—that there's a secret sauce, some magic intuition that can be deployed. Further, we want to believe that our manager taps into that magic. Brilliant managers do exist, but there are so few of them that you're essentially investing your money with a professional poker player by choosing an actively managed fund.

As Zweig observed during an appearance on my podcast, "One of the single hardest things any investor can do is not to pick securities that will outperform the market, but to pick *the managers* who can pick securities that will outperform the market."[9] Factor in human biases and the high fees, and actively managed funds just aren't worth it.

When I speak with large investors, people investing hundreds of millions or billions of dollars of other people's money, they tell me that they invest their own savings in passive index funds. The Nobel Prize–winning economist Richard Thaler has likewise said that his ". . . lazy strategy of doing very little, buying mostly stocks and then not paying attention has served [him] well."[10] If it works for him, and if it works for Warren Buffett, and if it works for Charley Ellis, and if it works for large, professional investors, it will work for you, too.

REBALANCING *YOURSELF*

My market timing incident in Rhode Island during the early 2000s was painful, but luckily, because I had done well during the downturn, I wasn't harmed by getting back in the market a little late. And as a learning experience, it was immensely valuable. I learned that I shouldn't try to outfox the market—I just didn't have that power. If I was to succeed, I had to back away, stay disciplined, and follow a proven strategy. As humbling as that shift was, I also found it empowering. Although I could falter by falling prey to my emotions, I also had the ability, should I choose to use it, to acknowledge my worst impulses and moderate them. All I needed to do was overcome my ego, know my limitations, correct for them, stop doing stupid-ass things, and I'd be okay. I needed to stop trying to control the world around me, and instead start controlling *myself*.

That, in fact, has been my message throughout this book. We all have the power to take hold of our financial destinies. We don't need geniuses by our side every minute. We don't need the latest, greatest app. We don't need some killer insight or analytic ability, and we certainly don't need big data. All we need is to stop ourselves from behaving like dopes. We need the self-awareness to understand our blind spots and how they wreak havoc, and then the discipline and commitment to say to ourselves "No, I won't buy that vacation home I can't afford—I'll rent instead," or "No, I won't let myself short my retirement in order to pay for college," or "No, I won't let myself buy a financial product I don't understand."

At times, we also need the honesty and humility to say "You know, I really don't know my ass from my elbow on this one, so I'm going to call in a professional who does." Where is it written that you have to be all-knowing to be smart? You don't! A good friend of mine, a master acupuncturist, once surprised me by telling me how she would turn to Western medicine if she had an irregular heartbeat. "Acupuncture is good for some things," she explained, "Western medicine for others." We should all be so open-minded, and go with what we know when it works for us and seek out professional help when it doesn't.

The key to financial happiness is to *get right with ourselves* around money. One place to begin is to part with the unrealistic expectations that so many of us harbor. We'll never achieve a sense of true comfort unless we can stop striving to be the richest guy or gal on our block, and focus instead on building lives that are, in a deeper sense, right for us. I sometimes joke with my trainer that he and I have the same job. He has clients coming to him and saying "Make me look twenty years younger. Make me look like a supermodel." And I've had some clients or callers who want me to make them independently wealthy overnight.

For the vast majority of people, such ambitions are unrealistic. You were born with your body and its limitations. No exercise or diet regimen will turn you into a slender supermodel. Likewise, your career choices, family situation, age, and so on place constraints on your finances. If you're a forty-year-old teacher making $60,000 a year, with two kids, a spouse who stays at home, and a $200,000 mortgage, I can't promise you that one day through some combination of savings and investing you'll be able buy your own Caribbean island.

But the ability to accept these limitations and work with them is a sign of emotional health and maturity, and it prevents us from giving in to our impulses and making stupid moves. Maybe it's okay to get a 6 percent return on our money instead of taking on more risk and aiming for 10 percent. Maybe it's okay to rent an apartment because buying doesn't make sense right now. Maybe it's okay *not* to solve every last money problem your adult children face and instead allow them to figure out how to manage their own financial lives.

Getting right with ourselves around money doesn't mean we have to be perfect. On the contrary, it means accepting our mistakes and rolling with them. Yes, we'll screw up from time to time—and that's okay. Returning to the diet analogy, you might occasionally indulge in some molten chocolate cake on Saturday night when you're out with your friends. Don't feel bad about that. When Monday rolls around, you can always start fresh and get back on track. With money, the very concept of "rebalancing" a portfolio assumes that the portfolio will become out of balance. That's fine, because you're performing this rebalancing on a regular basis. If you've made one of the thirteen mistakes covered in this book, take the opportunity right now to rebalance yourself, paying attention to the underlying emotions that led you astray. If you make mistakes in the future, you can always step back and get yourself right all over again.

I hope you'll make fewer mistakes going forward with this book in hand. But let's face it, sometimes you do need to fall flat on your face in order to learn important life lessons. If that's the case, don't let me stop you. Just remember that you're not terrible for messing up. You're not stupid. You're just human. You're entitled to a little self-pity, but after that, take back control. Make real changes in your life. Get organized. Plan. Save. Have those uncomfortable but necessary conversations with your kids and your parents. And for God's sake, learn to laugh a little. As I've found, it really does work wonders.

Thirteen *Smart* Things Smart People Should Do

Every Month . . .

- **Review your bank account and credit card statements:** Pay attention to your spending patterns. Is anything unusual or unexplained? Look out for unusual activity in your accounts that might suggest that you have been a victim of identity fraud.

- **Think about how you *feel* about your financial life:** Are you stressed out? Has a certain money issue been bothering you, even keeping you up at night over the past month? Did you veer off plan? Did you spend money unexpectedly? If so, take action to get back on track.

- **Think about pending purchases of financial products:** Did someone pitch you a product over the past month, like an insurance policy or a new mutual fund? If you're about to sign on the dotted line, take a few minutes to review the product and confirm that you fully understand it. If you don't understand it, seek the guidance of a fiduciary adviser.

- **Reflect on your behaviors around investments:** Did certain market moves you made freak you out? Did you deviate from your financial plan and try to time the market? If so, take stock, and recommit yourself to your financial plan and the passive investing philosophy.

- **Review your aging parents' financial situation:** Did anything change in your parents' lives that might require action on your part? If they suffered a health setback, what are the financial implications? What conversations do you need to have with them or other family members?

Every Quarter . . .

- **Review your investment and retirement accounts:** Don't perform a forensic accounting exercise here. Rather, just check in quickly to stay abreast of recent developments. If you're rebalancing manually, be sure to do this, but only on retirement accounts that are not taxable, so as not to create unnecessary tax consequences.

- **Change all passwords on your financial accounts:** Do I really need to nudge you on this? Um, yeah, I do.

Every Year . . .

- **Review your investments:** Are you comfortable with the level of risk you've taken on, and the returns you're making for that level of risk? Be realistic. If the market is up by ten percentage points, but your account is up by just five, don't get so upset if you've chosen to take on only moderate risk. Also, inquire whether fees on your account have changed. Be sure to rebalance your taxable accounts and consider whether you would like to make any tax-related moves, like taking losses against gains or making charitable gifts with highly appreciated securities.

- **Perform a tax audit:** Every year after tax time, review whether you encountered any surprises while preparing your taxes. Do you need to change your withholding for the upcoming tax year?

Doing so can free up money during the year to fund other goals or prevent a nasty surprise next year. Be sure to also check in before the end of the calendar year to determine whether you need to make any new charitable contributions or if you should convert a traditional IRA into a Roth IRA.

- **Secure your identity:** Go to annualcreditreport.com for a free review of your credit record. If you find a mistake, stay on top of it with the credit reporting agencies until the situation is rectified.

- **Check in on college planning for your kids:** Are you saving adequately for your kids' education? If they're in high school, have you spoken with them about their college choices and what options the family can realistically afford?

Every Three Years . . .

- **Review your homeowner and life insurance policies:** Did the value of your property change? Did you have more kids? Make sure you're adequately covered.

- **Review your estate plan:** Are your documents up-to-date? Have any changes occurred in your life or your family that might affect your plans? Do you need to change the guardian for your kids listed on your will or the beneficiaries of your retirement accounts?

Acknowledgments

I would like to thank Seth Schulman for his critical contributions to this book. I couldn't have done it without his steady guidance and gentle nudging. What started as a professional relationship quickly morphed into a personal one—I am lucky to count Seth as a friend.

My agent, Brian DeFiore, waited twelve years for me to get my act together and write this darned thing—I am forever thankful for his patience and judgment, not to mention his sense of humor. Brian helped shape this book from cover to cover.

Sara Weiss and the crew at Ballantine Books have been wonderful to me from the get-go and have been enthusiastic supporters of this project.

My dear friend Michael Goodman, CPA/PFS, CFP®, read early drafts of the manuscript and helped to keep me on my technical toes. Dr. Mithu Storoni, Dr. Jim Grubman, Dan Egan, and Sandy Jolley were kind enough to offer their time and expertise for this book.

Mark Talercio is the executive producer of my radio show and podcast, but he is so much more. He hates the limelight, which is why I am so happy to shine it on him. He makes my work life fun and fulfilling, and seamlessly organizes all aspects of it.

My friends and colleagues at CBS News have encouraged me to keep one foot in the world of personal finance and the other in hard news, something that is hard to do in this era of specialization.

Thanks to the thousands of friends, clients, callers, and viewers who graciously invited me into their intimate world of financial questions and mishaps.

Finally, I am blessed to have a family that has always been supportive and encouraging.

My partner in everything, Jackie, is my muse, my toughest editor, and my love. Without her, I would not be the person I am, nor would I have nearly as much fun along the way.

My number one cheerleader has always been my sister Kim, a constant source of strength and wisdom . . . and always my best audience. My brother-in-law Evan and I met on the floor of the Commodities Exchange in 1987. By introducing him to my sister, I secured access to a financial and philosophical Yoda for life.

My sister-in-law Pam and brother-in-law John have always been kind enough to listen to my ideas and weigh in with sound advice, sharp editing skills, and constructive feedback. I have known my friend Sherry for thirty-five years and we have been through every life-cycle event together, including the gestation of this book, from idea to finished product.

My mother, Susan, has put up with financial talk at the dinner table for almost forty years. In return, I inherited her ability to talk to anyone without judgment. She is my part-time stylist and full-time supportive and loving mom.

This book is filled with memories of my father, with whom I shared a bond that is indelible. Albie, I finally did it!

Notes

Dumb Thing #1

1. Sandy Jolley, phone conversation with author, December 12, 2017.
2. Here's a link to a description of "The Bet": https://www.cnbc.com /2018/02/16/warren-buffett-won-2-point-2-million-on-a-bet-and -gave-it-to-girls-inc.html.
3. David Robson, "Psychology: Why boredom is bad . . . and good for you," BBC, December 22, 2014, http://www.bbc.com/future/story /20141218-why-boredom-is-good-for-you.
4. See Tom Nichols, *The Death of Expertise: The Campaign Against Established Knowledge and Why It Matters* (New York: Oxford University Press, 2017).
5. Jason Zweig, "The special trick to find the right financial adviser," Jasonzweig.com, September 8, 2017, http://jasonzweig.com/the -special-trick-to-find-the-right-financial-adviser/.

Dumb Thing #2

1. As of this writing, the SEC has begun a process of upgrading the notion of suitability and creating a new standard called "best interest." It's not yet clear what "best interest" will mean, but likely it will be a stricter standard (and more protective of consumers) than "suitability," though not nearly as strict or protective as "fiduciary"

(Securities and Exchange Commission proposed rule, Release No. 34–83062; File No. S7–07–18 [2018], https://www.sec.gov/rules /proposed/2018/34–83062.pdf).

2. This guidance includes text that originally appeared in my blog: "F-Word Update Spring 2018," *Jill on Money,* April 2, 2018, https:// www.jillonmoney.com/blog/2018/4/2/f-word-update-spring-2018.

Dumb Thing #3

1. Andrew T. Jebb, Louis Tay, Ed Diener, and Shigehiro Oishi, "Happiness, income satiation and turning points around the world," *Nature Human Behaviour* 2 (January 2018), https://www.nature.com /articles/s41562–017–0277–0. These numbers varied regionally, tracking higher in wealthier areas.

2. Dr. Jim Grubman, interview with author, January 22, 2018.

3. Mithu Storoni, MD, PhD, in discussion with the author in New York City, August 29, 2017, and via telephone, February 2, 2018. The study she told me about is Archy O. de Berker, et al., "Computations of Uncertainty Mediate Acute Stress Responses in Humans," *Nature Communications* (March 29, 2016), doi: 10.1038/ncomms 10996 | www.nature.com/naturecommunication.

Dumb Thing #4

1. Adam Looney and Constantine Yannelis, "Borrowers with Large Balances: Rising Student Debt and Falling Repayment Rates," *Brookings Institution,* February 2018, https://www.brookings.edu /wpcontent/uploads/2018/02/es_20180216_looneylargebalances.pdf.

2. Jessica Dickler, "Student loans take a mental toll on young people," CNBC, October 17, 2017, https://www.cnbc.com/2017/10/17/student -loans-take-a-mental-toll-on-young-people.html.

3. Jessica Dickler, "Student loans take a mental toll on young people," CNBC, October 17, 2017, https://www.cnbc.com/2017/10/17/student -loans-take-a-mental-toll-on-young-people.html.

4. Chris Mueller, "High school students reflect on the stress in their lives at Teen Symposium in Appleton," *Post Crescent,* February 12, 2018, https://www.postcrescent.com/story/news/2018/02/12/high

-school-students-reflect-stress-their-lives-teen-symposium-appleton
/329645002/.

5. Andrew Dugan and Stephanie Kafka, "Student Debt Linked to Worse Health and Less Wealth," *Gallup*, August 7, 2014, http://news.gallup.com/poll/174317/student-debt-linked-worse-health-less-wealth.aspx.

6. "Is College Worth It?" *Priceonomics*, September 23, 2013, https://priceonomics.com/is-college-worth-it/.

7. "Whole Foods In Brentwood Sold Asparagus-Infused Water For $6 A Pop," CBS Los Angeles, August 5, 2015, http://losangeles.cbslocal.com/2015/08/05/whole-foods-sold-asparagus-infused-water-for-6-a-pop/.

8. Kevin Gray, "The Key Attributes Employers Seek on Students' Resumes," *National Association of Colleges and Employers*, November 30, 2017, http://www.naceweb.org/about-us/press/2017/the-key-attributes-employers-seek-on-students-resumes/.

9. "Finances in retirement: new challenges, new solutions," *Age Wave*, accessed June 14, 2018, http://agewave.com/what-we-do/landmark-research-and-consulting/research-studies/finances-in-retirement-new-challenges-new-solutions/.

10. "Older consumers and student loan debt by state," *Consumer Financial Protection Bureau*, August 2017, https://files.consumerfinance.gov/f/documents/201708_cfpb_older-consumers-and-student-loan-debt-by-state.pdf.

11. "Snapshot of Older Consumers and Student Loan Debt," *Consumer Financial Protection Bureau*, January 2017, https://www.consumerfinance.gov/data-research-reports/snapshot-older-consumers-and-student-loan-debt/.

12. Tony Kushner, *Angels in America: A Gay Fantasia on National Themes*, Part 2, "Perestroika" (London: N. Hern Books, 2006).

13. "Financial Aid and Student Loans with Kelly Peeler," *Jill on Money*, September 29, 2017, https://www.jillonmoney.com/blog/343-financial-aid-and-student-loans-with-kelly-peeler.

14. For more information, see my blog post on the topic: "How to pay for College," *Jill on Money*, April 4, 2017, https://www.jillonmoney.com/blog/how-to-pay-for-college.

15. For rankings, see "2,400 colleges + 27 data points = 711 Best Col-

leges for Your Money," *Time,* accessed June 14, 2018, http://time
.com/money/best-colleges/rankings/best-colleges/.

Dumb Thing #5

1. Monique Morrissey, "The State of American Retirement: How 401(k)s
   have failed most American workers," *Economic Policy Institute,*
   March 3, 2016, https://www.epi.org/publication/retirement-in-america
   /#charts.

Dumb Thing #6

1. Dan Egan, interview with author, January 17, 2018.
2. Larry Barrett, "Why So Many Adults, Children Don't Get Flu
   Shots," *Healthline,* February 11, 2016, https://www.healthline.com
   /health-news/why-so-many-adults-children-dont-get-flu-shots-0211
   16#4.
3. "Why People Don't Get Vaccinated," *Massachusetts Medical Society,* accessed June 14, 2018, http://www.massmed.org/patient-care
   /health-topics/colds-and-flu/why-people-dont-get-vaccinated-(pdf)/.
4. H. Kent Baker and Victor Ricciardi, "How Biases Affect Investor
   Behaviour," *European Financial Review,* February 28, 2014, http://
   www.europeanfinancialreview.com/?p=512. See also Vanessa Houlder, "Richard Thaler's Advice: Be a Lazy Investor—Buy and Forget," *Financial Times,* December 21, 2017.
5. Familiarity bias, in which investors "have a preference for familiar
   investments despite the seemingly obvious gains from diversifica-
   tion," may have also played a role. Quite often, biases can overlap
   and interact with one another to produce inferior decision-making.
   See H. Kent Baker and Victor Ricciardi, "How Biases Affect Investor Behaviour," *European Financial Review,* February 28, 2014,
   http://www.europeanfinancialreview.com/?p=512.
6. Akane Otani and Chris Dieterich, "As Dow Tops 25000, Individual
   Investors Sit It Out," *Wall Street Journal,* January 4, 2018, https://
   www.wsj.com/articles/as-dow-tops-25000-individual-investors-sit-it
   -out-1515099703.
7. "A Buy-and-Hold Strategy Can Serve Investors Well," *American*

Funds, DALBAR Investing Study, accessed June 14, 2018, https:// www.americanfunds.com/advisor/pdf/shareholder/ingefl-050_dalbar .pdf.

Dumb Thing #7

1. Colin Daileda, "This survey shows everyone reuses passwords," *Mashable*, February 28, 2017, https://mashable.com/2017/02/28 /passwords-reuse-study-keeper-security/#slKqMz1gB8qY.
2. Brady Porche, "Poll: 16 million Americans fear stolen cellphone more than identity theft," *Credit Cards*, February 25, 2018, https:// www.creditcards.com/credit-card-news/equifax-data-breach-cellphone -survey.php.
3. "Netsparker Cybersecurity Survey: 80 Percent of Americans at Risk," *Business Wire*, December 14, 2017, https://www.business wire.com/news/home/20171214005531/en/Netsparker-Cybersecurity -Survey-80-Percent-Americans-Risk.
4. Kenneth Olmstead and Aaron Smith, "Americans and Cybersecurity," *Pew Research Center*, January 26, 2017, http://www.pewinternet .org/2017/01/26/americans-and-cybersecurity/.
5. Adam Levin, *Swiped: How to Protect Yourself in a World Full of Scammers, Phishers, and Identity Thieves* (New York: Public Affairs, 2015), 193–194.
6. http://betteroffpodcast.com/ep-024-cybersecurity-and-hacking-with -kevin-mitnick/.
7. Dan Egan, interview with author, January 18, 2018.
8. Katherine Bindley, "How to Protect Yourself from an Online Dating Scam," *Wall Street Journal*, March 15, 2018, https://www.wsj.com /articles/how-to-protect-yourself-from-an-online-dating-scam-1521 129300.
9. The advice I give in this section draws on my blog posting on the topic: "Equifax Data Breach: What to Do," *Jill on Money*, September 8, 2017, https://www.jillonmoney.com/blog/equifax-data -breach.
10. Adam Levin, *Swiped: How to Protect Yourself in a World Full of Scammers, Phishers, and Identity Thieves* (New York: Public Affairs, 2015), 9.

11. "Fraud & Active Duty Alert Request Online," *Innovis,* accessed June 14, 2018, https://www.innovis.com/fraudActiveDutyAlerts /index.

Dumb Thing #8

1. Kathleen Elkins, "Here's how much the average family has saved for retirement at every age," CNBC, April 7, 2017, https://www .cnbc.com/2017/04/07/how-much-the-average-family-has-saved-for -retirement-at-every-age.html.
2. "How to Plan for Rising Health Care Costs," *Fidelity,* April 18, 2018, https://www.fidelity.com/viewpoints/personal-finance/plan -for-rising-health-care-costs.
3. "A summary of the 2018 annual reports," *Social Security,* accessed June 14, 2018, https://www.ssa.gov/oact/trsum/.
4. Gila Bronshtein et al., "The Power of Working Longer," *National Bureau of Economic Research,* Working Paper No. 24226 (January 2018), cited in Jeff Sommer, "Thinking About Retirement? Consider Working a Little Longer," *New York Times,* June 1, 2018, https:// www.nytimes.com/2018/06/01/business/thinking-about-retirement -consider-working-a-little-longer.html.

Dumb Thing #9

1. See my blog posting, "Ground Rules for Boomerang Kids," *Jill on Money,* June 1, 2016, https://tribunecontentagency.com/article/ground -rules-for-boomerang-kids/.
2. Dr. David Whitebread and Dr. Sue Bingham, "Habit Formation and Learning in Young Children," *Money Advice Service,* May 2013, https://mascdn.azureedge.net/cms/the-money-advice-service-habit -formation-and-learning-in-young-children-may2013.pdf.
3. For more, see the Consumer Financial Protection Bureau's "Resources for parents and caregivers," accessed June 14, 2018, https:// www.consumerfinance.gov/consumer-tools/money-as-you-grow/.
4. For more on these recommendations, please see Jill Schlesinger, "Personal Finance 101 for college kids," *Chicago Tribune,* August 16, 2017, http://www.chicagotribune.com/business/sns-201708162103—tms— retiresmctnrs-a20170816–20170816-story.html.

Dumb Thing #10

1. Genworth 2017 Cost of Care Survey: "Costs Continue to Rise Across All Care Settings," *Genworth,* September 26, 2017, http://newsroom .genworth.com/2017–09–26-Genworth-2017-Annual-Cost-of-Care -Survey-Costs-Continue-to-Rise-Across-All-Care-Settings.

2. See Jill Schlesinger, "Juggling Needs of Aging Parents, Children Who Need Financial Help," *Chicago Tribune,* June 14, 2018, http:// www.chicagotribune.com/business/success/jillonmoney/tca-juggling -needs-of-aging-parents-children-who-need-financial-help-20160912 -story.html.

3. Gila Bronshtein et al., "The Power of Working Longer," *National Bureau of Economic Research,* Working Paper No. 24226 (January 2018), http://www.nber.org/papers/w24226.

Dumb Thing #11

1. "Trust in Insurance: US Nationally Representative Sample: July 7–9 2017," *YouGov NY,* accessed June 14, 2018, http://d25d2506sfb94s .cloudfront.net/cumulus_uploads/document/foikfahv24/Trust%20 in%20Insurance%20Companies.pdf. See also: Paul Hiebert, "While Nearly Half of All US Adults Trust Insurance Companies, Most Find Their Language Confusing," *YouGov,* July 18, 2017, https:// today.yougov.com/news/2017/07/18/trust-in-insurance/.

2. Kimberly Lankford, "How Much Does Flood Insurance Cost?" *Kiplinger,* June 1, 2015 https://www.kiplinger.com/article/insurance /T028-C001-S003-how-much-flood-insurance-costs.html.

3. "Is Buy Term and Invest the Difference on Life Support?" *Nasdaq,* December 9, 2015, https://www.nasdaq.com/article/is-buy-term -and-invest-the-difference-on-life-support-cm552257.

4. See my blog post on the topic: "More Financial Vegetables: Life In-surance," *Jill on Money,* September 6, 2017, https://www.jillon money.com/blog/financial-vegetables-life-insurance.

5. Wenliang Hou, Wei Sun, and Anthony Webb, "Why Do People Lapse Their Long-Term Care Insurance?" *Center for Retirement Research at Boston College,* October 2015, http://crr.bc.edu/briefs /why-do-people-lapse-their-long-term-care-insurance/.

Dumb Thing #12

1. Nick DiUlio, "More Than Half of American Adults Don't Have a Will, 2017 Survey Shows," *Caring,* June 12, 2018, https://www.caring.com/articles/wills-survey-2017.

2. Brady Porche, "Financial Infidelity Poll: 31% Say Hiding Accounts Worse Than Cheating," *Credit Cards,* January 21, 2018, https://www.creditcards.com/credit-card-news/financial-infidelity-cheating-poll.php.

3. Information in this section also appears in my blog, Jillonmoney.com/blog. See also https://tribunecontentagency.com/article/pre-planning-eases-the-way-when-settling-an-estate-y/http://www.chicagotribune.com/business/sns-201610201500—tms—retires mctnrs-a20161020–20161020-story.html.

4. "Estate Tax Overview," mass.gov, accessed June 14, 2018, https://www.mass.gov/service-details/estate-tax-overview.

5. For my reflections on this interview, please see Jill Schlesinger, "Have the estate planning talk," *Jill on Money,* October 20, 2016, http://tribunecontentagency.com/article/have-the-estate-planning-talk/.

Dumb Thing #13

1. Peter Mallouk, *The 5 Mistakes Every Investor Makes and How to Avoid Them* (Wiley: 2014), 21.

2. Jason Zweig, *The Devil's Financial Dictionary* (New York: Public Affairs, 2015), 133.

3. Please see "Thinking in Bets with Annie Duke," *Better Off with Jill Schlesinger,* March 15, 2018, www.betteroffpodcast.com. I am roughly paraphrasing our conversation here.

4. Annie Duke, *Thinking in Bets: Making Smarter Decisions When You Don't Have All the Facts* (New York: Portfolio/Penguin, 2018), 62.

5. Bernice Napach, "Passive Investments Drive Record Fund Flows in 2017: Morningstar," *Think Advisor,* January 29, 2018, https://www.thinkadvisor.com/2018/01/29/passive-investments-drive-record-fund-flows-in-201/?slreturn=20180230152709.

6. Lance Roberts, "Opinion: Americans Are Still Terrible at Investing, Annual Study Once Again Shows," *Market Watch,* October 21,

2017, https://www.marketwatch.com/story/americans-are-still-terrible
-at-investing-annual-study-once-again-shows-2017–10–19.

7. The 2017 letter to investors is quoted in Trevor Hunnicutt and Jon-
athan Stempel, "Warren Buffett Rails Against Fee-Hungry Wall
Street Managers," *Reuters,* February 25, 2017, https://www.reuters
.com/article/us-berkshire-hatha-buffett-indexfunds/warren-buffett
-rails-against-fee-hungry-wall-street-managers-idUSKBN1640F1.

8. Charles D. Ellis, "The Loser's Game," *Financial Analysts Journal,*
January–February 1995, https://www.cfapubs.org/doi/pdf/10.2469
/faj.v51.n1.1865.

9. Please see, "Become an Intelligent Investor with Jason Zweig (Part
One)" *Better Off with Jill Schlesinger,* episode 009, March 2, 2017,
44 minutes, https://www.iheart.com/podcast/274-Better-Off-with
-Jill-28090565/episode/ep-009-become-an-intelligent-investor-2809
3122/.

10. Vanessa Houlder, "Richard Thaler's Advice: Be a Lazy Investor—
Buy and Forget," *Financial Times,* December 22, 2017.

Index

accredited investors, 10–11
aging foibles:
  house title transfers and,
    172–74
  liquid assets and, 173–74
  money gifts and, 174–75
aging in place, 164, 176–77
aging parents, care of, 163–81
  aging foibles and, 172–75
  care plan conversations and,
    175–80, 234
  health care costs and, 130, 136,
    165, 168, 177
  planning for aging and, 166–71
  sandwich generation and,
    165–66
aging plans:
  care schedule and, 177–78
  emotional costs and, 168–69
  exploring options and, 170–71,
    176
  family conversations about,
    167, 175–80

financing and, 168, 172, 177
  parents' desires and, 176–77
  problem solving and, 178–79
American Association of Retired
  People (AARP), 27
American dream, 83, 87, 94
American Stock Exchange
  (AMEX), xvii, 97
anchoring bias, 100
annuities, 3–4, 13–16, 212
antiques, 104–5

Baby Boomers, 87–88, 135
backdoor Roth IRAs, 125
balloon mortgages, 41
beneficiaries, 204–6
"Best Colleges for Your Money,
  The" article, 73
Big Five, 17–19
Big Short, The (Lewis), 81
Big Three, 31–32, 91–93,
  106
blind spot bias, 223, 229

blockchain technology, 222
Buffet, Warren, 12, 226–28

cash flow, 29–30, 35, 108
Certified Financial Planner Board
　of Standards, 27–28
Chartered Financial Analysts, 28
Cianci, Buddy, 217
cognitive biases, xviii, 99–105,
　110–11, 223, 229, 242n
college debt, 58–79
　borrowing benchmark and,
　　74–75
　cost-benefit analyses and,
　　61–63
　funding retirement first and,
　　68–72
　honest conversations and,
　　65–68
　loan repayment process and,
　　75–76
　pros and cons of, 59–60, 77–79
　smart decision-making and,
　　72–76
　value of private college and,
　　63–65
college education:
　federal and state grants for, 63,
　　73–74
　529 plans and, 21–22, 25, 68,
　　73
　NextGenVest service and, 73
　see also education savings
　　accounts
commodities market, 6, 108
　see also precious metals
computer passwords, 113–17,
　121, 212, 234

confirmation bias, xviii
consumer debt, 31–32, 92, 106
Consumer Financial Protection
　Bureau, 68
Coverdell Education Savings
　Accounts, 73
CPA Personal Financial
　Specialists, 28
credit reporting, 113, 121–22,
　235
crisis magnification effect, 96
currencies, 6, 222

data breaches, 113–14, 119,
　122
Devil's Financial Dictionary, The
　(Zweig), 219
digital technology, 115–19
disability insurance, xii–xiii, 185,
　194–95
divorce settlements, 94–95
DIYers, 29–31, 106–11, 201
Do-Not-Resuscitate orders, 210,
　215
dot-com boom/bust, 51, 82, 90,
　96, 217–18
Duke, Annie, 222–23

Eastwood, John, 13
Economic Policy Institute, 88
economy, xix, 6, 26, 43, 69, 81,
　96
education savings accounts,
　21–22, 25, 68, 73, 233
Egan, Dan, 99, 105–6, 117
Ellis, Charley, 226–28
emergency savings accounts, 31,
　92, 106

emotions, negative, xviii, 13–15, 36, 43–45, 67, 104–5, 148–55
  see also money issues
employee benefits, 194–95
end-of-life planning, 200–207
  beneficiaries and, 204–6
  cemetery plots and, 212
  child guardians and, 207
  death certificates and, 213
  funeral expenses and, 200, 213
  living trusts and, 201
  obituaries and, 211
  organ donations and, 203
Equifax data breach, 113–14, 119
estate planning, 207–14, 235
  see also legal documents
estate taxes, 207–8
exchange traded funds (ETFs), 6–7

familiarity bias, 242*n*5
fear, xviii, 13–15, 36, 44–45, 152–55
Federal Trade Commission (FTC), 118, 122
fiduciary responsibility, 25–29
55+ communities, 170, 180
financial advice, 21–38
  correcting mistakes and, xviii–xix
  criteria for needing, 31–35
  DIYers and, 29–31
  fiduciary responsibility and, 25–29
  financial products and, 19–20
  reality checks and, 35–38

Financial Analysts Journal, 226
financial industry, 26–27
financial literacy, 159–60
financial mistakes:
  advice to counter, xviii–xix
  examples of, xi–xvi
  forgiveness for making, xx
  high costs of, xvi, xix
  reasons for, xvii–xix
financial products, 3–20
  annuities, 3–4, 13–16
  asking questions and, 17–19; *see also* Big Five
  financial advice and, 19–20; *see also* financial professionals
  gold and, 5–8
  hedge funds and, 10–12
  investment classes and, 108
  lack of knowledge and, 12–17
  regular review of, 233
  reverse mortgages and, 8–10
financial professionals:
  Certified Financial Planner Board of Standards and, 27
  fiduciary vs. suitability standards, 25
  legal obligations of, 20–28
  professional certifications and, 25, 28
financial security basics, 31–32, 91–93
  see also Big Three
financial stress, 46–47, 60, 70
  see also fear
529 plans, 21–22, 25, 68, 73
floating rate funds, 12
flood insurance, 183–85, 188

401(k) plans, 71, 101, 125, 128, 212
full retirement age and (FRA), 134

get-rich-quick schemes, 105
Girls Inc. of Omaha, Nebraska, 12
gold, as financial investment, 5–8
gold standard, 6
government grants, 63, 73–74
Great Depression, 43
Great Recession, xix, 96
greed, xviii, 13
Grubman, Jim, 43–44, 46, 52, 150, 154

Hammerle, Virginia, 213
health care costs, 130, 136, 165, 168, 177
health care proxies, 209
hedge funds, 10–12
home ownership, 80–95
    financial security basics and, 91–93
    optimism bias and, 83–86
    real estate myths and, 82–83, 85–91
    renting vs. buying and, 94–95
    This Old House (TV show) and, 90
    vacation homes and, 80–82, 207
    see also real estate industry
homeowner's insurance, 89, 183, 235
house flipping, 86–87

Housing and Urban Development Department, U.S., 8
housing expenses, 91–92, 183
housing market, 44–45
Hurricane Irma, 163, 183

identity protection, 112–24
    changing passwords and, 113–17, 121, 212, 234
    checking credit reports and, 113, 121–22
    guarding Social Security nos. and, 112–17, 120
    limiting social media use and, 120–21
    staying abreast of scams and, 116–18, 121–22
identity theft:
    data breaches and, 113–14, 119, 122
    prevention measures and, 120–24, 233
    scams and, 112–13, 116–18, 121–22
    Swiped (Levin) and, 114, 243n
Index Revolution, The: Why Investors Should Join It Now (Ellis), 226
inflation, 6, 129, 189
institutional investors, 10–11
insurance, 182–98
    disability insurance and, xii–xiii, 185, 190, 194–95
    flood insurance and, 183–85, 188
    homeowner's insurance and, 89, 183, 235

insurance mistakes and,
188–97
insurance self-check and,
196
life insurance and, 23–24, 110,
188–94, 235
long-term care and, 168, 177,
185–88, 195
risk protection and, 186–88
insurance companies, 15–16,
184–87
Internal Revenue Service (IRS),
12, 29–31, 112–13, 118,
122
intestate, *see* wills and estates
investing, steps to:
allocate assets and, 108
create financial plan and,
106–8
mind "Big Three" and, 106
revisit allocation and,
109–10
stick to plan and, 108–9
investing mistakes, 220–23
investing success:
market timing and, 223–28
passive approach and, 98, 103,
109, 220, 225–26
risk assessment and, 105–11
investment property, 58–59,
88–89, 108

Jill on Money blog, ix
job market, 64–65, 70
Jolley, Sandy, 9–10, 18
Joneses, keeping up with the,
103–5, 149, 152
junk bond funds, 12, 17

Kushner, Tony, 70

Labor Department, U.S., 26
legal documents, 209–14
document filing and, 210
Do-Not-Resuscitate orders
and, 210, 215
health care proxies and, 209
letters of instruction and,
209
power of attorney and, 209
trusts and, 209–10
Lehman Brothers, 96–97
letters of instruction, 209
Levin, Adam, 114, 120, 243*n*
Lewis, Michael, 81
life insurance:
changing needs and, 109–10,
193–94, 235
permanent vs. term and,
23–24, 188, 191–93
policy lapses and, 195–96
underestimating need for, 185,
188–90
lifestyle:
early retirement and, 126–28,
138–40
lifestyle choices and, 56, 111,
182–83
needs vs. wants, 39, 133–35,
142, 147–48
you only live once (YOLO)
and, 144
liquid assets, 18, 173–74, 212
living trusts, 201
long-term care insurance (LTCI),
168, 177, 185–88, 195
loss aversion, 100

Marathon Oil, xvii, 98, 102
market timing, xi, 217–32
  blockchain technology and,
    222
  classic mistakes and, 220–23
  real estate industry and, 90–91
  rebalancing and, 228–31
  Rhode Island guru and,
    217–18, 228
  short-term movements and,
    219–20
  wise investing and, 223–28
Medicaid, 172, 177
Mitnick, Kevin, 115–16
Mobil Corporation, 98
money blogs, ix
money gifts, 174–75, 208
money issues, 146–62
  money conversations and,
    161–62
  money emotions and, 149–55;
    see also negative emotions
  parenting tips and, 155–60
  possible effects of, 35, 44–46
  root causes of, 42–44, 53,
    102–3
  see also money values; self-
    awareness
Money, 73
money obsession, 34, 37–38,
  44–45, 153
money secrets, 47–49, 204
money values, 39–57, 146–49
  having "enough" and, 54–57
  needs vs. wants, 39, 133–35,
    142, 147–48
  overvaluation of money and,
    40, 42–48, 52

preoccupation with money
  and, 40, 48–50; see also
  money obsession
spending habits and, 146–49
strategies toward health and,
  41, 50–54
mortgages, 8–10, 41
mutual funds, 11, 101

National Association of Colleges
  and Employers (NACE), 65
National Association of Personal
  Financial Advisors (NAPA),
  28
National Flood Insurance
  Program, 183
natural disasters, 163, 183
negative emotions, xviii, 13–15,
  36, 43–45, 59, 67, 104–5
New York Stock Exchange
  (NYSE), 7
NextGenVest, 73

Obama, Barack, 26–27
optimism bias, xviii, 83–86
organ donations, 203

parenting, money and:
  childhood jobs and, 158
  financial literacy and, 159–60
  healthy attitudes and, 160–62
  helping kids out and, 158–59
  money problems and, 157–58
  "snowplow" parents and,
    154–55
  transparency and, 156–57
passive investing, 98, 103, 109,
  220, 225–26

password protection, 113–17, 121

peace of mind, 72, 110–11, 189

Peeler, Kelly, 73

pensions, 134–36, 212

personal finances:
  annual review of, 234–35
  monthly review of, 233–34
  quarterly review of, 234

power of attorney, 209

precious metals, 5–8

private colleges, 63–65

professional certifications, 25, 28

Quinn, Jane Bryant, 219

real estate industry:
  estate taxes and, 207–8
  market timing and, 90–91
  property values and, 44–45, 49
  real estate myths and, 82–83, 85–91; *see also* home ownership
  reverse mortgages and, 8–10
  tenants by entirety and, 204

reality checks, 13, 35–38, 129
  see also self-awareness

rebalancing, 227–31

recency bias, 100–105, 110

renting:
  investment properties and, 58–59, 88–89, 108
  real estate myths and, 82–83, 85–91
  rent-stabilized apartments and, 92–93
  vs. home ownership, 94–95

restraint bias, xviii

retirement age, 59, 136–38

retirement calculations, 34–35, 107, 132–36

retirement funding:
  401(k) plans and, 71, 101, 125, 128, 212
  college debt and, 68–72
  maxing out contributions and, 31, 92, 106
  pensions and, 134–36, 212
  Roth IRAs and, 125, 135, 212, 235
  Social Security and, 127–29, 134–36

retirement gradations, 140–42

retirement lifestyle, 126–28, 138–40

retirement preparation, 125–45
  financial planners and, 142–43
  long-term planning and, 128–32
  retirement age and, 59, 136–38
  retirement calculations and, 34–35, 107, 132–36
  retirement gradations and, 140–42
  retirement lifestyle and, 126–28, 138–40

reverse mortgages, 8–10

Rhode Island, 217–18, 228

risk assessment, 96–111
  cognitive biases and, 99–103
  self-worth and, 103–5
  steps to investing and, 105–11

risk assessment questionnaire, 107

risk tolerance, 104–10
Roth IRAs, 125, 135, 212, 235

sandwich generation, 165–66
Securities and Exchange
    Commission (SEC), 10, 227,
    239n
self-awareness, 49–54, 155–56,
    229–30, 233
self-worth, 42–43, 103–5
"snowplow" parenting, 154–55
social media use, 120–21
    see also digital technology
Social Security:
    protecting ID nos. and,
        112–17, 120
    as retirement income, 127–29,
        134–36
spending addictions, 35, 44
spending choices, 131–32
spending habits, 54–56, 146–49,
    233
state taxes, 130, 210
stock market:
    2018 crash and, 220–21
    American Stock Exchange
        (AMEX) and, xvii, 97
    crisis magnification effect and,
        96
    dot-com boom/bust and, 51,
        82, 90, 96, 217–18
    excessive risk taking and,
        101–4
    investment advice and, 224–25
    Lehman Brothers bankruptcy
        and, 96–98
    New York Stock Exchange
        (NYSE) and, 7

Storoni, Mithu, 46–47
stress, 46–47, 60, 70
Stress-Proof: The Scientific
    Solution to Protect Your
    Brain and Body (Storoni),
    46
suitability standards, 25
Swiped: How to Protect
    Yourself in a World Full of
    Scammers, Phishers, and
    Identity Thieves (Levin),
    114, 243n

tax audits, 234–35
tax fraud, 112–13
tax incentives, 21–22, 85–87
tax reform, 44, 87
tax refunds, 33–34
tax scams, 118, 122
technology industry:
    digital technology and,
        115–19; see also identity
        theft
    dot-com boom/bust and, 51,
        82, 90, 96, 217–18
Thaler, Richard, 228
Thinking in Bets (Duke), 223
30 percent rule, 91–92
This Old House (TV show),
    90
Treasury Inflation-Protected
    Securities (TIPS), 6
Trustees of the Social Security
    and Medicare Trusts,
    136
trusts, 209–10

U.S. Steel, xvii, 98

vacation homes, 80–82, 207

wills and estates, 199–216
  end-of-life planning and,
    200–207
  estate planning basics and,
    209–14

legal process and, 200, 203–4,
    213
life changes and, 203–6
money secrets and, 204
workaholics, 39–40

Zweig, Jason, 15, 219, 228

PHOTO: JOHN FILO, CBS NEWS

JILL SCHLESINGER is an Emmy-nominated and Gracie Award–winning business analyst for CBS News, a weekly guest on NPR's *Here and Now,* and a Certified Financial Planner. She writes a weekly syndicated column, *Jill on Money,* and serves as the host of the nationally syndicated radio show and podcast *Jill on Money.*

jillonmoney.com
Facebook.com/JillonMoney
Twitter: @jillonmoney
Instagram: @jillonmoney

ABOUT THE TYPE

This book was set in Sabon, a typeface designed by the well-known German typographer Jan Tschichold (1902–74). Sabon's design is based upon the original letter forms of sixteenth-century French type designer Claude Garamond and was created specifically to be used for three sources: foundry type for hand composition, Linotype, and Monotype. Tschichold named his typeface for the famous Frankfurt typefounder Jacques Sabon (c. 1520–80).